The Role of Cognates in the Teaching of French

American University Studies

Series II
Romance Languages and Literature

Vol. 94

PETER LANG
New York · Bern · Frankfurt am Main · Paris

Petra Hammer and Gerald S. Giauque

The Role of Cognates in the Teaching of French

PETER LANG
New York · Bern · Frankfurt am Main · Paris

Library of Congress Cataloging-in-Publication Data

Hammer, Petra
The role of cognates in the teaching of French.
(American university studies. Series II, Romance languages ; vol. 94)
1. Romance languages – Study and teaching. 2. Romance languages – Cognate words. 3. French language – Cognate words – English. 4. English language – Cognate words – French. I. Giauque, Gerald S. II. Title. III. Series.
PC36.H36 1988 440'.07 88-860
ISBN 0-8204-0761-5
ISSN 0740-9257

CIP-Titelaufnahme der Deutschen Bibliothek

Hammer, Petra:
The role of cognates in the teaching of French / Petra Hammer and Gerald S. Giauque. – New York; Bern; Frankfurt am Main; Paris: Lang, 1988.
(American University Studies: Ser. 2, Romance Languages and Literature; Vol. 94)
ISBN 0-8204-0761-5

NE: Giauque, Gerald S.:; American University Studies / 02

Table of Contents

1. Introduction..1

PART I

A PSYCHOLOGICAL FRAME OF REFERENCE FOR SECOND

LANGUAGE ACQUISITION..5

2. A Review of Three Methodologies in Second Language Teaching.......7

3. A Child's First Language Acquisition and the Concept of Distanciation..13

4. The Acquisition of Word Meaning..17

5. The Relationship Between First Acquisition and Second Language Learning..24

6. A Bilingual Language Model..29

PART II

COGNATES WITH THE ENGLISH LANGUAGE..33

7. The Meaning Component of Words and Cognate Study..................35

8. Deceptive Cognates..39

9. The Extent of "Good" Cognates..42

10. Frequency Ratings of the English-French Cognates................47

11. Foreign Language Vocabulary Study..52

PART III

THE UTILITY OF COGNATES..55

12. The Appropriate Age Levels at Which to Study a Second Language with Cognates..57

13. The Experimental Testing of the Utility of Cognates in Second Language Acquisition..60

14. Suggestions for Further Research Dealing with Cognate Study......69

15. The Efficiency Aspect of Cognate Study....70
16. The Interrelationship of Language....72
17. Towards an International Language....76
18. English-French Cognate Bibliography....76
19. English-German Cognate Literature Review and Bibliography....80
20. English-Spanish Cognate Literature Review and Bibliography....81
21. Dravidian Cognates Bibliography....87

PART IV

TRANSFER OF SIMILARITIES....89

22. Transfer of Commonalities Between Related Languages....91
23. Oral Recognition of English-French Cognates....96
24. Design of an English-French Cognate Unit....100
25. Objectives of the Teaching Material in the Cognate Unit....104
26. Teaching Suggestions for the English-French Cognate Unit....108
27. A copy of the English-French Cognate Unit....111

Lesson One....113
Lesson Two....121
Lesson Three....125
Lesson Four....132
Lesson Five....135
Lesson Six....139
Lesson Seven....146
Appendix A....153
Appendix B....159
Appendix C....167

Introduction

The relative ease of rapid transportation and communication, due to modern technology, entails a greater need for second language acquisition, since language barriers may be a disadvantage on interpersonal, social, political, economic and scientific grounds. Unfortunately, the ease with which contact with different language groups is possible is not matched by equal facility of second language acquisition; too often there exists a great discrepancy between the amount of time spent on second language study and the proficiency attained.

Among the various approaches in second language teaching and the research which surrounds it, efforts have been directed toward research on several mnemonic techniques for learning second language vocabulary: Bower (1970) analyzed the loci method as a mnemonic device; Ott, Butler, Blake and Ball (1973) investigated the effect of interactive image elaboration on the acquisition of second language vocabulary; and Atkinson (1975) suggested a mnemonic keyword method.

As increasing numbers of individuals need or wish to learn a second language while employed, developing an efficient method becomes of paramount importance. A primary objective in new methods of learning a second language must be to decrease the ratio of the time expended to the proficiency attained. Increased efficiency of method will not only attract more students to language learning, but will also minimize the expenditure of time and money involved.

The Michel Thomas Language Center (1976) advertised that in an introductory course in Spanish or French of 20 to 25 hours in length, "students achieve functional proficiency in speaking and reading in the present tense, and have a working vocabulary of 2,000 words." In a basic proficiency course, lasting 50 to 55 hours, "students achieve functional proficiency in speaking, reading and writing in the five most commonly used verb tenses: present, past, future, conditional and imperative. They will have a working vocabulary of 3,000 words."

In comparison with the Michel Thomas language program the Curriculum Guide for French (1974) for the Province of Alberta, Canada proposes the learning of "900 passive and 300 active words for level one" (p. 21). This cannot be necessarily equated with a school year as a school year amounts to 60 hours of French instruction for elementary pupils, 70 hours for junior high school students and 125 hours for senior high school students in the Edmonton Public School System.

The discrepancy of suggested achievement in school language learning and the Michel Thomas method may not be completely explained by the conditions and characteristics of the learner in two different situations. The Michel Thomas method is in effect a cognate approach to the study of interrelated languages like English, French and Spanish.

Michel Thomas relies on two rules in his method of instruction: first, the learner has to be put at ease, for too much anxiety can cripple learning. Second, it is not the student but the teacher who is responsible for ensuring that learning occurs. It is promised that no memorization, no learning by rote, no drill, no textbooks and no homework are necessary, and that usable language proficiency is achieved within a very short time.

This claim that functional proficiency in a second language may be attained within 25 to 55 hours may be valid, if one notes that the English and French languages share approximately 11,000 words (Hammer & Monod, 1976) and the English and Spanish languages approximately 4,000 (Nunn & Van Scroy, 1949). The learner is taught relatively little new information but rather how to apply knowledge of his first language to a second and related language. Thus, if the cognate approach is a viable economic private enterprise, it should be possible to apply a cognate approach in second language learning of related languages in a school or university setting.

References

Atkinson, R.C. Mnemotechnics in Second-Language Learning. American Psychologist, Vol. 30, 1975, 821-828.

Bower, G.H. Analysis of a Mnemonic Device. American Scientist, Vol. 58, 1970, 596-510.

French as a Second Language. Tentative Curriculum Guide, The Department of Education, Edmonton, Canada, 1974.

Hammer, P. & Monod, M. English-French Cognate Dictionary. University of Alberta, Edmonton, Canada, 1976.

Michel Thomas Language Center, "Bilingual/Bicultural Training, Spanish, French, English, Price List." Beverly Hills, 1185 Beverly Drive, California, U.S.A., 1976.

Nunn, Marshall E. & Van Scroy, Herbert A. *Glossary of Related Spanish-English Words.* University; Alabama: *University of Alabama Studies, No. 5, July 1949.*

Ott, C.E., Butler, D.C., Blake, R.S. & Ball, J.P. The Effect of Interactive-Image Elaboration on the Acquisition of Foreign Language Vocabulary. *Language Learning*. Vol. 23, 1973, 197-206.

Setzler, H.H. & Clark, R.E. Research Briefing. *Educational Technology*, August 1976, 43-44.

PART I

A PSYCHOLOGICAL FRAME OF REFERENCE FOR SECOND LANGUAGE ACQUISITION

A Review of Three Methodologies in Second Language Teaching

Second language teaching methodologies have been influenced to some extent by linguistic and psychological research findings. Three second language teaching methods, the grammar-translation, also known as the traditional approach, the audio-lingual method and the cognitive code-learning approach will serve to illustrate this point.

The name "grammar-translation" method illustrates the emphasis accorded to the study of some rules of syntax, paradigms of morphological forms and the application of these in translation. As Smith (1970: 4) noted:

> . . . emphasis on grammar can be traced to the influence of eighteenth century grammarians who assumed the existence of a universal grammar founded in universal reason and embodied in its purest state in the Greek and Latin of classical literature.

Grammar lessons and translations of reading material were the focus of this type of second language teaching. Coleman's study (1929) recommended the single objective of developing reading proficiency as being realistically attainable under typical classroom conditions. It should be noted that the grammar-translation method pre-dated the widespread use of the tape recorder.

The introduction of the audio-lingual method into second language school teaching about 1950 incorporated theoretical constructs and insights in the field of psychology. The behavioristic school of psychology, with Skinner as the exponent in the analysis of operant behavior conditioning, brought the application of shaping, overlearning, reinforcement, conditioning, stimulus and response within the realm of second language teaching.

The audio-lingual habit theory advanced by Nelson Brooks (1966) espoused the tenets of structural linguistics. The origins of structural grammar may be found in de Saussure's (1916) contention that language is a form and not a substance, the contributions of Sapir (1921) and Bloomfield (1933) who described the languages of the American Indians, the study of information models and research in machine translation. Structural linguistics may also have been, in part, a reaction against traditional grammar, which was criticized as failing to take into account the language of today, imposing a norm determined by the styles of the great writers of the past, describing only the written language and emphasizing the study of morphology while neglecting to present an analysis of many important and frequent sentence constructions. In contrast, structural grammar is descriptive, not prescriptive. The investigation of a linguistic corpus is inductive as was the compilation of Le Français Fondamental (1959), for example.

The audio-lingual method used behavioristic psychology as the psychological basis and structural grammar as the linguistic one. In audio-lingual language teaching, emphasis was placed on imitation, practice and repetition of selected language material. The language laboratories made it possible to provide native language models to the second language learner for imitation and extensive structure drills. Unlike the grammar-translation method, the audio-lingual method placed emphasis on the spoken language. Johnston and Seerly (1958: 15) observed "language is speech. The written form comes later, consideraby later, in the progression of language learning which is first hearing and speaking and then reading and writing." Second language teaching, according to the proponents of the audio-lingual method, was aimed at maintaining the natural order of language learning, that is, listening, speaking, reading and writing. Speech was regarded as behavior and thus the behavioristic theories of learning appeared to apply.

As the audio-lingual habit theory became prevalent in second language teaching, drawbacks of the oral approach were noted by Chastain and Woerdehoff (1968), Woodsworth (1973) and Smith (1970). Ausubel (1964: 420) identified the following as disadvantages of the audio-lingual method for adolescents:

> 1) the rote learning of phrases; 2) inductive rather than deductive learning of grammatical generalizations; 3) avoidance of the mediational role of the native language; 4) presentation of the spoken form of the language before the written form; and 5) insistence on exposing the beginner to the 'natural speed rendition' of the spoken language.

The audio-lingual method was not found to be uniformly effective for second language students across all grades.

The most recent of the three approaches mentioned, the cognitive code-learning method, may be regarded as being partly a reaction against the audio-lingual habit method and partly an alignment with transformational linguistics. Carroll (1965) suggested that the cognitive code-learning method is based on a modified, up-dated grammar-translation method. In this method language learning is treated as an intellectual discipline. Carroll (1965: 278) summarized this method as follows.

> . . . learning a language is a process of acquiring conscious control of the phonological, grammatical, and lexical patterns of a second language, largely through study and analyses of these patterns as a body of knowledge. The theory attaches more importance to the learner's understanding of the structure of the foreign language than to his facility in using that structure, since it is believed that, provided the student has a proper degree of cognitive control over the structures of the language, facility will develop automatically with use of the language in meaningful situations.

In the cognitive code-learning method, exercises are designed to teach grammatical understanding of the concepts being introduced. Prior to any practice with the structure, deductive explanation of grammar is given and all four language skills are practised from the beginning of the course.

Transformational grammar, as first described by Chomsky (1957) in <u>Syntactic Structures</u>, provided a new and descriptive mechanism for grammars. The descriptive mechanism went no further than previous grammatical systems in providing useful information for the second language teacher (Marckworth, 1977). Transformational generative grammar provided excellent syntactic descriptions, but these were not useful to the second language learner.

Lawler and Selinker (1971) criticized the utility of transformational generative grammar for the cognitive code-learning method because 1) individual differences among speakers are not considered, 2) the "ideal speaker--listener relationship" is not practical in second language teaching and 3) the time factor in learning a second language is not considered.

In summary, no single method in second language teaching was found to be a panacea. Authors such as Cook (1969) and Belasco (1970: 42) suggested combining elements of different methods. These authors did not assume ". . . that a cognitive approach is mutually exclusive with a verbal-behavior approach." Furthermore, it appears that the grammar-translation method emphasized reading, the audio-lingual method, speech, and the cognitive code-learning method, all language skills.

What has been omitted from consideration in the methods reviewed appears to be the developmental aspect of the child. Smith (1970: 6) pointed out: "Education, in general, and mastery of a second language, in particular, are longitudinal processes; the appropriate manner in which they are to be studied should be longitudinal."

Questions

1. Which one of the three methodologies do you personally prefer? Please state the reasons for your choice.
2. What are the psychological and lingusitic bases of the grammar translation method?
3. Trace the relationship between technological advances and second language teaching methods.
4. Why is research in psychology of interest to second language instruction?
5. What are the weaknesses and strengths of the grammar translation, audio-lingual and cognitive code-learning methodologies respectively?
6. Design your own teaching methodology on the basis of your analysis in question 5.
7. Write a 500 word paper on error analysis in second language teaching. Be prepared to discuss its merits and weaknesses.
8. What is the utility of contrastive linguistics in second language teaching?
9. Why should a second language be taught in schools? Please list your arguments.

References

Ausubel, D. Adults Versus Children in Second Language Learning: Psychological Considerations. Modern Language Journal, Vol. 48, November 1964, 420-424.

Belasco, S. C'est la guerre? Or can Cognition and Verbal Behavior Co-Exist in Second Language Learning. Modern Language Journal, Vol. 54, 1970, 395-412.

Bever, T.G. The Cognitive Basis for Linguistic Structures. 279-362 in John R. Hayes, ed., Cognition and the Development of Language. John Wiley and Sons, New York, 1970.

Bloomfield, L. Language. H. Holt & Company, New York, 1933.

Brooks, N. Language Learning: The New Approach. Phi Delta Kappan, Vol. 47, March 1966, 357-359.

Buteau, M.F. Student's Errors and the Learning of French as a Second Language: A Pilot Study. International Review of Applied Linguistics in Language Teaching, Vol. 8, 1970, 133-145.

Carroll, J.B. The Contributions of Psychological Theory and Educational Research to the Teaching of Foreign Languages. Modern Language Journal, Vol. XLIX, May 1965, 273-281.

Chastain, K. The Audiolingual Habit Theory Versus the Cognitive Code-Learning Theory: Some Theoretical Considerations. International Review of Applied Linguistics in Language Teaching, Vol. 7, 1969, 97-106.

Chastain, K. Behavioristic and Cognitive Approaches in Programmed Instruction. Language Learning, Vol. 20, 1970, 223-235.

Chastain, K. A Methodological Study Comparing the Audio-Lingual Habit Theory and the Cognitive Code-Learning Theory--A Continuation. Modern Language Journal, Vol. 54, 1970, 257-266.

Chastain, K. & Woerdehoff, F.J. A Methodological Study Comparing the Audio-Lingual Habit Theory and the Cognitive Code-Learning Theory. Modern Language Journal, Vol. 52, 1968, 268-279.

Chomsky, N. Syntactic Structures. Mouton & Co., The Hague, 1957.

Clark, H.H. The Primitive Nature of Children's Relational Concepts. 269-278 in John R. Hayes, ed., Cognition and the Development of Language. John Wiley and Sons, New York, 1970.

Coleman, A. The Teaching of Modern Foreign Languages in the United States. The MacMillan Company, New York, 1929.

Cook, V.J. The Analogy Between First and Second Language Learning. International Review of Applied Linguistics in Language Teaching, Vol. 7, 1969, 207-216.

Le Français Fondamental. Chilton Co.,--Book Division, Philadelphia, 1959.

Henning, G.H. Remembering Foreign Language Vocabulary: Acoustic and Semantic Parameters. Language Learning, Vol. 23, 1973, 185-196.

Hok, R. Cognitive and S-R Learning Theory Reconciled. International Review of Applied Linguistics, Vol. 10, 1972, 263-269.

Johnston, M.C. & Seerley, C.C. Foreign Language Laboratories in Schools and Colleges, U.S. Department of Health, Education and Welfare, Office of Education, Washington, D.C., 1958.

Lakoff, R. Transformational Grammar and Language Teaching. Language Learning, Vol. 19, 1969, 117-140.

Lawler, J. & Selinker, L. On Paradoxes, Rules, and Research in Second Language Learning. Language Learning, Vol. 21, 1971, 27-43.

Marckworth, L. Personal Communication. The University of Alberta, Edmonton, 1977.

Mueller, T.H. The Effectiveness of Two Learning Models: The Audio-Lingual Habit Theory and the Cognitive Code-Learning Theory. 113-122 in P. Pimsleur and T. Quinn, eds., The Psychology of Second Language Learning, Cambridge University Press, Cambridge, 1971.

Richards, J.C. Error Analysis and Second Language Strategies. Language Sciences, in press (1971).

Sapir, E. Language, Harcourt, Brace & World, New York, 1921.

Saussure, F. de. Course in General Linguistics. Philosophical Library, New York, 1916/1959.

Selinker, L. The Psychologically Relevant Data of Second Language Learning. 35-43 in P. Pimsleur and T. Quinn, eds., The Psychology of Second Language Learning, Cambridge University Press, Cambridge, 1971.

Smith, P.D., Jr. A Comparison of the Cognitive and Audiolingual Approaches to Foreign Language Instruction. Center for Curriculum Development, Philadelphia, 1970.

Stern, H.H. First and Second Language Acquisition. 57-66 in H.H. Stern, ed., Perspectives on Second Language Teaching. Modern Language Center Publications, No. 1, Toronto: The Ontario Institute for Studies in Education, 1970.

Wardhaugh, R. The Contrastive Analysis Hypothesis. TESOL Quarterly, Vol. 4, 1970, 123-130.

Woodsworth, J.S. On the Role of Meaning in Second Language Teaching. Language Learning, Vol. 23, 1973, 75-88.

A Child's First Language Acquisition and the Concept of Distanciation

According to Werner and Kaplan (1963) the child advances through a sequence of distanciations of the addressor and addressee, the addressor and referent (object) and the addressor and symbolic vehicle (language). In terms of symbol formation and communication, the principal components comprising the symbol situation are two persons, the addressor and the addressee, and by what channel a message is transmitted, be it through gesture, facial expression and/or use of the symbolic vehicle, that is, language.

The addressor-addressee relationship widens as the child matures. The initial fusion of the infant-mother relationship is gradually superseded by peer relationships and eventually generalized others. With the development of language, the child comes to establish stable relations between objects and his own body and can thus rise out of the undifferentiated nature of the addressor-referent (object) relationship. The earlier media of representations, like bodily movements of the child, become more and more replaced by vocal utterances and, with the use of the symbolic vehicle, the addressor can distance himself from direct, pragmatic operation upon things. As the distance between the addressor and the symbolic vehicle becomes greater, the symbolic vehicle reflects less egocentricity and idiosyncracy. Concomitantly, with the addressor-symbolic vehicle distanciation, the distance between the symbolic vehicle and the referential object develops. Instead of treating the name as if it were the object, vehicle and referent become distinct as to their substantial nature.

By placing a time dimension on this model, with the developmental stages as the dependent variable, each of the principal components (addressor, addressee, symbolic vehicle and referent) undergoes changes from undifferentiated globality to distanciation and differentiation. It is assumed that this distanciation process of the addressor and symbolic vehicle is not unique for a given language, but rather constitutes a developmental sequence of a general nature.

The acquisition of language is a gradual process which may be examined with particular reference to Piaget's (1969) cognitive stages. The sensori-motor stage, extending from birth to approximately the second year of life, corresponds in language acquisition to the mastery of all the vowels and two thirds of the consonants (Bar-Adon & Leopold, 1971). One and two-word sentences occur during the second year of life. During the early part of what Piaget terms the pre-operational stage, continuing approximately from the second to the seventh year of age, the greatest improvement in clarity of articulation occurs. Practically all speech is comprehe sible after three and a half years. It has been observed that by the age of three years and eight months, on the average, children use all the basic sentence structures (statement, question, command) used by adults (Menyuk, 1963; Slobin, 1963; Brown, Cazden and Bellugi-Klima, 1964). During the stage labeled as the concrete operational, which, according to Piaget, encompasses the period from seven to eleven years of age, language development advances to the point where the child can think logically enough to solve problems involving "concrete" objects and events. The final stage, called the formal operational, generally develops during the eleventh to the fifteenth years. A distanciation with respect to the symbolic vehicle (language) appears to be required before the young adolescent becomes able to solve hypothetical problems, complex verbal problems and to use scientific reasoning. The distanciation process within language appears to correlate positively with the cognitive developmental stages.

The distanciation process with respect to the addressor (child) and the symbolic vehicle (language) is characterized by a differentiation between word and sentence, between sound and meaning and between symbol and referent. Concerning the differentiation process between words and sentences, students of child linguistics, psychologists, and philosophers have often noted the holophrastic nature of early verbal symbolizations. Sully (1897), Stern (1924), Leopold (1939) and Bruner (1975), among others, refered to the self-contained phonetic utterance or word as "one-word sentence." The one-word sentence is thought to represent an undifferentiated linguistic whole. It is out of this undifferentiated whole that words and sentences emerge. Research findings have demonstrated that lexicalization and syntactic structurization appear to be interdependent. Werner and Kaplan (1952: 103) found that as word meanings become less holophrastic and more syncretic, and fluid, sentence structures become more stable. Piaget (1955: 135) observed the same phenomenon. The child of six years of age ".

. . ignores isolated words and deals with whole sentences, understanding them or altering them as they stand without analyzing them." The differentiation between words and sentences is aided once the child is taught how to read. Watts (1944: 64) noted that "familiarity with print helps (the child) to know words as separate elements of his language."

Another distanciation process within the symbolic vehicle occurs when the child comes to distinguish between sound and meaning. At first, the child does not separate the phonetic forms of words from their meanings; rather, as Piaget (1955: 251) noted, the word, to the child, is an integral part of the object it denotes. To the question "Have words any strength?" Piaget recorded that a child answered that they had if they denoted things that had strength, but not otherwise.

It is postulated that the distanciation process between the symbol and the referent is related to the degree of verbal abstractness. For example, Sully (1897) and other researchers in child language development have noted how literally children interpret the figurative and metaphorical use of our language. Werner and Kaplan (1963), discussed at least three degrees of "distance" between the symbol and the referent. At the level of "minimal distance" the vehicle directly pictured that which it represented. Naturalistic onomatopoetic depictions, whereby children imitate the noises or sounds of objects and/or persons, for example, "boom" referring to thunder, are illustrations of designatory vocal imitations. At a level of "intermediate distance" the vehicle functions in a "concrete metaphoric" way in the representation of the referent. Here, unlike the depiction of sonic properties of events, visual properties are rendered linguistically. For example, physiognomic depiction of the variations of length are expressed by variations of sound durations. At a third degree of distance the vehicle functions as an "alluding metaphor" (Werner and Kaplan, 1963: 454). Conventional representation of the world using the linguistic medium reflects the highest degree of material differentiation between the symbolic vehicle and the referent. Increased mastery of the abstract nature of language is thus related to the developmental process.

Questions

1. Define the distanciation process within language.
2. In what order does the distanciation process occur within language?
3. When is the distanciation process completed?

References

Bar-Adon, B., & Leopold, W. F. (eds.) Child Language, Prentice-Hall, Inc., Englewood Cliffs, New Jersey, 1971.

Brown, R., Cazden, C., & Bellugi-Klima, U. The Child's Grammar from I to III. 382-412 in Child Language. (eds., Bar-Adon, B., & Leopold, W. F.) Prentice-Hall, Inc., Englewood Cliffs, New Jersey, 1971.

Bruner, J. S. The Ontogenesis of Speech Acts. Journal of Child Language, Vol. 2, 1975, 1-19.

Leopold, W. F. Speech Development of a Bilingual Child. Evanston: Northwestern University Press, 4 vols., 1939.

Menyuk, P. Syntactic Structures. 407-422, in Child Language. (eds., Bar-Adon, B., & Leopold, W. F.) Prentice-Hall, Inc., Englewood Cliffs, New Jersey, 1971.

Piaget, J. The Language and Thought of the Child. Translated by M. Gabain, A Meridian Book, New York, 1955.

Piaget, J., & Inhelder, B. The Psychology of the Child. Basic Books, Inc., Publishers, New York, 1969.

Slobin, D. I. Grammatical Development in Russian-Speaking Children. 343-348 in Child Language. (eds., Bar-Adon, B., & Leopold, W. F.) Prentice-Hall, Inc., Englewood Cliffs, New Jersey, 1971.

Stern, W. Psychology of Early Childhood. George Allan and Unwin Ltd., London, 1924.

Sully, J. Children's Ways. Appleton-Century-Crofts, New York, 1897.

Watts, A. F. The Language and Mental Development of Children. Harrap, London, 1944.

Werner, H., & Kaplan, E. The Acquisition of Word Meanings: A Developmental Study. Vol. XV, Serial No. 51, No. 1, 1950. Society for Research in Child Development, Inc., Evanston, Illinois, 1952.

Werner, H., & Kaplan, B. Symbol Formation. Clark University, John Wiley & Sons, Inc., New York, 1963.

The Acquisition of Word Meanings

An examination of the processes of word meaning acquisition shows that word meanings evolve. At the pre-symbolic stage the global context of the child's experiences between himself, other people and the referential object appears to be fused. This is supported by the conclusions of Werner and Kaplan (1952; 1968), who suggested that the micro-genetic process of transforming "felt" meanings into appropriate linguistic expression to others follows an orderly, sequential pattern. At first meanings are felt or suffered rather than cognitively apprehended. The early vocalizations of the child are embedded in a context of concrete action and affect where words by themselves carry little or no meaning. Child language investigators agree that a child's conception of the meaning of words does not coincide with that of an adult. It is the adult who assumes the meaning intended by the child's first words (Taine, 1877; Preyer, 1882: Sully, 1897; Ach, 1971). Gradually, the diffuse and interpenetrating sentiments and meanings become embodied to some degree in personal, idiomatic, and contextualized gestures and verbalizations. Child language investigators have suggested that due to their limited verbal expressive ability, children enlarge the meaning of words (Tiedemann, 1787; Taine, 1877; Preyer, 1882; Sully, 1897; Leopold, 1939) and invent their own (Taine, 1877; Stern, 1924; Leopold, 1939). Increasingly, as experience is shaped more and more to facilitate communication with others, there is a progressive differentiation and articulation of connotations. Eventually, lingualization in the developing person becomes increasingly detached from imagery and gesture and becomes dominant over these more personal and covert media. Finally, communication about experience becomes more and more directed toward, and facilitated by, the communal lexicon and syntax (Werner & Kaplan, 1963: 242).

The learning of word meaning by children develops from coarse early semantic classifications. A gradual refinement of the semantic system occurs as prescribed by the child's environment. Proper names appear among the first lexical items which have exact meanings (Leopold, 1939). Later, an increase in vocabulary enables the developing child to differentiate among and to specify events in his environment. Werner and Kaplan (1963: 99) noted that the process of _differentiation_ and _specification_, whereby a vocal form, first global and nonspecific, becomes increasingly function-specific and conforming to the speech of socialized normal adults, is a gradual process. As the child grows up, the distance between the domain of concrete, perceptual motor experiences and the abstract levels of language usage is reflected in the lexical conceptualization of generality. Instead of being context specific, the word is used to refer to class concepts.

The coincidence of age agreement between Piaget's cognitive stages and Werner and Kaplan's word meaning acquisition study is noteworthy. At approximately eleven to twelve years of age the transition from the concrete operational stage to the formal operational stage is postulated to begin. For the same age group, Werner and Kaplan (1952: 1963) found a change in performance on the Word-Context Test. Prior to eleven years the request to the child to define verbal concepts, for example, "what is a bottle?", the reply was in terms of concretely contextualized action. A bottle was defined as "There is lemonade in it." However, twelve or thirteen year old children define "bottle" in terms of relatively context-free general thing names, as for example, "a bottle is a container into which all kinds of liquids go." Werner and Kaplan (1963: 188) quote a study by Barnes (1896-1897) which examined the definitions of children from six to fifteen years of age. Barnes found that definitions formulated in terms of concrete action declined from 82 percent at the 6-year level to 33 percent at the fifteen-year level. Barnes noted that it is still quite common at age ten for children to give more than fifty percent of their definitions in concrete terms.

Werner and Kaplan (1952) investigated experimentally the processes underlying the acquisition of word meaning through verbal contexts. A Word-Context Test was designed wherein children from eight-and-a-half to thirteen-and-a-half years were asked to give an "adequate" or "suitable" meaning to an unknown (artificial) word, embedded in six different sentence-contexts.

> The sentences are exposed progressively and cumulatively, that is, the first, the first and second, and so on. As each additional context is exposed, the subject is required to endow the artificial word with a meaning, to indicate how that meaning fits each of the previous contexts. Ideally, the subject is directed towards the formulation of a word meaning that will be semantically and grammatically insertable into each of the sentence-

> contexts without alteration or transformation of the structures of the sentence-contexts (Werner & Kaplan, 1952: 82).

Werner and Kaplan (1952) concluded on the basis of their study that the process of establishing a stable, relatively general meaning for words, a meaning which transcends specific significances of a word in different contexts, is a long and difficult one.

Similarly, Vygotsky (1962: 52-81) noted the developmental aspect in word meaning acquisition as it relates to concept formation. He identified three developmental phases in the process of concept formation: syncretic, complex and conceptual thinking. Syncretic thinking, continuing from approximately three to seven years of age, is characterized by subjective impression and syncretic images of the child. According to Vygotsky (1962), word meaning is no more than the representation of a group of individual objects depicted as a visual image in the child's mind. In complex thinking, the bonds established between objects are concrete and factual rather than abstract and logical. Complex thinking occurs approximately during the period between the seventh and the eleventh years. Vygotsky (1962: 69) noted that "word meanings as perceived by the child refer to the same objects the adult has in mind, which ensures understanding between child and adult, but that the child thinks the same thing in a different way, by means of different mental operations." Finally, conceptual thinking, as characterized by the ability to abstract or isolate single traits from a concrete whole and to analyze and synthesize the abstracted elements, results in a network of concepts of various degrees of abstractness and generality. Thus, Vygotsky (1962: 74-75) claimed that ". . . a name is never a concept when it first emerges (but) . . . rather an image, a picture, a mental sketch of a concept . . ." When true concepts are formed, the word ceases to serve as the arbitrary referencing function in the forming of a concept and becomes instead an abstract symbol of the concept. Conceptual thinking emerges in children around eleven to thirteen years of age.

The three basic phases of concept formation represent, according to Vygotsky (1962), "an intellectual process in the true sense" rather than a mere recording of "the child's knowledge and experience, or his linguistic development." Vygotsky (1962: 58) wrote that "the development of the processes which eventually result in concept formation begins in earliest childhood, but the intellectual functions that in a specific combination form the psychological basis of the process of the concept formation ripen, take shape, and develop only at puberty." The developmental sequence is invariable. Concept formation progresses from the undifferentiated and syncretic thinking of the very young child to the abstract, analytic and synthetic thinking of the adolescent and adult. However, as Vygotsky (1962: 75) pointed out, "it should be noted that even the normal adult, capable of forming and using concepts, does not consistently operate with concepts in his thinking . . . the adult constantly shifts from conceptual to concrete, complexlike thinking."

It is suggested that the acquisition of word meanings may parallel conceptual meaning acquisition. Although investigators of child language acquisition hesitate to talk about conceptual knowledge of words at an early age of the child, Church and Stone (1973: 224) noted that "the language that a child learns contains a number of subvocabularies, refering to special, logically related 'domains' of experience." They listed time-related words such as "day," "night," "first" and "now;" spatial vocabulary including "up," "down," "on;" a special vocabulary of shape and color names. These subvocabularies identified by Church and Stone may represent a conceptual framework that is modified as the child progresses through the cognitive developmental stages postulated by Piaget. The conceptual meaning acquisition of these subvocabularies may be further developed in school, where particular subject matter is presented in an orderly, sequenced, and articulated manner. Vygotsky (1962: 85) noted that "instruction is one of the principal sources of the school child's concepts and is also a powerful force in directing their evolution; it determines the fate of his total mental development."

Studies in education and psychology assure us that the growth of human intellect is tied to the number of acquired concepts. Thus, without conceptual understanding, a word will not necessarily carry with it conceptual knowledge. However, concepts come to be associated with words. Wüster (1959) described the relationship of words and concepts as follows: "Denn ohne sprachliche Zeichen (Wortsymbole) gäbe es keine Begriffe und kein richtiges Denken. Umgekehrt wären Wörter ohne Begriffe . . .'leere

Worthülsen'--nur ein Gegenstand der Akustik" (p. 621). (Without words, conceptual and abstract thinking would not be possible. Words without concepts would be empty word shells, just an object of noise.) Vygotsky described the relationship poetically. "A word devoid of thought is a dead thing, and a thought unembodied in words remains a shadow" (1962: 153).

For children learning their first language, the relationship of words and concepts may be depicted as two planes at right angles to each other. In adulthood, depending upon the size of the person's functional vocabulary, word meanings and concepts are like two parallel planes each holding the other in place. Thus, as the child acquires conceptual structure, stability is provided for word meanings. Werner and Kaplan (1963: 19) similarly maintained that ". . . an object as a meaningful entity issues from, and remains linked to, an underlying process of schematization. If this bond breaks, meaning is lost."

According to Cassirer (1944), words express emotion since man's contact with symbols is never in isolation from the continuum of human emotion. The relationship of word and affect may be such that the amount and type of emerging affect could depend upon the conceptual content of the word. This may be illustrated by word types: technical words, for example, probably have the lowest degree of affective content while curse words probably have the highest.

Werner and Kaplan (1952) identified two sequential levels in the acquisition of word meanings. They noted that during the early years the child learns the meaning of verbal symbols predominantly in concrete situations: through handling of objects in the presence of adults, direct pointing and naming. At an advanced level, the meaning of a word is inferred from the cues of the verbal context.

Vygotsky (1962) also identified two levels in the development of word meanings. He described the meaning acquisition of words during the first level in a manner similar to that of Werner and Kaplan (1952). The concepts embodied in concrete words refer to ". . . a dependent component of perceptual, object-determined thought" (p. 112). However, then, unlike Werner and Kaplan (1952), Vygotsky did not emphasize the process of meaning acquisition, but rather the product, suggesting that the second level in the development of word meaning is characterized by "generalized abstract conceptualization" (p. 112).

In summary, Werner and Kaplan (1952, 1963), Piaget (1969) and Vygotsky (1962) appear to agree that there is an essential difference between the adult's conceptual thinking and the forms of thought characteristic of the young child. The distanciation process (Werner and Kaplan, 1963) within the first language appears to be related and intimately linked to the cognitive development (Piaget, 1969) and concept formation (Vygotsky, 1962). Concepts, formulated on a purely abstract plane without reference to any concrete situation or impression, require a degree of linguistic manipulation which may be possible only when a certain degree of distanciation is achieved. The word appears to be an integral part of the developing processes leading to concept formation and cognitive development.

Questions

1. How long does it take for the child to acquire word meanings?
2. List the developmental phases in word meaning acquisition according to Werner and Kaplan (1952) and Vygotsky (1962)?
3. What is the relationship between words and concepts and words and affect? How do words, concepts and affect interrelate?
4. What is in your opinion the benefit of studying first language acquisition although you are specializing in second language teaching?

References

Ach, N. Über die Begriffsbilding. Wissenschaftliche Buchgesellschaft, Darmstadt, 1971.

Barnes, E. A Study in Children's Interest. in: Studies in Education, Stanford University, 1896-1897.

Cassirer, E. An Essay on Man. Doubleday, Garden City, New York, 1944.

Church, J., & Stone, L. J. Childhood and Adolescence: A Psychology of the Growing Person. Third Edition, Random House, New York, 1973, 216-231.

Leopold, W. F. Speech Development of a Bilingual Child. Evanston: Northwestern University Press, 4 vols., 1939.

Preyer, W. History of the Development of Speech. 29-31 in Child Language. (eds., Bar-Adon, B., & Leopold, W. F.) Prentice-Hall, Inc., Englewood Cliffs, New Jersey, 1971.

Stern, W. *Psychology of Early Childhood*. George Allan and Unwin Ltd., London, 1924.

Sully, J. *Children's Ways*. Appleton-Century-Crofts, New York, 1897.

Taine, H. Acquisition of Language by Children. 20-26 in *Child Language*. (eds., Bar-Adon, B., & Leopold, W. F.) Prentice-Hall, Inc., Englewood Cliffs, New Jersey, 1971.

Tiedemann, D. Observations on the Development of the Mental Faculties of Children. 13-17 in *Child Language*. (eds., Bar-Adon, B., & Leopold, W. F.) Prentice-Hall, Inc., Englewood Cliffs, New Jersey, 1971.

Vygotsky, L. S. *Thought and Language*. The M. I. T. Press, Cambridge, 1962.

Werner, H., & Kaplan, E. *The Acquisition of Word Meanings: A Developmental Study*. Vol. XV, Serial No. 51, No. 1, 1950. Society for Research in Child Development, Inc., Evanston, Illinois, 1952.

Werner, H., & Kaplan, B. *Symbol Formation*. Clark University, John Wiley & Sons, Inc., New York, 1963.

Wüster, E. Die Struktur der sprachlichen Begriffswelt und ihre Darstellung in Wörterbüchern. *Studium Generale*, Vol. 12, 1959, 615-627.

The Relationship Between First Language Association and Second Language Learning

Second language acquisition appears to be directly pertinent to the distanciation process between words and sentences, between sound and meaning and between symbol and referent. In second language teaching, words and syntax must explicitly be pointed out to the learner. Vocabulary learning in second language study helps to establish the verbal unit of thought, that is, the word. With second language learning the object-word link becomes severed. That the name is not inherent in the object may be realized by learning that the same referent, for example "stone," is rendered by different phonetic forms as "pierre," "piedra" and "Stein" in the French and German languages. Leopold (1939: 98) who studied the speech development of a bilingual child noted that ". . . one of the advantages of bilingualism is that the child was at no time the slave of words; she always focused her attention on the sense behind the phonetic configurations."

It is likely that the distanciation process within the first language becomes complete with the transition to the formal operational stage. However, this distanciation process may be aided and possibly accelerated with second languge acquisition during elementary school years. Ianco-Worrall (1972) duplicated the finding of Leopold's (1939) observation. The bilingual child separated the sound and meaning of words at an earlier age than a unilingual child. What is reflex-like in the first language is consciously acquired in the second language. As the linguistic and the semantic aspects of speech merge from opposite directions (Vygotsky, 1962), a similar relationship is suggested between first and second language acquisition. If the reciprocal relationship between first and second language acquisition be an accurate assumption, second language acquisition could contribute to a better command of the native language and to the overall intellectual development of a child.

The reciprocal relationship between first and second language acquisition can also be observed in the process of word meaning acquisition. In first language acquisition, the process of word meaning acquisition follows a sequence of affective, denotative and conceptual meaning. However, in a second language learning situation, word meanings are not necessarily previously "felt" meanings, as in first language acquisition. Word meanings are acquired in a specific verbal context and denotative may precede affective word meaning acquisition in second language study.

Understanding the denotative meaning of words alone, however, does not necessarily ensure communication or understanding. For example, the denotative meaning of "thrifty," "tight," and "stingy" is "reluctant to spend more money than necessary;" however, the emotions and attitudes associated with the three adjectives, that is, the connotative meanings are very different. As Rapoport (1975: 128) pointed out, "the choice of the 'right word' or expression in speaking and in writing is often a matter of choosing a word with culturally accepted psychological connotations appropriate for the occasion." Learning the affective meaning of words in a second language appears to follow the acquisition of denotative and/or conceptual meaning which is the reverse of what happens when a child acquires his first language.

It is hypothesized that the two levels identified in the process of word meaning acquisition are also applicable to second language study. A concrete object to which a word refers may be explicitly pointed out or shown. However, associating objects with concrete nouns may result in a prohibitively slow vocabulary acquisition technique in second language teaching and learning. Furthermore, depending upon the level of verbal abstractness achieved by the students, it appears reasonable to suspect that students come to rely more on inferring word meanings from verbal contexts.

In a reciprocal relationship between first and second language acquisition, on the one hand, it is suggested that second language acquisition could contribute to the achievement of conscious control over one's first language; on the other hand, a good command of one's own language is suggested to aid and contribute to the mastery of a related second language. Second language teaching should take into consideration the linguistic and cognitive developmental level of the learner. To the extent that learners have acquired learning principles in their first language applicable to second language learning, knowledge of these may aid in learning a second and related language. For example, if a learner is capable of inferring the meaning of words from cues of the verbal context, he should be able to apply this principle in second language study.

The proposed reciprocal relationship between first and second language acquistion, wherein second language learning may aid the distanciation process within the first language, and the proposed complementary relationship between first and second language acquisition, wherein competence in the first language may be applicable and transferable to a second and related language, appear to arise from different conditions of learning, different functions of speech and different characteristics of the learners. First language learning begins at birth in an insulated environment where the significant persons in the child's experience speak approximately the same language. Growing up, as J.R. Firth (1964) pointed out, means growing up into language, taking possession of it as a tool of living. While first language acquisition is generally unplanned, it is, nevertheless, an example of successful learning.

Controlling and directing the child's behavior is another dimension of early first language development not common in second language acquisition. At first the adult regulates the child's actions with verbal descriptions and directives which later the child will do himself. Luria (1959) noted that the verbal ability and the directive function of speech do not coincide. For example, the child may learn the word "no" long before he uses it in its directive function. Luria and Bain (1976) found that from two to two-and-a-half years of age the child finds it difficult to coordinate internal control with external commands. The directive function of speech starts to regulate behavior during the third and part of the fourth years of life.

The unplanned, successful learning conditions present in the child's first language acquisition, and the mastery of the directive function of speech to regulate his behavior, cannot be entirely reproduced in second language acquisition when this learning occurs in a school environment. Second language learners at school generally have acquired a basic knowledge of their mother tongue; in addition, the second language learner is literate. The characteristics of learners, their ages, reasoning ability and competence in the first language must be taken into consideration while at the same time employing, in so far as possible, the learning concepts that facilitated initial language acquisition.

The conditions of learning a second language, the directive function of speech and the characteristics of the learner are different in first and second language acquisition, yet the processes of first and second language acquisition are only variants within the indivisible process of language development.

Different values for learning a second language have been identified. In this context Goethe maintained: "He who does not know a second language does not truly know his own." Vygotsky (1962) pointed out that "What the child does unconsciously in his own language, he learns consciously in his second language." Bain (1974) wrote:

> Words encapsulate the mind. And any single linguistic history is arbitrary. The unilingual thus becomes a victim of a particular tyranny. Personal emancipation resulting from active participation in alternate world views is the practical motive for the efficient study of other languages.

The different values attached to learning a second language as noted by Goethe, Vygotsky and Bain may stem from the observation that second language study affects first language acquisition in different ways at different stages in the linguistic and cognitive development of the learner. From a longitudinal examination of first language acquisition, another possible value for learning a second language could be that second language study aids the distanciation process in the first language.

Questions

1. How could second language study aid the distanciation process in the first language?
2. What is meant by a reciprocal relationship between first and second language acquisition?
3. What is meant by a complementary relationship between first and second language acquisition?
4. When does the reciprocal relationship between first and second language acquisition cease to exist?
5. What is the optimum age for second language acquisition? How could you determine this?
6. When does the complementary relationship between first and second language acquisition begin?
7. On the basis of what you have learned about first language acquisition and, in particular, word meaning acquisition, what would you take into consideration in second language teaching?
8. What are some differences between first and second langauge acquisition?

References

Bain, B. Verbal regulation of cognitive processes: a replication of Luria's procedures with bilingual and unilingual infants. Child Development, Vol. 47, 1976, 543-546.

Bain, B. Course outline for Psychology of Bilingualism. The University of Alberta, Edmonton, 1974.

Firth, J.R. The Tongues of Men and Speech. Oxford University Press, London, 1964.

Ianco-Worrall, A.D. Bilingualism and Cognitive Development. Child Development, Vol. 43, 1972, 1390-1400.

Leopold, W.F. Speech Development of a Bilingual Child. Evanston: Northwestern University Press, 4 vols., 1939.

Luria, A.R. The Directive Function of Speech in Development and Dissolution. Word, Vol. 15, 1959, 341-352, 453-464.

Rapoport, A. Semantics. Thomas Y. Crowell Company, New York, 1975.

Vygotsky, L.S. Thought and Language. The M.I.T. Press, Cambridge, 1962.

A Bilingual Language Model

Traditionally the components of language have been described as phonetics, syntax, and lexicon. These components appear to interact in a unique way for each language system. For a unilingual person, phonetics, lexicon and syntax interact in the lingual communication process. The ability to pronounce is a necessary precondition for oral communication. With the rules of syntax, words are combined into sentences. Lexicon can be the smallest possible unit of communication, that is, it is the smallest unit of speech that has meaning, when taken by itself, but it has the largest number of members. Phonetics is the smallest language component, syntax is larger and lexicon constitutes the largest component in language, since there need not be a limitation on thought and knowledge finding expression through words.

It is suggested that during the acquisition of a second language, the phonetic system, the syntax and the lexicon of the second language become integrated with the first language counterparts. With related languages, some degree of overlap in syntax, phonetics and lexicon exists. The interplay of the language elements occurs between phonetics and lexicon, and syntax and lexicon. Words remain in one pool, representing semantic correlation and differentiation within the same language and across languages. Using this model, Steiner's statement seems to be applicable: "The (bi-or) polyglot mind undercuts the lines of division between languages by reaching inward, to the symbiotic core" (Steiner, 1975: 119).

It should be noted that, in this bilingual model, no distinction is made between coordinate and compound bilingualism (Ervin & Osgood, 1954). The coordinate and compound bilingual distinction appears to be justified only in so far as it refers to the setting and manner in which the second language is acquired. Coordinate bilinguals acquire their two languages in a culturally distinctive context; compound bilinguals acquire the facility in two languages in a single cultural or linguistic setting. The coordinate/compound dichotomy of the means of acquisition of bilinguality may lead to the assumption that two processes of language development exist rather than one.

Fluency in two languages may cancel the distinction of coordinate and compound bilingualism. In tests on translations, the scores of coordinate and compound bilinguals did not reveal statistically significant differences (Lambert, Havelka & Crosby, 1958). Ervin and Osgood (1954: 145) noted that ". . . the very process of two-way translating tends to transform a coordinate system into a compound system." There are additional data that cast some doubt on the usefulness of these terms to describe psychological functions: Kolers (1963: 299) found that subjects "with nearly identical linguistic histories respond differently, while others with different histories respond similarly." It appears that the coordinate/compound dichotomy reflects the experience of the individual and associations which she/he attaches to words, whether intralingual or interlingual.

Vygotsky (1962: 121) advanced the thesis that "word meanings evolve (and demanded that) this insight must replace the postulate of the immutability of word meanings." Steiner (1975: 94) also noted that "words are not the embodiment of invariant mental operations and fixed meanings." Through the acquisition and integration of concepts for which no counterparts are available in the native language, the semantic aspect of words of a bilingual or multilingual individual may become modified and unlike that of any unilingual person. In addition, it is probable that this discrete semantic field of a bi- or multilingual individual occurs irrespective of the coordinate/compound bilingual dichotomy. Evidence for this postulate may be cited from bilingual studies dealing with the influence of bilingualism on perception and meaning: Rosenzweig (1961) performed a study comparing word-association responses in English, French, German, and Italian. He found that across languages similar associations tend to occur among words of similar meaning; this occurred regardless of differences of verbal forms. Ervin (1961) investigated possible semantic shifts of bilinguals: she examined the color-naming of Navajo bilinguals in comparison with two monolingual groups and found that the categories of color used by the Navajo bilinguals differed systematically from the monolingual norms. She concluded that the bilinguals had integrated the color systems of both Navajo and English.

Preston and Lambert (1969) examined the functional relations between a bilingual's two languages by employing a bilingual version of the Stroop Color-Word Task. Two sets of processes, color naming versus word reading, were placed in competition by representing, for example, the word "green" in black color. The results of the experiment indicated ". . . that activation of a set of processes in one language does not make the other language system totally inoperative" (Preston & Lambert, 1969: 301). The integration of two languages may explain the instances of deviation from the norms of either language. In this way the deviations which occur in the speech of bilinguals may be a result of their familiarity with more than one language.

The perception of differences among word meanings in the course of learning a second language, may be responsible for the anomie the learner experiences (Lambert et al. 1963). Differences are rarely perceived as neutral and value judgments are attached if the individual is affected by the difference. The perception of differences between languages may inhibit the realization of the similarities between different language groups. It is only at a later stage of second language competence where the similarities are perceived. At this point, a higher level of generalization is attained. This is where the promise of second language learning becomes materialized: "So viel Sprachen einer kann, so viel mal ist er ein Mensch" (Erdmann, 1925: 125). (As many languages as one knows, so many people does one become.)

Questions

1. List the components of language.
2. Which one is the largest language component and which one is the smallest?
3. List the characteristic(s) of a coordinate bilingual person.
4. List the characteri tic(s) of a compound bilingual person.
5. What are the distinctive features of a bilingual or multilingual person?
6. What are the similarities and differences between a unilingual and bilingual person?

References

Erdmann, K.O. Die Bedeutung des Wortes. Vierte Auflage, H. Haessel Verlag, Leipzig, 1925.

Ervin, S.M. Semantic Shift in Bilingualism. American Journal of Psychology, Vol. 74, 1961, 233-241.

Ervin, S.M. & Osgood, C.E. Second Language Learning and Bilingualism. Journal of Abnormal and Social Psychology, Vol. 49, 1954, 139-146.

Kolers, P. Interlingual Word Associations. Journal of Verbal Learning and Verbal Behavior, Vol. 2, 1963, 291-300.

Lambert, W.E., Havelka, J., & Crosby, C. The Influence of Language Acquisition Contexts on Bilingualism. Journal of Abnormal and Social Psychology, Vol. 56, 1958, 239-244.

Lambert, W.E., Gardner, R.C., Barik, H.C. & Tunstall, K. Attitudinal and Cognitive Aspects of Intensive Study of a Second Language. Journal of Abnormal and Social Psychology, vol. LXVII, 1963, 358-368.

Preston, M.S., & Lambert, W.E. Interlingual Interference in a Bilingual Version of the Stroop Color-Word Task. Journal of Verbal Learning and Verbal Behavior, Vol. 8, April 1969, 295-301.

Rosenzweig, M.R. Comparisons among Word-Association Responses in English, French, German, and Italian. American Journal of Psychology, Vol. 74, 1961, 347-360.

Steiner, G. After Babel. Oxford University Press, New York, 1975.

Vygotsky, L.S. Thought and Language. The M.I.T. Press, Cambridge, 1962.

PART II

COGNATES WITH THE ENGLISH LANGUAGE

The Meaning Component of Words and Cognate Study

An investigation of the extent and limits of semantic overlap of vocabularies in two languages may be clarified by examining the elements of words. A word may consist of three separate but interrelated meaning components: denotative, connotative and conceptual. For example, the denotative meaning of the word "dog" refers to a common domestic animal, the affective meaning depends on whether the individual has had pleasant or unpleasant experiences with dogs generally, and the conceptual meaning, as studied in biology, may be "a carnivorous mammal (*canis familiaris*) of the family Canidae, kept in a domesticated state by man since prehistoric times." In addition, it is not uncommon for a word to have multiple denotative meanings. For example, "dog," in mechanics, refers to "any of various devices, usually of simple design, for holding, gripping, or fastening something." Ultimately, the extent to which the three meaning components of a word are known will influence the degree or extent of understanding.

Paulhan, quoted by Vygotsky (1962: 146), noted that the sense of a word is a "dynamic, fluid, complex whole, which has several zones of unequal stability. . . . A word in a context means both more and less than the same word in isolation: more, because it acquires new content; less, because its meaning is limited and narrowed by the context." According to Paulhan, the sense of a word is "the sum of all the psychological events aroused in our consciousness by the word. Meaning is only one of the zones of sense, the most stable and precise zone. Meaning remains stable throughout the changes of sense."

Although words from two languages may coincide with respect to one of the meaning components, be it affective, denotative, connotative or conceptual, it is unlikely that word meanings are identical in every aspect. In addition, the meaning of a word varies with the concreteness or abstractness of its referent. Words in two languages may not have identical meanings; even within the same language, no two human beings share an identical associative context. Steiner (1975: 198) advanced the thesis that both intralingual and interlingual understanding require a form of translation: "All communication 'interprets' between privacies." Werner and

Kaplan (1963: 50), who discussed the general nature of developmental changes in the symbolic process, noted:

> . . . we do not believe that consensus with respect to the meanings of verbal symbols requires identity of connotations in the different participants: the only requirement is that the connotations evoked in both addressor and addressee occupy a comparable position within each individuals' personal network of meanings.

A second language learner is confronted with the formidable task of acquiring the vocabulary or lexicon of the second language, that is, the denotative, conceptual, connotative and purely affective meanings of words. This task may be facilitated if the learner is able to apply the system of meanings he already possesses in his first language. More rapid learning of a new vocabulary may be achieved if learning is guided from the known to the unknown. By linking the second language vocabulary to the first language, similarities, differences and relationships can be noted. If cognates, or words with similar or identical spelling and similar meaning, are to be efficiently employed in second language learning, the semantic foundation of the first language can and should serve as a basis. With the presence of already prepared and developed meanings of words, the phonetic form of a second language word may be coupled to the meaning of the first. In second language learning, words need not be linked to an object-determined perception if the learner is familiar with equivalent words in his first language; rather, the words of one language may simply be linked with words of another. This linking of words between languages is possible to the extent that word meanings overlap. Learners do not need to build a conceptual framework totally separate from that of their first language; rather they can add to and integrate their first language system with the second language.

Wüster (1959) maintained that,

> Ein richtiges Verstañdnis, eine richtige Handhabung der fremden Sprache, ein Denken in dieser Sprache aber ist nicht möglich, wenn man sich nicht das Begriffssystem dieser Sprache als Ganzes zu eigen gemacht und wenn man nicht die zahllosen Unterschiede des fremden Begriffsystems gegenüber der eigenen Muttersprach erfasst hat (Wüster, 1959: 623).

> (A real understanding, a correct manipulation of a foreign language, a thinking in this language is not possible if one has not acquired the conceptual system

> of this language as a whole and if one does not understand the innumerable differences between the foreign language conceptual system and that of the mother tongue.)

According to Schopenhauer, as cited by Erdmann (1925), a benefit to the learner of a second language, is the possibility of acquiring concepts which do not exist in the mother tongue:

> Indem man also bei Erlernung einer fremden Sprache ganz neue Sphären von Begriffen in seinem Geiste abstecken müsse, erlerne man nicht bloss Wörter, sondern erwerbe Begriffe. Aus diesem Grunde ist die Aneignung mehrerer Sprachen . . . ein tief engreifendes Bildungsmittel (p. 129).
>
> (By learning a second language one acquires an understanding of totally new concepts rather than a simple understanding of words. By increasing the number of concepts through second language learning, second language learning constitutes a profound means of education.)

If subject matter is to be taught in a second language, it is necessary to determine the extent to which words and concepts go hand in hand, and the extent to which students already possess the concepts in their first language but lack the vocabulary to express them in their second. In many cases a secondary school or college student or an adult learner will have attained the concept of an English-French cognate word. Thus, cognate study at these levels may greatly facilitate the acquisition of the conceptual system of the second language.

It may be hypothesized that, by emphasizing cognates to second language learners, there may be initially a _rapprochement_ of the meaning of the cognate words, followed by a differentiation or nuanciation. The acquisition of word meaning in a second language through cognates may parallel the organismic development of moving from a ". . . state of relative globality and undifferentiatedness towards states of increasing differentiation and hierarchic integration" (Werner & Kaplan, 1963: 7). Initially the English-French cognate meanings may be substantially fused with each other but, as the second language study continues, progressive differentiation may occur and, simultaneously, word meanings may be linked or integrated. The broad meaning may be grasped first; a realization of the finer shades and differences of the cognate meaning may follow.

Questions

1. Define denotation, connotation and concept.
2. How do you know that another individual understands what you say?
3. Write a 500 word essay on Steiner's statement: "All communication 'interprets' between privacies."
4. Could this statement apply to second language teaching? How?
5. How would you perceive the meaning acquisition of cognates?

References

Erdmann, K.O. *Die Bedeutung des Wortes*. Vierte Auflage, H. Haessel Verlag, Leipzig, 1925.

Steiner, G. *After Babel*. Oxford University press, New York, 1975.

Vygotsky, L.S. *Thought and Language*. The M.I.T. Press, Cambridge, 1962.

Werner, H., & Kaplan, B. *Symbol Formation*. Clark University, John Wiley & Sons, Inc., New York, 1963.

Wüster, E. Die Struktur der sprachlichen Begriffswelt und ihre Darstellung in Wörterbüchern. *Studium Generale*, Vol. 12, 1959, 615-627.

Deceptive Cognates

Deceptive cognates, or words which, because of their similarity of spelling with English words, might mislead the unwary as to their meaning, have been of interest to translators and second language teachers alike. In order to prevent misunderstandings in translations between the English and French speakers which can ". . . en politique internationale entraîner les plus catastrophiques conséquences" (Boillot, 1956: 7), several word lists of deceptive cognates have been compiled: Boillot published Le Vrai Ami du Traducteur in 1930; Jules Derocquigny investigated deceptive cognates in 1931 in Autres Mots Anglais Perfides; Maxime Koessler and Jules Derocquigny compiled a word list of French-English deceptive cognates entitled Les Faux Amis ou Les Pièges du Vocabulaire Anglais in 1946. About 500 deceptive cognates are listed in this work which incorporates illustrations of cases where deceptive cognates have been incorrectly translated. But since their dictionary of provides examples taken from translations of pre-twentieth century English literature, Koessler and Derocquigny's work has, except for its historical and scholarly interest, little practical value for second language teaching in the classroom.

Charles Downer (1927) investigated deceptive cognates and compiled a list of these words for students of French. He abandoned the idea of compiling a book of deceptive cognates as he found it impossible to make such a work complete and perfectly accurate, and because the English and French languages were infuencing each other so rapidly that semantic distinctions, which formerly could be made with positive assurance, were no longer valid. However, 20 years later, Robert Seward published a Dictionary of French Deceptive Cognates which was not specifically intended for translators but, as the author states, ". . . this list has been made partly as a suggestion to the makers of notes and vocabularies for the classroom texts" (1947: 7). His dictionary, although not specifically compiled for school use, could be employed in the teaching and learning of French as a second language.

Deceptive cognates constitute a potential source of misunderstanding and confusion. Unfortunately, there seems to be a void in the literature dealing with deceptive cognates as they relate to negative transfer. Where there has been an attempt to resolve this void, researchers disagree. Osgood (1949) studied the phenomenon of transfer in human learning and proposed a paradigm with respect to negative transfer. The empirical law associated with this paradigm was expressed in the following way:

> Where stimuli are functionally identical and responses are varied, negative transfer and retroactive interference are obtained, the magnitude of both decreasing as similarity between the responses increases (Osgood, 1949: 135).

This paradigm appears to be applicable to deceptive cognates. However, Debyser (1971: 53) claimed that deceptive cognates are probably the least enduring types of interference between two languages because ". . . les effets au niveau du message sont trop perturbateurs pour ne pas être rapidement corrigés." Current literature has failed to reconcile the two positions. As Scatori (1932) suggested, deceptive cognates have received too little attention.

The deceptiveness of English-French cognates may be visualized along a continuum, that is, cognates differ with respect to the degree with which semantic shifts have occurred in the two languages. Bugelski and Cadwallader (1956), who re-examined Osgood's empirical laws on transfer, noted that when dealing with a given stimulus, the most devastating thing may not be a shift to a very different response, but a shift to a response that is only slightly different. For example, Chantal (1969: 41) listed the main meanings for the word <u>application</u> in English and standard French (SF).

English	Standard French (SF)
1. The application of a theory	1. application d'une théorie
2. application of a poultice	2. application d'un cataplasme
3. application for a job	3. ---------------------

and noted "whereas English and SF share meanings 1 and 2, SF <u>application</u> does not have meaning 3 of its English counterpart, which is rendered by 'candidature'." It may be more difficult for a native French speaker to detect when an English speaker uses a French word with a meaning it has acquired from an English cognate than an incorrect vocabulary choice.

Questions

1. How do you define deceptive cognates?
2. List three examples of deceptive cognates.
3. What strategy would you devise to minimize the potential source of misunderstanding and confusion through deceptive cognates?

References

Boillot, F.F. *Le vrai ami du traducteur anglais-français et français-anglais*. Les Presses universitaires de France, Paris, 1930.

Boillot, F.F. *Le Second Vrai Ami du Traducteur*. Editions J. Oliven, Paris, 1956.

Bugelski, B.R., & Cadwallader, T.C. A Reappraisal of the Transfer and Retroaction Surface. *Journal of Experimental Psychology*, Vol. 52, 1956, 360-366.

Chantal, R. de. The French Language in Canada. in Chantal et al., *The French Language and Culture in Canada* Being the *Hurd Memorial Lectures, 1966-1969*. Delivered at Brandon University, Brandon, Manitoba, 1969, 27-51.

Debyser, F. Comparaison et interférence lexicales. *Le Français dans le Monde*, Nos. 78-85, juin 1971, 51-57.

Derocquigny, J. *A Contribution to the Study of the French Element in English*. Le Bigot Bros. Printers & Publishers, Lille, 1904.

Derocquigny, J. *Autres Mots Anglais Perfides*. Vuibert, Paris, 1931.

Downer, C.A. Deceptive Cognates. *Le Petit Journal*, December 1924.

Downer, C.A. Pitfalls in the French Vocabulary. *Le Petit Journal*, November 1927.

Koessler, M., & Derocquigny, J. *Les Faux Amis*. Librairie Vuibert, Paris, 1946.

Osgood, C.E. The Similarity Paradox in Human Learning: A Resolution. *Psychological Review*, Vol. 56, 1949, 132-143.

Scatori, S. Deceptive Cognates in Spanish. *Modern Language Journal*, Vol. 16, 1932, 396-401.

Seward, R.D. *Dictionary of French Deceptive Cognates*. Bates College, S.F. Vanni, New York, 1947.

The Extent of "Good" Cognates

The English and French languages have not only a common genetic source, but, moreover, have long enjoyed political, cultural, scientific and literary contact and share, with respect to lexis, an extensive vocabulary. Vocabulary similarities exist as a result of 1) the use of Latin and Greek loan-words in the form of radicals, prefixes, and suffixes in the English and French languages, 2) the Norman influence, dating from the eleventh century, which enriched the English language with many French words, 3) the terminology of modern technology common to both English and French, and 4) common lexical borrowings from other languages.

Examining the influence of English on French from a purist's point of view, Bonnaffé compiled the dictionary *L'anglicisme et l'anglo-américanisme dans la langue française* (1920). Paul Barbier (1921) studied loan-words from English in eighteenth century French and described the influence of eighteenth century English on written French (1922). Mackenzie (1939) investigated "les relations de l'Angleterre et de la France d'après le vocabulaire." He identified 4,500 anglicisms found in French and 6,000 gallicisms found in English and determined the points in time when these cultural, technical or scientific terms were introduced into English or French. Mackenzie further showed that French influence has been considerable in the language of the sciences; this, he concludes, is particularly evident in medicine, geology and chemistry as attested by lexical borrowings.

The potential value of cognates, or words which have the same or similar spelling and meaning in two or more languages, as a means of effecting more economical second language vocabulary learning has been recognized and researchers have undertaken the task of determining the extent of the French element in English. Eddy (1926:271) investigated the French element in English "to secure information as to the potential value of French for increased control over the English vocabulary, with the ultimate purpose of paving the way for utilization of this value by English-speaking students of French." She examined the etymological origins of the 10,000 words in Thorndike's *The Teacher's Word Book* (1921) and found that 3,868 or 39 percent of the words have entered the English language directly from French.

However, Eddy made no distinction between source words recognizable and unrecognizable in form by high school students, nor did she determine whether or not these words are familiar to high school students.

Gragg (1942) studied the contribution of high school Latin, French and Spanish to English vocabulary building. Based upon a study of the relationships of words close enough in form and meaning to assist students in learning the new English words through transfer, he found that the potential contribution for French is 38 percent, of which 29 percent have related words in pre-high school English. Gragg concluded that "students of foreign language in the high school have two bases for understanding new words: That of related words in pre-high school English, and that of related words in the foreign language" (Gragg, 1942: 622).

Chirol (1973) undertook a semantic analysis of approximately 2,500 French words used in English. She wrote:

> . . . nous empruntons à l'étranger des choses qui nous font défaut et nous paraissent particulièrement utiles, pratiques, enviables, ou bizarres, curieuses, comiques (p. 13) . . . ce que l'anglais emprunte à la France à travers ses mots c'est un art-de-vivre et un savoir-vivre (Chirol, 1973: 32).

Chirol maintained that French technical and scientific vocabulary was completely assimilated in English. However, where the vocabulary refers to "un art-de-vivre (mode, cuisine, arts, relations sociales, etc.)" (Chirol, 1973: 29), the words tended to keep identifying features of their French origin. She explained this phenomenon:

> Historiquement, la français a été la langue de la noblesse anglo-normande; par la suite il est resté celui des cours et de la diplomatie; cet héritage reste visiblement inscrit dans nos inventaires et plus encore dans les contextes où s'inscrivent ces mots. (Le mot "français") apparaît comme la marque d'une culture d'importation qui est l'apanage d'une élite mais absolument refusée par le 'peuple'. Le mot "français" est un produit de luxe, d'importation étrangère et qui n'a pas cours sur le marché indigène (Chirol, 1973: 26-27).

The extent of commonality of vocabulary between the English and French languages was determined by a systematic review of the Larousse Dictionnaire Moderne Francais-Anglais (1960). This review resulted in a word list of 10,993 English-French cognates with the same or similar spelling and meaning (Hammer & Monod, 1976). Deceptive cognates or words which have the same spelling in the two languages but different meanings, were excluded from the list using Les Faux Amis (1946) by Koessler and Derocquigny and Seward's Dictionary of French Deceptive Cognates (1947).

For the purpose of language study, cognates are words that are similar or identical in form and meaning in two or more languages. Loan words, or words which have been borrowed from one language for use in another, are treated as cognates if they are similar in form and meaning. For example, English and French both adopted the word "malaria" from the Italian language. If two words have the same origin but are now so different that speakers of the two languages do not identify them as similar, they are not considered cognates. The term similar is restricted here to include items that have the "same" meaning in both languages in ordinary use. Similar in form refers either to a change of one letter in the spelling of the French and English word, for example, oncle-uncle, avantage-advantage, or to the following regularities among others if the spelling of the English and French words are otherwise the same:

Nouns

1.	French -té (542)	= English -ty
	qualité	quality
2.	French -ie (533)	= English -y
	industrie	industry
3.	French -re (339)	= English -er (or) -re
	mètre	meter
	centre	center
	agriculture	agriculture
4.	French -isme (302)	= English -ism
	communisme	communism
5.	French -nce (274)	= English -nce (or) -ncy
	fréquence	frequence, frequency
6.	French -iste (259)	= English -ist
	journaliste	journalist
7.	French -eur (160)	= English -or (or) -er
	acteur	actor
	employeur	employer
8.	French -cien (10)	= English -cian

	électricien		electrician
9.	French -ion (1,176)	=	English -ion
	omission		omission
	aviation		aviation
	Verbs		
10.	French -er (829)	=	English: drop -er (or) -r
	confesser		to confess
	commencer		to commence
11.	French -ier (107)	=	English -y
	varier		to vary
	Adjectives		
12.	French -ique (605)	=	English -ic
	classique		classic
13.	French -if, ive (196)	=	English -ive
	collectif		collective
14.	French -eux, euse (161)	=	English -ous
	curieux		curious
15.	French -é (104)	=	English -ed
	sacré		sacred
16.	French -tiel, elle (16)	=	English -tial
	confidentiel		confidential

The numbers in parentheses indicate the frequency of the cognates within each word-ending similarity class. For example, there are 542 cognates which have the French "-té" and English "-ty" ending. The cognates with these sixteen word-ending regularities account for 5,613 of the 10,993 words in the cognate list. These cognate word-ending regularities include at least ten cognates, they are easily recognized, and there are almost no spelling exceptions.

Questions

1. Do you think the extent of the French element in English justifies a cognate approach? Please support your answer.
2. Have you relied on or made use of cognates in your own second language study?

3. If your answer was "no" to question 2 could you give any reasons why not?
4. What could be some disadvantages of cognate study?

References

Barbier, P. Review of Edouard Bonnaffé's Dictionary. *The Modern Language Review*, Vol. 16, January 1921, 90-94.

Barbier, P. Loan-Words from English in Eighteenth Century French. *The Modern Language Review*, Vol. 16, January 1921, 138-149, and 252-264.

Barbier, P. Some Notes on English Influence in the Vocabulary of Written French. *The Modern Languages Journal*, Vol. 4, October 1922, 139-146.

Bonnaffé, E. *Dictionnaire Etymologique et Historique des Anglicismes*.

Bonnaffé, E. Anglicismes et mots d'influence anglaise. *The French Quarterly*. Manchester, September 1922, 164-171.

Chirol, L. *Les "mots français" et le mythe de la France en anglais contemporain*. Editions Klincksieck, Paris, 1973.

Dubois, M.-M. *Dictionnaire Moderne Français-Anglais*. Librairie Larousse, Paris, 1960.

Eddy, H.M. The French Element in English. *The Modern Languages Journal*, Vol. X, 1926, 271-280.

Gragg, D.B. The Contribution of High-School Latin, French, and Spanish to English Vocabulary. *Journal of Educational Psychology*, Vol. 33, November 1942, 615-622.

Hammer, P., & Monod, M.J. *English-French Cognate Dictionary*. The University of Alberta, Edmonton, 1976.

Koessler, M., & Derocquigny, J. *Les Faux Amis*. Librairie Vuibert, Paris, 1946.

Mackenzie, F. *Les relations de l'Angleterre et de la France d'après le vocabulaire*. Paris, 1939.

Seward, R.D. *Dictionary of French Deceptive Cognates*. Bates College, S.F. Vanni, New York, 1947.

Thorndike, E.L. *The Teacher's Word Book*. Teachers College, Columbia University, New York, 1921.

Frequency Ratings of the English-French Cognates

Word-count studies and word frequency lists reflected the effort of researchers to determine a possible basic vocabulary for the functional teaching of French. The compilation of _Le Français Fondamental, (Premier et deuxième degré)_ in 1959 was an example. Its aim is ". . . qu'il fournit des moyens d'expression suffisants, . . . en vue de l'acquisition du "français complet." Jean-Guy Savard and Jack Richards compiled a word list with "les indices d'utilité du vocabulaire fondamental français" (Savard & Richards, 1970) and Mackey, Savard and Ardouin (1971) investigated "le vocabulaire disponible du français." The purpose of constructing these word lists was to determine the utility and availability of the French vocabulary necessary to communicate at a basic level in French.

Since English vocabulary power of students differs and English-French cognates are useful only to the extent that the student knows their meaning in English, the selection of English-French cognates for different grade levels is of paramount importance. To facilitate the cognate selection for school use the authors applied the frequency and utility index for French words of _Le Français Fondamental Premier Degré, Les indices d'utilité du vocabulaire fondamental français_ by Savard and Richards (1970) and _Le vocabulaire disponible du français_ by Mackey, Savard and Ardouin (19701) to the cognate list. The 1,445 lexical items listed in _Le Français Fondamental, Premier Degré_ contained 171 cognates on the authors' list. These words are identified in the English-French cognate dictionary with two capital F's in brackets [FF].

Savard and Richards (1970) examined the 3,300 lexical items listed in _Le Français Fondamental,_ and added to the indices of frequency and distribution of words their availability and valence which were combined in one index, that of utility of the French words. Of the 3,300 lexical items examined by Savard and Richards (1970) 1,072 are contained in the cognate list. These are identified witha capital S in brackets [S].

Mackey _et al_ (1971: 38) examined _Le vocabulaire concret et usuel des enfants français et acadiens._ About 5,000 words were collected from approximately 700 students between the ages of nine and twelve from about twenty different classes in about twelve schools in Acadia. Students were asked to write twenty words for each of the following centers of interest:

> 1) Les parties du corps, 2) les vêtements (homme et femme), 3) la maison (sans les meubles), 4) les meubles, 5) la nourriture, 6) les objets sur la table, 7) la cuisine, 8) l'école, 9) l'éclairage et chauffage, 10) la ville, 11) le village, 12) les moyens de transport, 13) les travaux des champs, 14) les animaux domestiques, 15) les amusements, 16) les métiers (Mackey _et al_, 1971: 21).

1,104 words from Mackey _et al_'s list contained in the English-French cognate word list are identified with a capital M in brackets [M].

Of the English-French cognates rated with Savard _et al_ (1970) and Mackey _et al_ (1971)'s French frequency word lists, 404 words were contained in both their lists. Of the lexical items listed in _Le Français Fondamental, Premier Degré_ 106 were contained in Savard _et al_'s word list and 94 in Mackey _et al_'s. Thus, 1,837 English-French cognates are of high frequency and utility in French.

It should be noted that the criteria of high frequency and high utility in French does not necessarily mean that these words are frequent in English. The vocabulary of Acadian French-speaking children was used to compile Mackey _et al_'s word list. Thus, only words common to children's vocabularies were included. The cognates identified with Mackey _et al_'s word list may be useful for English-speaking children of the same age group who study French as a second language.

For the English-French cognate dictionary the frequency ratings of the English cognate words were also established using Kucera and Francis' (1967) _Computational Analysis of Present-Day American English_. Unlike the frequency ratings of the French word lists cited earlier, the aim of Kucera and Francis' study was not to determine a basic vocabulary or the "most common" words of English but rather to compile a corpus of printed American English published in a single calendar year (Kucera & Francis, 1967: xviii). The corpus is composed of 500 samples of roughly equal length, that is, 2,000 words drawn from 15 genres, ranging from ". . . the sports page of the newspaper to the scientific journal and from popular romantic fiction to abstruse philosophical discussion" (Kucera & Francis, 1967: xix). The authors stated:

> The alphabetical list of the Corpus contains a complete listing of all the 50,406 distinct graphic words that occur in the corpus (p.3). The first one hundred most

> frequent words of the Corpus account for only 0.198 percent of the types (words) in the Corpus . . . (and) low frequency words occurring no more than ten times include 42,487 words and constitute 84.29 percent of the total number of different words in the Corpus (Kucera & Francis, 1967: 295).

The authors drew the reader's attention to the following delimitations of their word list:

> no distinction is made between homographs and homologs (p. xxi) (and that) the _Hapax legomeno_ is sensitive to some quantitative constrains of corpus size and probably also to qualitative genre influences (Kucera & Francis, 1967: vii).

It may be added that frequently used words can be expected to have a variety of meaning. Word counts, however, list only the frequency of spellings and generally ignore semantic variations.

The English word frequency ratings are noted in the English-French cognate dictionary with the English word. The letters Ku refer to Kucera and Francis' word list, followed by three figures separated by dashes. Following the system used by Kucera and Francis, the first figure gives the actual frequency of occurrence of the word in the Corpus. The second figure designates the number of genre subdivisions in which the word occurs, and the third figure gives the number of samples in which the word is found. Approximately forty-five percent or 4,929 of the English cognate words are rated with this reference. Of the English-Franch cognates rated with Kucera's word list 262 are rated with Savard's system, 269 are rated with Mackey's and 4 are rated with the system employed in _Le Français Fondamental_ French frequency ratings.

An examination of the English-French cognates reveals the following interesting characteristics: 1,837 cognates are of high frequency in French as rated with _Le Français Fondamental_, and in Savard's and Mackey's frequency ratings. The English frequency ratings of the cognates indicate that these words occurred predominatnly only once in Kucera's Corpus as the ratings 1-01-001 shows. The cognates in this list appear to comprise three strata: the 1,837 high frequency cognates in French, the 4,929 cognates rated with the English frequency ratings and the remaining 4,227 cognates not rated with any of the frequency lists applied.

Many of the ten thousand nine hundred ninety three (10,993) distinct cognates contained in the English-French cognate dictionary may be used in different contexts and their meanings overlap in different realms. For example, the sense of the French word "conversion" used in ecclesiastical, mathematical, financial or philosophical contexts may be expressed by the English word "conversion", and the adjective "harmonique" may be used to express the sense of the corresponding English word in musical or mathematical contexts. Including their number would likely exceed 10,993.

An analysis and frequency count of the English-French cognates was performed to identify in which contexts meanings overlapped. This analysis revealed that:

1174 are medical terms
377 are chemistry terms
338 are ecclesiastical terms
235 are botany terms
219 are jurisprudence terms
217 are zoology terms
210 are music terms
206 are mathematic terms
201 are military terms
198 are geography terms
177 are physics terms
170 are grammar terms
151 are electricity terms
150 are colloquial terms
126 are technology terms
115 are philosophy terms
112 are culinary terms
104 are sports terms
100 are art terms
93 are commerce terms
89 are finance terms
88 are architecture terms
78 are nautical terms
74 are astronomy terms
58 are theatre terms
57 are aviation terms
41 are agriculture terms
30 are automobilism terms
27 are radiophony terms
24 are heraldry terms
16 are geology terms
14 are railway terms
10 are cimematography terms
2 are popular terms

This listing, however, does not account for the number of terms which are cognates within two or more categories.

An alphabetical listing of the English-French cognates rated with *Le français fondamental*, *Les indices d'utilité du vocabulaire français* and *Le vocabulaire disponible du français* is presented in appendix C. For further information about the respective English and Franch word frequency studies applied to the cognate list, the reader is referred to:

Kucera, H., and Francis, N.W. *Computational Analysis of Present-Day American English*. Providence, Brown University Press, 1967.

Le Français Fondamental, (Premier Degré). Institut Pédagogique National, Ministère de l'Éducation Nationale, Direction de la Coopération, Paris, 1959.

Mackey, W.F., Savard, J.-G., and Ardouin, P. *Le Vocabulaire disponible du français*, Marcel Didier (Canada) Ltée. Montréal, 1971.

Savard, J.-G., & Richards, J. *Les indices d'utilité du vocabulaire fondamental français*, Les Presses de l'Université Laval, Québec, 1970.

Foreign Language Vocabulary Study

Research should be directed towards determining how one can learn a foreign language with a minimum effort. There is no royal road to fluency in a language, however, some strategies may be better than others, depending on the language skills to be acquired and the ability of the learner. A minimum vocabulary of individual words and a minimum of grammatical rules, i.e., rules about how words change and how to arrange them in a sentence, are the essential components of a foreign language program for self-expression or for receptive comprehension.

Depending on the language skills to be acquired, learning to read, learning to express oneself in speech or in writing, and learning to follow the course of ordinary conversation represent different problems and require different teaching and learning strategies. Bodmer (1944: 151) summarized the essential differences between the skill required for wide reading and the skill required for proficient self-expression as follows:

> To express ourselves correctly we need to have a *ready* knowledge of a *relatively* small number of words -- fifteen hundred or two thousand at most -- and a *precise knowledge* of the *essential* grammatical conventions of *straightforward statement.* To read widely without a dictionary, we need a *nodding acquiantance* with a relatively *large* vocabulary *(fifteen thousand* words may be given as a rough estimate), and a general familiarity with a *wide range* of grammatical conventions, which we can recognize at sight, if meaningful (Bodmer, 1944: 15).

Oral recognition of ordinary conversation appears to be acquired last since the need for oral recognition does not arise in an acute form unless we are living in the country where the language is habitually spoken. Anyone who can read, write or speak can learn to understand a language when he or she hears it spoken incessantly.

The problem of how to determine a minimum vocabulary has been examined from a statistical analysis used in compiling and examining word lists, a semantic analysis of words and a comparative study of cognates and international words of various languages. Word-count studies and word frequency lists reflect the effort of researchers to determine a possible basic or minimum vocabulary for the functional teaching of a foreign language. From frequency counts, the proportion of words belonging to the various parts of speech was also determined. A semantic analysis of words by C. K. Ogden resulted in a word list of approximately 850 words which are needed in order to define something for which you do not already know the right word. The interrelationship among the Indo-European languages has been examined with reference to English.

> A random sample of one word from each of the first thousand pages of the Concise Oxford Dictionary gives the following figures: words of Romance (Latin, French, Italian, Spanish) origin 53.6 percent, Teutonic (Old English, Scandinavian, Dutch, German) 31.1 percent, and Greek 10.8 percent (Bodmer, 1944: 30).

For speaking and writing the required mimimum vocabulary was estimated to be about fifteen hundred words. Bodmer (1944: 18) suggested that a vocabulary of less than two thousand words is sufficient for fluent self-expression in any European tongue. For reading novels the vocabulary has been estimated to be fifteen thousand.

A possible strategy for vocabulary acquisition could proceed in the following manner based on the various vocabulary analyses. First concentrate your effort on pronouns, determiners, auxiliaries, prepositions and conjunctions. They are essential words in sentences, are not the sort of words of which the meaning can be guessed, are relatively few in number (approximately 200 words), and occur frequently. Bodmer (1944: 214) wrote that with 150 such words for ready use, which can be learned at the rate of ten new words in two weeks, you will have at your disposal at least 25 per cent of the total number of words you use when you write a letter. Word frequency counts can be used as a first step toward the selection of a reading vocabulary but the limitations of word frequency counts should be kept in mind: frequency counts of words vary according to the kind of language material selected, and frequency counts do not necessarily take semantic variations into considerations. For a speaking or writing vocabulary, a semantic selection of words may be more appropriate. Bodmer (1944: 508) suggested that word economy depends on judicious selection of general terms and descriptive periphrases for specific uses. To use this principle, the components must be elements of the basic minimum of essential words and the juxtaposition of parts must sufficiently indicate the meaning, for example, theater - playhouse. Bodmer (1944: 510) wrote:

> By combining sixteen fundamental verb substitutes (come, get, give, go, keep, let, make, put, seem, take, be, do,

> have, say, see, send) with other essential items of the word list Basic English thus provides an adequate Ersatz for four thousand verbs in common use (e.g., to go on, to make up, to get on).

Finally, words which look alike or similar in two or more languages and usually have an area of common meaning, may be guessed more easily in print than in speech.

Questions

1. How would you match foreign language skills to be acquired with the ability of the learner?
2. How have vocabularies been examined? List three methods employed in conducting foreign language vocabulary analyses.
3. What strategy would you devise for foreign language vocabulary learning?
4. What would you do with cognates and international words in your foreign language class? Support your method with evidence.

References

Bodmer, F. The Loom of Language. W.W. Norton & Company, Inc., New York, 1944.

Lademann, N. Zur Problematik der Einheit von Denken und Sprechen bei der Erarbeitung fremdsprachiger lexikalischer Kenntnisse und ihre Realisierung mit Hilfe visuell-bildlicher Unterrichtsmittel, Arbeitsbericht Nr. 47, Martin-Luther Universität, Halle-Wittenberg, 1977.

PART III

THE UTILITY OF COGNATES

The Appropriate Age Levels at Which to Study a Second Language with Cognates

Knowledge of one's first language may facilitate, through transferable elements, the acquisition of a related second language. However, the degree of complementary relationship may depend, not only upon the extent of commonality between two related languages, but also upon the degree of cognitive development of the student.

To exploit similarities of related languages, the appropriate age levels for cognate learning may be that of students in secondary school years. University students and interested adults could also profit from studying a second language using a cognate approach. These tentative conclusions are based on the assumption that high school students and educated adults could benefit most from cognate study because of the characteristics of the learner (he or she is older, more mature, and, generally, has a greater attention span, power of analysis and language competence). Moreover, the younger child mimics well, but as the child becomes able to learn and apply rules, cognate language analysis provides explanations which will help him to recognize and to remember facts of a language for a considerable length of time.

Piaget, as quoted by Wadsworth (1971), identified two processes, assimilation and accommodation, which account for the cognitive growth and development of the human being. Schemata, which develop over time and with experience, are intellectual structures into which events are organized according to common characteristics as they are perceived by the organism. Awareness of similarities and differences appears to be essential for the formation of concepts. Assimilation, according to Piaget, is the cognitive process by which the individual person adds new perceptual matter or stimulus events into existing schemata or patterns of behavior. It accounts for the growth of schemata. Accommodation, according to Piaget is the creation of new schemata or the modification of old schemata. Accommodation thus accounts for the change of schemata.

These two processes, assimilation and accommodation, appear to operate in second language acquisition, where assimilation may be equated with the acquisition of similarities, and accommodation with the acquisition of differences. Claparède's (1916) law specified the order in which the two processes operate, that is, awareness of differences precedes the awareness of likeness, or accommodation precedes assimilation. Vygotsky (1962: 88) explained this sequence of Claparède's law by suggesting that "the awareness of similarities requires a more advanced structure of generalization and conceptualization than awareness of dissimilarities." If this assumption is correct, this argument would provide another reason to use high school and post high school students as the appropriate age group for cognate study.

In order to arrive at a determination of the appropriate age levels for studying French through the use of cognates, the following learning concepts are assumed: 1. words that are frequently used in French are words of high utility; 2. if these words also have cognates in English, they will be most appropriate for teaching utilitarian French to Anglophone students; and 3. if these words are in common usage among various age groups of French speakers, they will not be too advanced for English speaking high school or university students.

The frequency and utility of cognates in the Hammer and Monod (1976) list were determined using the studies of Mackey, Savard and Ardouin (1971) and those of Savard and Richards (1970). It should be noted that the criteria of high frequency and high utility in French does not necessarily mean that these words are frequent in English. However, it is assumed that the English-French cognates identified with Mackey *et al.*'s and Savard and Richards' word lists correlate positively with the vocabulary knowledge in English of secondary and university students.

Questions

1. What is the appropriate age group for cognate study?
2. How was the appropriate age group for cognate study determined?
3. The benefit a student could derive from cognate study depends on two factors. Please list them.
4. State Claparède's law and illustrate it with an example.

References

Claparède, E. *Psychologie de l'enfant et pédagogie expérimentale*. Septième édition, Librairie Kundig, Genève, 1916.

Hammer, P., & Monod, M.J. English-French Cognate Dictionary. The University of Alberta, Edmonton, 1976.

Mackey, W.F., Savard, J.-G., & Ardouin, P. Le vocabulaire disponible du français, Marcel Didler (Canada) Ltée., Montreal, 1971.

Savard, J.-G. & Richards, J. Les indices d'utilité du vocabulaire fondamental français, Les Presses de l'Université Lavel, Québec, 1970.

Vygotsky, L.S. Thought and Language. The M.I.T. Press, Cambridge, 1962.

Wadsworth, B.J. Piaget's Theory of Cognitive Development, David McKay Company, Inc., New York, 1971.

Experimental Testing of the Utility of Cognates in Second Language Acquisition

On the basis of similarity in spelling and meaning, researchers have suggested that there should be a high transfer value of French words to the corresponding words in English. However, the actual amount of transfer can only be determined by scientific and systematic experimentation. Verifying studies in this area of transfer remain few.

Limper (1932) performed a study dealing with student knowledge of some English-French cognates. The purpose of his study was to determine whether or not French words in English are recognized by a large percentage of students; he intended to help textbook writers to determine which words have to be listed in a glossary accompanying a reading text. He chose 1,499 words from the Vander Beke's French Word Book (1929) which have the same or similar spelling and meaning as the corresponding English words, and he then designed simple-recall tests. Students were asked to write the English word which the French word suggested to them. Words whose English cognates did not appear in the first five thousand words of the Thorndike (1921) list were arranged in multiple choice tests to determine whether students knew the English meaning of the French word (Limper, 1932: 41). These tests were administered to grade nine, grade eleven and first year college students in a number of schools in the mid-west of the United States. The sample was composed totally of students who had not studied French previously. Limper found that the recognition of cognates cannot be taken for granted, nor can it be assumed that their cognate meanings are understood. Both factors could limit the possible utility of cognates in second language instruction and learning.

West (1934) addressed the same issue. He explained that the degree to which cognates may be recognized and understood depended upon the context, the age of the student, his vocabulary power in his mother tongue and upon the amount of practice he has had with cognates. West advocated that students should be taught to guess the meaning of unfamiliar lexical items but to do so cautiously and wisely.

Although English-French cognates received some atention in the past, little research has been done recently. Eichler (1972) investigated the effects of cognate usage on foreign language speaking proficiency (German, French and Spanish). Specifically, he sought to answer the question: "Is there a difference in effectiveness between cognate and conventional usage as measured by the French MLA pre- and post-speaking tests giving scores in mimicry, oral reading, direct response, and free description?" (Eichler, 1972: 7). No statistically significant differences were found in the analyses, but mean differences in favor of the cognate group were observed on the free description variable. Eichler wrote that "any definite conclusions based on effectiveness relative to cognate usage would be premature. In view of the movement of the free description cores in the direction projected by the research hypothesis, it was felt that additional time might eventually have produced significant differences" (Eichler, 1972: 63).

In 1975 a study (Hammer, 1975) was conducted to determine whether grade ten students were able to utilize English-French cognates in listening and reading comprehension of French. As part of the study, students were taught the phonemic and spelling alterations influencing English-French cognates.

Seventy-four students with four years of French, comprising three intact grade ten classes, participated. Each intact class was randomly assigned to one of the three possible groups: Group A, the control group, Group B, which received instruction in the oral recognition of cognates, and Group C which received instruction involving the written recognition of cognates. The pretest - posttest control group design (Campbell & Stanley,

It was found on the pretest that without any prior cognate training, the three group means on the written cognate recognition test (WCRT) were within a very close range 19.58, 19.44, 19.52 whereas there was a larger range among the group means on the oral cognate recognition test (OCRT) 17.21, 18.88 and 18.00 respectively. This observation supported Hammer's theoretical assumption and that of Mackey (1972), that written cognates, which share the graphemic, lexical and semantic realm in two vocabulary systems, are more uniformly identified than orally presented cognates which share the lexical and semantic realm but are more difficult to identify because of phonetic differences. In silent reading of the WCRT, phonetic differences may not figure as predominantly as in the OCRT.

Statistically significantly improved performances on the oral and written cognate posttests were found for the experimental groups but not for the control group. In addition, the written cognate recognition group performed statistically significantly better, not only on the written cognate post test, but also on the oral cognate post test. The reverse transfer effect from the oral recognition of cognates to reading recognition and comprehension of cognates was not found.

To determine whether there is any relationship between English vocabulary power, as measured with the Quick-Scoring Vocabulary Test (QSVT), and the ability to recognize cognates in an oral and/or a written setting, the test scores on the QSVT, WCRT and OCRT were correlated. The correlations of the QSVT and the cognate tests were statistically significant with one exception. The correlation of the QSVT and WCRT posttest for Group B (the oral cognate recognition group) was not statistically significant. It appears, therefore, that English vocabulary power is not the only necessary precondition for cognate usage in the oral acquisition of a second and related language. It was strongly suggested, however, that it is helpful in conjunction with the ability to recognize cognates.

In summary, agreement has been found on the following points in studies dealing with English-French cognates: 1. the ratio of cognates to deceptive cognates is approximately eleven to one; 2. cognates are regarded as an efficient vocabulary acquisition device; and 3. cognates are suggested to be most useful in reading a second language.

To test the effectiveness of cognate study a University experiment was conducted with second year French students. A control and an experimental group were required. The experimental treatment used in the study consisted of an English-French cognate unit which contains a systematic exposition of cognates, French excerpts to practice the recognition of and comprehension with cognates, ten example words for each of the ten cognate word-ending regularities and a short review of some of the characteristics of some parts of speech. Fifteen minutes per lesson of class time in a week were devoted to the unit. The seven lessons of the cognate unit were covered in a period of six weeks from October 22, to December 1, 1976. The MLA French reading test, Form LA and Form MA, served as the pre- and posttest measures. An English reading test, Jewell's (1969) Reading Comprehension Test for Senior High School Students in Large Urban Areas in Alberta, was selected as a covariate.

No statistically significant mean differences between the two groups on the French reading pre- and posttest were found nor did the control and experimental group means differ statistically significantly on the Jewell English reading test. Conclusions concerning cognates as an efficient approach to second language vocabulary acquisition must be tentative and must be viewed in terms of two possible limitations. First, the test used, the MLA French reading test, is not a cognate measuring instrument. Secondly, it is probable that first and second language learning do not correspond to a straight learning curve but rather conform more closely in form to a parabola. This explanation holds that, initially, in second language study, reading is hampered by unfamiliar vocabulary and syntax. However, as the student advances in his second language study, unfamiliar lexical items and syntax decrease and a positive relationship of reading in two languages emerges.

To determine the possible relationship between English reading compehension ability, as measured with Jewell's test, and French reading comprehension ability, as measured with the MLA reading rest, the scores of these tests were correlated. For the 38 students in second year French, low negative to moderately high positive correlation coefficients were found. None were statistically significant. Apart from the idiosyncrasy of the students in the control and experimental group and the relatively small sample size, the observed fluctuating correlation coeffcients for the Jewell English reading test and the French MLA reading pre- and posttest may be a result of different emphasis accorded to reading in previous French instruction. The observed correlation coefficients of the scores in the university experiment suggested that there was little relationship between the English and French reading tests.

An experiment testing the efficiency of cognate study was also conducted with grade ten students. The experiment started April 13, 1977 with the pretest administration of the French MLA reading test Form LA and the Jewell English reading test and concluded with the French MLA reading test Form LB on June 6, 1977. The students in the experimental groups received a copy of the English-French cognate unit while the students in the control groups did not. A delayed written cognate recognition test part 1 (WCRT 1) was administered June 22, 1977, two weeks following the conclusion of the experiment proper.

Two teachers with two French II classes each participated in the study. Teacher number one had 36 French II students who are in their fourth year of French study. One intact class of 18 students was randomly assigned to the control group and the other class of 18 students was assigned to the experimental group. Teacher number two had 30 French II students, of which one intact class of 15 students was randomly assigned to the control group and the other class to the experimental group. One lesson per week of the English-French cognate unit was assigned. The teacher clarified grammar points in the cognate unit. The questions at the end of each lesson in the cognate unit were corrected in class at the end of each week.

As in the university experiment, the possible relationship of English reading comprehension ability, as measured with Jewell's test, and French reading comprehension ability, as measured with the MLA reading test Form LA and LB, was examined by correlating the scores of these tests. The correlation coefficients for the English and French reading tests fluctuated for the control and experimental groups of both teachers. Whether a difference in emphasis on the reading skills during previous French instruction of the students in the control and experimental groups may have caused the fluctuations is speculative. The fluctuations may also have been due to the small sample for which the correlation coefficients were calculated. The results were too inconclusive to postulate a curve-like relationship between first and second language acquisition.

The between group mean differences on the French MLA reading test, Form LA and LB, and the Jewell English reading test of the control and experimental groups of teachers number one and two were tested for statistical significance. No statistically significant mean differences were found for the control and experimental groups of teachers one and two on the French MLA reading test, Form LA and LB serving as pre- and posttest, although the experimental groups of both teachers scored a higher mean on the French MLA reading posttest than their respective control group counterparts. Since the French MLA reading test is not exlusively a cognate measuring instrument, the results appear to be limited by the test used to assess the efficiency of the cognate approach.

The within group mean difference for the control and experimental groups of teachers number one and two was also tested for statistical significance. The within group mean difference on the French MLA reading pre- and posttest was statistically significant at the 0.01 level for the control group and at the 0.003 level for the experimental group of teacher number one. The control group of teacher number two had no statistically significant pretest/posttest mean difference nor did the mean difference for the experimental group reach statistical significance. Thus, student rates of learning for teachers number one and two differed.

The written cognate recognition test Part 1 (WCRT 1) was used as a delayed posttest for the control and experimental groups of teacher number one and teacher number two. The mean difference on the WCRT 1 for the control and experimental group of teacher number one reached a probability level of 0.07 which fell short of being statistically significant at the 0.05 level. On the WCRT 1, which is a cognate measuring instrument, the experimental group had a higher mean than the control group. Thus, after a delayed period of two weeks the cognate studying effect resulted in a mean difference between the control and the experimental group at the 0.07 level of significance. For teacher number two the delayed WCRT 1 posttest mean difference between the control and experimental group did not even approach statistical significance. Since the students of teacher number two had no statistically significant improved pretest/posttest gain, it appears likely that students may not have learned enough about cognates during the seven week experiment to apply this cognate knowledge on a delayed written cognate recognition test.

The same experiment, procedures, experimental curriculum and grade level were performed with a third grade ten teacher. However, the French MLA reading test Form LA and LB was replaced with a written cognate recognition test, Part 1 (WCRT 1) serving as the pretest and Part 2 (WCRT 2) as the posttest.

For the students in the control and experimental group, statistically significant positive correlation coefficients were found on the Jewell English reading test and the WCRT 1 and 2. Thus, a high test score on the

Jewell English reading test tended to correlate with a high score on the WCRT. The mean difference between the scores of the control and experimental group on the WCRT 1, which served as pretest, was not statistically significantly different. However, with the WCRT 2, which served as posttest, the experimental group had a statistically significantly higher mean than the control group. Thus, the experimental group studying the English-French cognate unit performed statistically significantly better than the control group when a cognate measuring instrument was employed.

The cognate approach to second language teaching is more than a methodology in isolation. Rather, it is an approach that can be used in conjunction with any second language teaching methodology. The commonalities between languages are not necessarily recognized by all students and should be pointed out explicitly when a cognate approach is incorporated. The definition of cognates and their characteristics is factual information which may reinforce the unconscious strategy of some students, or may open new avenues to students who have not noticed the similarities. It is particularly at the secondary and university levels that teachers may find optimum utility in the cognate approach.

University students scored a higher mean on the Jewell English reading test and the French MLA reading test Form LA than grade ten students. It appears probable that for university students some of the material included in the cognate unit used in this study was too simple. The definition of cognates and their characteristics presented in the cognate unit may be interesting, factual information. The review of some characteristics of the parts of speech and the excerpts could be omitted for university students who know this material and have no difficulty recognizing cognates.

The implications of two findings of the study not directly related to the hypotheses investigated are worthy of mention. A statistically significant difference between teacher number one and two, as measured by students' scores on the MLA French reading posttest, was found in the study with grade ten students. A possible explanation for the teacher difference was that one teacher was a native French speaker and the other was not. The statistically significantly better test performance of the students of a native French-speaking teacher in comparison with a non-native French-speaking teacher appears to be consistent with Ach's (1971) criteria of word meaning acquisition. According to Ach, it is the functional purpose of communication between human beings which leads to meaning acquisiton" (p. 303). (Das Funktionelle Moment der Verständigung zwischen zwei Menschen ist es das zur autochtonen Bedeutungsverleihung führt.) A native French-speaking teacher may not only speak more French during the class, but the student may also be impelled to gain understanding through that language.

The other finding not directly related to the hypotheses under study was that a statistically significant difference at the the 0.001 level was found for high versus low pretest scores. Students who had a high pretest score did not perform statisticaly significantly better on the posttest. However, for students with a low pretest score it was found that the level of probability is one in a thousand that a student will improve statistically significantly on the posttest. Possible explanations for this finding may be that test results show the student how well he has mastered the subject material. In addition, if the test score is low, parents may impose restrictions until better test results are achieved. Also, higher test scores of peers may motivate a student to work harder and to do better. Then too, it is possible that the cognate approach provided a new and more efficient learning avenue for this low scoring group.

The most important implication of the results of the present study was that university and grade ten students using the English-French cognate unit had a higher mean score than the control groups on a standardized French reading test, the MLA Form LB, serving as the posttest, and a statistically significantly higher mean on the WCRT posttest. The lack of a statistically significant mean difference for the control and experimental groups on the French MLA posttest was not considered necessarily to indicate a shortcoming of the English-French cognate unit, but rather the short duration of the experiment may have been responsible. It may be noted that only the students in the experimental group of teacher number one, who spent approximately twice the amount of personel time on the cognate unit than the students in the experimental group of teacher number two, had a statistically significant pretest/posttest mean difference on the French MLA reading test.

Questions

1. How would you test the possible utility of cognates?
2. What are the limitations of cognate study? Can you list more than four?
3. In what language skill are cognates most useful? Justify your answer.
4. What is the ratio of "good" cognates to "deceptive" cognates?
5. Could you suggest reasons for the dearth of experimental studies to verify the utility of cognates?
6. List three implications of a cognate approach to second language teaching.
7. State the two findings which were not directly related to the hypotheses investigated.
8. Would you adopt a cognate approach to second language acquisition? Please support your decision.

References

Campbell, D.T., & Stanley, J.C. Experimental and Quasi-Experimental Designs for Research. Rand McNally College Publishing Company, Chicago, 1973.

Eichler, J. The Effects of Cognate Usage on Foreign Language Speaking Proficiency. Ph.D. Thesis, University of Wyoming, 1972.

Hammer, P. The Role of English-French Cognates in Listening and Reading Comprehension in the Learning of French as a Second Language. M. Ed. Thesis, the University of Alberta, Edmonton, 1975.

Hammer, P. Cognates as an Efficient Approach to Second Language Acquisition, unpublished Ph.D. Thesis, The University of Alberta, Edmonton, 1978.

Hammer, P., & Monod, M.J. English-French Cognate Dictionary. The University of Alberta, Edmonton, 1976.

Limper, L.H. Student Knowledge of Some French-English Cognates. The French Review, Vol. VI, 1932-33, 33-49.

Mackey, W.F. Principes de didactique analytique, traduite et mise à jour par Lorne Laforge, Librairie Marcel Didier, Franch,, 1972.

Thorndike, E.L. The Teacher's Word Book. Teachers College, Columbia University, New York, 1921.

Vander Beke, G.E. French Word Book. The Macmillan Company, New York, 1929.

West, M.P. Note on the Inferability of Cognates. High Points, Vol. 16, November 1934, 23-25.

Suggestions for Further Research Dealing With Cognate Study

On the basis of the studies reviewed, the theory presented on the dynamics of first and second language acquisition, and the experimental testing of the efficiency of the cognate approach, the following points for further investigation are suggested.

1. The theoretical framework for the study of English-French cognates needs to be tested for its correctness and accuracy.

a) It would be interesting to determine through experimentation when the distanciation process within the first language occurs.

b) It would be useful to verify through experimentation whether the distanciation process may be aided and accelerated with second language study.

c) Further empirical examination would be desirable to determine the degree of semantic shift in a bilingual or multilingual individual.

2. The studies should be repeated with a larger sample and different teachers to confirm or disconfirm the findings.

3. The studies should be replicated, increasing and standardizing the time exposure for each experimental group.

4. The correlation coefficients between the French MLA reading test and the Jewell English reading test varied for the university and grade ten students participating in the 1977 study. It would be interesting to determine the relationship of students' reading ability in two languages at different stages in the linguistic development of first and second language acquisition.

5. It would be interesting to test empirically which of the elements of the cognate unit contributes most to possibly increased efficiency in the process of second language acquisition: a) the information students receive about cognates, b) the amount of time students practice the recognition of cognates and memorize the cognate word-ending regularities and c) the review of some characteristics of the parts of speech and their arrangements in sentences.

6. It is desirable that, before undertaking further research on the efficiency of the cognate approach, a cognate comprehension measuring instrument, incorporating scales for both written and oral comprehension, should be developed and tested.

The Efficiency Aspect of Cognate Study

The observations of a productivity consultant attending a recital of Schubert's Unfinished Symphony may have some relevancy for examining the cognate approach in second language study.

> A. For considerable periods, the four oboe players had nothing to do. That number should be reduced and their work spread over the whole orchestra.

As the oboe contribution can be assimilated by the entire orchestra, cognate contribution to second language acquisition could be assimilated throughout the entire high school second language program. The cognate approach is not a methodology in its own right. Rather it can complement any French programs used in the schools.

> B. All twelve violins were playing identical notes; this seems unnecessary duplication, and the staff of this section should be drastically cut.

To ignore the linguistic and cognitive competency of the learner who embarks on the study of a related second language is wasteful. To the extent that the learner has acquired learning principles in his first language applicable to second language learning, he should apply them in second language study.

> C. Much effort was absorbed in the playing of the demisemiquavers; this seems an excessive refinement and it's recommended that all notes should be rounded off to the nearest semiquaver.

When emphasizing the similarities of the English and French languages, it is likely that semantic distinctions and nuances may be disregarded. Refinement is a product of time and dedication but has a less important place in the initial stages of acquiring functional second language proficiency.

> D. No useful purpose is served by repeating with horns the passage that has already been handled by the strings. If all such redundant passages were eliminated the concert could be reduced from two hours to twenty minutes. If Schubert had attended to these matters he would probably have been able to finish his symphony (Grayson, 1976: 20).

By emphasizing similarities through the cognate approach, second language teaching and learning may result in less non productive repetition and, at the same time, may stimulate a broadening of vocabulary acquisition through association. Thus, if second language acquisition can be accelerated, it may be desirable to pursue a cognate approach as a salutary adjunct to our second language learning programs.

References

Grayson, C. J. The World of Mankind: Four Points of View. Public Relations Journal, Vol. 32, October 1976, 20-24.

Lawrence, D. H. The Evaluation of Training and Transfer Programs in Terms of Efficiency Measures. Journal of Psychology, Vol. 38, 1954, 367-382.

The Interrelationship of Languages

The origin and the development of the multiplicity of languages have been topics of speculation for generations and various hypotheses concerning them have been advanced. The development of language may have followed lines similar to those of the language development of the twins studied by Luria and Yudovich (1959). Just as the closely knit companionship of these twins revealed the embeddedness of names in contexts-of-action and forestalled any pressure towards communication with the surrounding world, so the variations within a primordial language (_Ursprache_) may have occurred due to pressures of communication within a group of people. The multiplicity of languages has been explained in evolutionary terms as follows: ". . . over long stretches of time, societies and cultures split apart and, through accretion of particular experience, evolved their own local speech habits" (Steiner, 1975: 56). Spatio-temporal distance between tribes or communities may have promoted the multiplicity of languages. Without the convenience of rapid transportation and communication, tribes only one or two hundred kilometers apart may have existed in virtual isolation.

If the development of man is a result of an evolutionary process, it is possible that one language was the source of the many languages found in the world today. Just as the different races on our planet may be biological adaptations to particular climatic and geographical circumstances, so different languages may be the result of adaptations to particular needs of groups of people. It has also been theorized that the physiological changes of different races resulted in or was the source of the proliferation and diversity of languages. Whatever the origin of the multiplicity of languages may have been, different languages could be regarded as evolutionary developments towards the best possible means of communication.

Linguistically it is just as difficult to determine whether there existed a primordial language, or _Ursprache_. Tentative support for the possibility of an _Ursprache_ was provided by Sir William Jones (1786) who showed the relationship and derivation of Roman, Greek, Germanic and Persian from Indic. This language was supposedly spoken in the late Stone Age, probably in eastern Europe, by a people or group of peoples of unknown and perhaps mixed race. It is assumed that the primitive Indo-Europeans were a nomadic, cattle-raising people, who, in the western areas of their range (e.g., Greece and Rome), established an agricultural economy. Dialects accompanied their migrations into India, Persia, Greece, Rome and the western borders of Europe, where they were in use at the time of first recorded history. At the beginning of this period the parent speech was highly inflected, as are Sanskrit and Greek, but as languages evolved, there has been a general tendency toward the analytic type, as in French or English. A similar relationship of the Indo-European to other families of languages, such as Finno-Ugric or Semitic, while possible, has not yet been demonstrated.

It has been demonstrated in comparative and historical language studies that, if languages are related, they share phonological, morphological, syntactic and semantic features derived from a common inheritance. Variations between languages are due to internal develpments and contacts with other languages. The areas of commonness probably decrease proportionately to the length of time separation. Changes within a language due to internal developments may lead to a divergence from the source language. Similarly, contacts with other languages may promote adoptions from other languages, or may lead to change in a convergent direction. Hamann, as early as 1761, noted the close kinship of linguistic and monetary exchanges between neighboring language groups. His studies also indicated that language relationships may evolve due to the influence of time and proximity. Technological changes in reducing spatio-temporal distance in communication, transportation and economic cooperation may favor the convergence of the multiplicity of languages.

Kieckers (1931) listed almost 3,000 living languages. Bodmer (1944) wrote that the 2,000 million people on this globe speak approximately 1,500 different languages. Taylor (1976: 8) noted that if we count only the languages used by over one million speakers, the number is reduced to 140. According to Bodmer (1944) only about 30 of them are each spoken by more than 10 millions. The reported statistics are tentative and depend upon whether political or linguistic criteria are used to determine language boundaries. The daily speech of nearly half of the world's population belongs to the Indo-European family, and covers most of the territory of Europe, India, North and South America, and a part of Asia Minor.

The language of international communication in Europe was Latin, the medium of scholarship. For more than 1,000 years Latin made learned Europeans a single fraternity. After the Reformation, the rise of nationalism encouraged the use of vernaculars. The eclipse of Latin meant that there was no single vehicle of cultural intercourse between the learned academics of Europe.

Bodmer (1944: 452) noted that nearly 300 years ago it began to dawn upon a few human minds that language, instead of being left to the hazards of a slow evolution, could be intelligently interfered with and directed toward a desirable goal. Artificial languages were experimented with and the number increased since the nineteenth century. Of the attempted and introduced artificial languages the outstanding are such as Volupük by M. Schleyer, Esperanto by L. L. Zemenhof, Idiom Neutral by W. Rosenberger, Ido by de Coutrat and others, Novial by O. Jespersen, and Basic English by C.K. Ogden. Where the single aim of an international language had been to cater to the needs of international scholarship, the needs of international trade and internationally organized labor has become tenfold more clamorous. Modern technology is a supernational culture which ministers to the common needs of human beings, while linguistic differences lead to a leakage of intellectual energy which might otherwise be enlisted to make the potential plenty of modern science available to all mankind (Bodmer, 1944).

Questions

1. According to the authors, what principle may have influenced the multiplicity of languages?
2. What conditions may favor the emergence of an international language?

References

Bodmer, F. The Loom of Language, W.W. Norton & Company, Inc., New York, 1944

Firth, J.R. The Tongues of Men and Speech, Oxford University Press, London, 1964.

Herder, J.G. Essay on the Origin of Language. (trans. A. Gode), in On the Origin of Language. Frederick Ungar Publishing Co., New York, 1966, 87-103.

Humboldt, W.V. Man's Intrinsic Humanity: His Language (1830-1835). (trans. M Cowan), in Humanist Without Portfolio. Wayne State University Press, Detroit, 1963.

Jones, W. Third Anniversary Discourse of the President of the Royal Asiatick Society. Complete Works, Vol. I-II, London, 1799

Kieckers, E. Die Sprachstämme der Erde. Carl Winters Universitätsbuchhandlung, Heidelberg, 1931.

Luria, A.R. & Yudovich, F.I. Speech and the Development of Mental Processes in the Child. Staples Press, London, 1959.

Steiner, G. After Babel. Oxford University Press, New York, 1975.

Towards an International Language

The English language became world-wide through conquest, colonization, and economic penetration. If historical circumstances favor the adoption of a living one as a world language, Anglo-American could be selected since it has a high proportion of cognate and international words. A cognate bibliography dealing with a variety of languages is presented below in an effort to help create teaching material to further the development of an international language for peaceful collaboration between nations. It should be noted that in the context of this chapter, the meaning of "cognate" has been extended and refers to any word identical or similar in spelling and meaning in two or more languages.

English-Arabic Cognate Bibliography

Zughoul, M.R. Lexical Interference of English in Eastern Province Saudi Arabia. Anthropological Linguistics, Vol. 20, No. 5, May 1978, 214-225.

English-Hebrew Cognate Bibliography

Fishman, J.A., Cooper, R.L., & Conrad, A.W. The Spread of English: The Sociology of English as an Additional Language. Newbury House, Rowley, Massachusetts, 1977.

English-Chinese Cognate Bibliography

Chan, M., & Kwok, H. A note on English Words in Hong Kong Cantonese. A paper presented at the 5th International Congress of Applied Linguistics, August 21-26, Montreal, 1978.

English-Finnish Cognate Bibliography

Sajavaara, K., & Lehtonen, J. The Finnish-English Contrastive Project: Status and Progress Report. Jyväskylä Contrastive Studies 6, University of Jyväskylä, 1978, 7-30.

Sajavaara, K., Lehtonen, J., Leskinen, H., Pulkkinen, P., P. Räsänen, A., & Hirvonen, T. Influence of English on Modern Finnish: Preliminary Report on a Research Programme. Jyväskylä Contrastive Studies 6, University of Jyväskylä, 1978, 31-51.

English-French Cognate Bibliography

Barbier, P. Review of Edouard Bonnaffé's Dictionary. The Modern language Review, Vol. 16, January 1921, 90-94.

Barbier, P. Loan-Words From English in Eighteenth Century French. The Modern Language Review, Vol. 16, January 1921, 138-149, and 252-264.

Barbier, P. Some Notes on English Influence in the Vocabulary of Written French. The Modern Languages Journal, Vol. 4, October 1922, 139-146.

Behrens, D. Über Englisches Sprachgut im Französischen, Giessen, 1927.

Bell, V.F. A Comparison of Common Words in English and in French. Unpublished Master's thesis, University of Iowa, 1935.

Bodmer, F. The Loom of Language, W.W. Norton & Company, Inc., New York, 1944.

Boillot, F.F. Le Vrai ami du traducteur anglais-français et français-anglais, Les Presses universitaires de France, Paris, 1930.

Boillot, F.F. Le Second Vrai Ami du Traducteur. Editions J. Oliven, Paris, 1956.

Bonnaffé, E. L'anglicisme et l'anglo-américanisme dans la langue française, Paris 1920.

Bonnaffé, E. Dictionnaire Etymologique et Historique des Anglicismes.

Bonnaffé, E. Anglicismes et mots d'influence anglaise. The French Quarterly. Manchester, September 1922, 164-171.

Chirol, L. Les "mots français" et le mythe de la France en anglais contemporain. Editions Klincksieck, Paris, 1973.

Clarke, G.A., & Charpentier, A. Manuel lexique des difficultés linguistiques du français, G.G. Harrap and Co., London, 1931.

Derocquigny, J. A Contribution to the Study of the French Element in English. Le Bigot Bros. Printers & Publishers, Lille, 1904.

Derocquigny, J. Autres Mots Anglais Perfides, Vuibert, Paris, 1931.

Downer, C.A. Deceptive Cognates. Le Petit Journal, December 1924.

Downer, C.A. Pitfalls in the French Vocabulary. Le Petit Journal, November 1927.

Eddy, H.M. The French Element in English. The Modern Languages Journal, Vol. X, 1926, 271-280.

Eichler, J. The Effects of Cognate Usage on Foreign Language Speaking Proficiency. Ph.D. Thesis, University of Wyoming, 1972.

Gragg, D.B. The Contribution of High-School Latin, French, and Spanish to English Vocabulary. Journal of Educational Psychology, Vol. 33, November 1942, 615-622.

Hammer, P. The Role of English-French Cognates in Listening and Reading Comprehension in the Learning of French as a Second Language. Unpublished M. E. Thesis, the University of Alberta, Edmonton, 1975.

Hammer, P. Cognates as an Efficient Approach to Second Language Acquisition. unpublished Ph.D. Thesis, The University of Alberta, Edmonton, 1978.

Hammer, P. The Utility of Cognates in Second Language Acquisition. Unpublished paper presented at the Fifth International Congress of Applied Linguistics, Montréal, August 21-26, 1978.

Hammer, P. What's the Use of Cognates? unpublished document, Edmonton, Alberta, June 1978.

Hammer, P., & Monod, M.J. English-French Cognate Dictionary. Unpublished document, The University of Alberta, Edmonton, 1976.

Hammer, P., & Monod, M. English-French Cognates: A Re-examination. Alberta Modern Language Journal, Vol. 15, No. 1, Fall 1976, 23-41.

Hammer, P., & Monod, M. The Role of English-French Cognates in Listening Comprehension. Audio-Visual Language Journal, Vol. 16, No. 1, Spring 1978, 29-32.

Ilbek, J. A Case of Semantic Interference. The French Review, Vol. 41, 1967-1968, 368-376.

Koessler, M., & Derocquigny, J. Les Faux Amis. Librairie Vuibert, Paris, 1946.

Limper, L.H. Student Knowledge of Some French-English Cognates. The French Review, Vol. VI, 1932-33, 37-49.

Mackenzie, F. Les relations de l'Angleterre et de la France d'après le vocabulaire, Paris, 1939.

Morrissey, M.D. The Use of Cognates in Foreign Language Learning. A paper presented at the 5th International Congress of Applied Linguistics, Montreal, August 21-26, 1978.

Pellisier, E. French Roots and their Families, MacMillan and Co., London, 1886.

Riley, M.A. Vocabulary Device in French. High Points, Vol. XIV, Number 7, September 1932, 45-46.

Ross, L. The Use of International Words as Phonetic Exercises with Particular Reference to Self-Instructional Language Laboratory Courses. The Audio-Visual Language Journal, Vol. 10-11, Spring 1973, 25-28.

Rubel, R. The Influence of the Study of French on the Interpretation of English Vocabulary. Master's Thesis, College of the City of New York, New York, 1935.

Sacks, N.P. English Historical Grammar and the Teaching of French. The French Review, Vol. 28, October 1954, 57-61.

Seward, R.D. Dictionary of French Deceptive Cognates. Bates College, S.F. Vanni, New York, 1947.

Taylor, I. Similarity Between French and English Words -- A Factor to Be Considered in Bilingual Language Behavior? Journal of Psycholinguistic Research, Vol. 5, No. 1, 1976, 85-94,.

West, M.P. Note on the Inferability of Cognates. High Points, Vol. 16, November 1934, 23-25.

English-German Cognate Literature Review

The historical relationship between the German and English languages is partly obvious and partly obscured by sound changes. Authors like Kern (1902), Chamberlin (1905), Goedsche (1932), Ryder (1950) and Hammer (1957) who dealt with English-German cognates emphasized mainly the utility of cognates in second language teaching. Kern (1902, 1908) and Chamberlin (1905) consider the amount of memorizing reduced by cognate study worth the effort. In addition, Chamberlin (1905) thinks that words are better learned if they overlap in form and meaning in two languages and that the knowledge of etymological meanings may lead to a better understanding of the words. Ryder (1950) advocates the study of German-English cognates as valid and interesting *per se*.

In order that English students learning German as a second language may benefit from English-German cognates, the High German Sound Shift must be taught. Kern (1908) lists consonant changes such as

English "d"	= German "t"
word	Wort
English "th"	= German "d"
thorn	Dorn

Ryder (1950) provides a summary of sound changes for the consonants. He notes however, that ". . . the vowel situation is far more complicated than the consonantal" (Ryder, 1950: 7) The cognate method should not be limited to the study of the change of form. Due attention must also be given to the change of meaning of cognates.

English-German Cognate Bibliography

Chamberlin, W.A. The Comparative Study of Words in Foreign Languages. *The School Review*, Vol. XIII, 1905, 315-323.

Goedsche, C.R. A First German Lesson for College Students. *German Quarterly*, Vol. V, 1932, 153-160.

Hammer, C. Stress the German-English Cognates. *The Modern Language Journal*, Vol. 41, 1957, 177-182.

Kern, P.O. The Linguistic Aspect of the Question. *The School Review*, Vol. X, 1902, 60-68.

Kern, P.O. The Study of Cognates as an Aid in the Acquisition of a Vocabulary. *The School Review*, Vol. XVI, 1908, 109-112.

Morgan & Strothmann. Shorter German Reading Grammer. Ginn, Boston, 1952.

Orr, J. Three Studies on Homonymics. Edinburgh University Press, Edinburgh, 1962.

Ryder, F.G. A Suggestion for Elementary German. Language Learning, Vol. 3, June 1950, 3-13

Schach, P. Semantic Borrowing in Pennsylvania German. American Speech, Vol. 26, 1951, 257-267.

Weineck, O. Third German Reader. F.W. Christern, New York, 19. . .

Wilss, W. Der Einfluss der englischen Sprache auf die deutsche seit 1945. Beiträge zur Linguistik und Informationsverarbeitung, Heft 8, R. Oldenbourg Verlag, München, 1966, 30-48.

English-Italian Cognate Bibliography

Altrocchi, R. Deceptive Cognates, Italian-English and English-Italian. University of Chicago Press, Chicago, 1935.

English-Polish Cognate Bibliography

Welna, J. Deceptive Words. A study in the Contrastive Lexicon of Polish and English. Papers and Studies in Contrastive Linguistics (ed. J. Fisiak), Vol. 7, Poznan, 1977, 73-84.

English-Russian Cognate Bibliography

Akulenko, V.V. et al. (eds.). English-Russian and Russian-English dictionary of misleading words. Sovetskaja Enciklopedia, Moskva, 1969.

Borovsko, Z. I. Inostrannye yazyki v Shkole. 1972, 6, 47-55.

English-Serbo-Croation Cognate Bibliography

Ivir, V. Serbo-Croat-English false pair types. SRAZ, Vol. 25-26, 1968, 149-159.

English-Spanish Cognate Literature Review

During the 1930's and 1940's ten publications on English-Spanish cognates appeared, of which Johnston (1939, 1941), Kendrick (1943), Bolinger (1948), Nunn and Van Scroy (1948), and Anthony (1949) studied related Spanish-English words and Scatori (1932), Jones (1935), Stevens (1943) and Reid (1948) examined the deceptive cognates.

Johnston (1939, 1941) investigated the cognate relationship between English and Spanish vocabularies as a basis for instruction and compiled a cognate word list of high frequencey words based on the first 300 words of the

Buchanan and Thorndike word books. She did not determine the semantic developments of the cognates in her frequency list; that is, to what extent and in what realm the English-Spanish cognate meanings overlap. She emphasized the value of cognates as a means of effecting more economical vocabulary learning, especially relevant and useful in second language reading, and also contributing to understanding the vocabulary in the mother tongue. Word formations and phonetic characteristics could also be studied with cognates. Johnston suggested that students' ability to recognize full or partial cognates should be studied. She wrote:

> Cognate relationships could be utilized to better advantage in teaching and the time devoted to word study could be concentrated on real difficulty if it were known how much inferential power to assume on the part of students of different ages and stages of advancement (Johnston, 1939: 154).

Kendrick (1943) examined the cognate word list compiled by Johnston (1939) and performed a semantic study of these cognates in Spanish and English. She found that "the majority of cognates have enough meaning in common to make them an extremely valuable means of learning vocabulary" (Kendrick, 1943: 241). She advocated that students need to be trained in cognate recognition. Time spent looking up words like generoso or acusar is wasted if an appropriate English cognate fits the context. Bolinger (1948) published an article on identical cognates in English and Spanish in which he emphasized that students take a keen interest in guessing the English cognates.

Nunn and Van Scroy (1949) published a Glossary of Related Spanish-English Words which contains a list of some four thousand items from the common body of words in Spanish and English. The authors also give a list of and a warning about false cognates. They mention two types: "those which have an accidental similarity with no etymological distinction" and "those which have a common root but have developed different shades of meaning in the two languages". The authors write that "errors of the second type are more frequent". Thus, the study of cognates cannot be restricted to that of change in form; semantic shifts of cognate words should also be examined.

Authors such as Scatori (1932), Jones (1935), Stevens (1943) and Reid (1948) were concerned with deceptive cognates. Similarity in form (spelling) but differences in meaning can cause misunderstanding. Scatori (1932) lists nearly a hundred Spanish forms that resemble an English word sufficiently to confuse students.

Jones (1935) based his "deceptive doubles" on Spanish words which have identical or similar spelling in both English and Spanish but different meanings in the two languages respectively. Jones collected during several years "about three hundred of these twin words--with a difference" (Jones, 1935: 16). He noted that his list is "only a tenth of the size of the Terry list of safe words" (p. 16). Jones advocated that his students continue to guess the meaning of unfamiliar words on the basis of spelling similarities because the chances of correctly guessing the meaning is greater than that of incorrectly guessing. Jones thought that the "context usually serves to indicate the absurdity of the apparent resemblance (of deceptive doubles)" (Jones, 1935: 16).

Stevens (1943) examined deceptive cognates in Spanish with respect to textbook vocabularies. He noted that deceptive cognates are not indicated in glossaries. Stevens (1943) wrote: "The beginning student who is forced to rely upon the accuracy of the vocabulary in his book will produce some awkward, misleading, or completely incorrect translations" (p. 116). Second language learners must be taught to cultivate a general readiness to expect words to change their meanings with their contexts and how to guess meanings of unfamiliar words. Stevens lists approximately 30 Spanish deceptive cognates.

Reid (1948) proposed the compilation of a list of Spanish deceptive cognates useful "not to the professional purist or to the translator of technical material, but to the average intermediate or advanced student of the language" (Reid, 1948: 280). He included a list of approximately 125 truly deceptive cognates, i.e., English words whose real or apparent cognates in Spanish *ordinarily* have a significantly different meaning.

The ground work for English-Spanish cognates has been performed. The proportion of good to deceptive cognates has been determined at ten to one (Jones, 1935). The selection of high frequency English-Spanish cognates has been performed by Johnston (1930). The similarity of meanings of English-Spanish cognates has been found to warrant cognate usage in second language teaching (Kendrick, 1943). Nunn and Van Scroy (1949) list some four thousand English-Spanish cognates to facilitate second language vocabulary acquisition. Unfortunately studies which would determine the ability of students at a given age or grade level to recognize cognates and to know their meaning are lacking. Thus, statements such as "Cognates, by permitting the student to acquire vocabulary without great effort, enable the student to concentrate on grammatical and pronunciation matters" (Anthony, 1949: 131) have to be regarded tentatively until necessary research has been performed.

Anthony (1952-53) qualified the definition of cognates by saying that cognates defined as words which have a related form and meaning in two or more languages and which have a common ancestor may be of interest to linguists but not to second language teachers, who are concerned with the language as it is spoken today. He included in the definition of cognates any words that have sufficient correlation in meaning and form in the two languages regardless of origin (p. 79). Anthony pointed out that the utility of a cognate depends on its recognizability. He suggested the teaching of English-Spanish cognates because he regarded cognates as a method of rapid expansion of vocabulary for the language student. For the selection of cognates for teaching purposes, Anthony suggested the frequency and usefulness of each individual cognate as a possible selection criterion. Another possibility could be to teach the English-Spanish correspondences which are quite common, as for example: "Spanish -cion is often equivalent to English -tion" (p. 81). Anthony reasoned that once students have grasped the generalization and classification of cognates into patterns, transferring its application to numerous other words would be quite possible. Students should have the opportunity to practice cognate recognition.

Once the spelling alterations of orthographically and semantically similar words have been explained, cognates are useful for reading purposes. For pronunciation Wilkins and Hoffman (1964) regard cognates as a problem. The authors write:

> Items which are spelled alike in two languages, but where the spelling corresponds to two different sound systems, are a source of difficulty because the similarity often elicits a response first from the native language rather than from the target language (Wilkins & Hoffman, 1964: 39).

They used English-Spanish and English-French cognates in testing pronunciation and found statistically significant mean test score differences among the courses at the 0.01 level of significance. The more semesters of Spanish language studies a student had had, the better was his performance on the cognate word pronunciation task.

Kessler (1969) examined the relative difficulty of learning to pronounce cognate and non-cognate words in a second language. She found that at the beginning levels of Spanish study, cognates were more difficult to pronounce correctly than non-cognates. Kessler regards the cognate test as a valid measure of the student's pronunciation ability. Furthermore, these scores correlated with the number of years the student had spent learning to speak the second language. Thus Kessler's study (1969) also confirms Wilkins and Hoffman's use of cognates to test pronunciation.

Eichler (1972) who investigated the effects of cognate usage on foreign language speaking proficiency notes that although overall speaking proficiency gains were not significantly affected by the treatment, free description was most markedly affected by the cognate approach.

English-Spanish Cognate Bibliography

Anthony, E.M. Book Reviews. Language Learning, Vol. 2, 1949, 130-132.

Anthony, E.M. The Teaching of Cognates. Language Learning, Vol. IV, 1952-53, 79-82.

Bolinger, D.L. Identical Cognates in English and Spanish, Hispania, Vol. 31, 1948, 271-279.

Eichler, J. The Effects of Cognate Usage on Foreign Language Speaking Proficiency. Ph.D. Thesis, University of Wyoming, 1972.

Gragg, D. B. The Contribution of High-School Latin, French, and Spanish to English Vocabulary. Journal of Educational Psychology, Vol. 33, November 1942, 615-622.

Hagerty, T.W., & Bowen, I.D. A Contrastive Analysis of a Lexical Split: Spanish hacer to English do/make/ etc. in R. Nash (ed.), Reading in Spanish-English Contrastive Linguistics, I, Inter American University Press, Puerto Rico, 1973, 1-71.

Johnston, M.C. Cognate Relationship Between English and Spanish Vocabularies as a Basis for Instruction. Ph.D. Thesis, The University of Texas at Austin, 1939.

Johnston, M.C. Spanish-English Cognates of High Frequency. Modern Language Journal, Vol. 25, 1941, 405-417.

Jones, W.K. Deceptive Doubles: Twin Words--With a Difference. Modern Language Journal, Vol. 20, 1935, 15-18.

Kendrick, E.J. A Semantic Study of Cognates in Spanish and English. Ph.D. Thesis, The University of Illinois, Urbana, 1943.

Kessler, L.W. The Relative Difficulty of Learning to Pronounce Cognate and Non-Cognate Words in a Second Language. M.A. Thesis, University of California, Los Angeles, 1969.

Macaulay, R.K.S. Vocabulary Problems for Spanish Learners. English Language Teaching, Vol. 20, No. 2, 1966, 131-136.

McHale, C.F. Spanish Don'ts. New York, 1939.

Mosēl, J.N. Embarrassing Moments in Spanish. New York: Frederick Ungar Publishing Company, 1945.

Nash, R. Spanglish: Language Contact in Puerto Rico. American Speech, No. 45, 1974.

Nash, R. Englanol: More Language Contact in Puerto Rico. American Speech, No. 46, 1974.

Nash, R. Phantom cognates and other curiosities in Puerto Rican Englanol. Monda Lingvo - Problemo, Vol. 5, No. 15, 19, 157-167.

Nunn, M.E., & Van Scroy, H.A. Glossary of Related Spanish-English Words. University: Alabama: University of Alabama Studies, Number 5, July 1949.

Reid, J.T. Deceptive Demons. Hispania, Vol. 31, 1948, 280-297.

Scatori, S. Deceptive Cognates in Spanish. Modern Language Journal, Vol. 16, 1932, 396-401.

Stevens, L.C. Textbook Vocabularies and Deceptive Cognates in Spanish. Modern Language Journal, Vol. 27, 1943, 116-118.

Terry, T.P. Short Cuts to Spanish. Houghton, Mifflin, Boston, 1920.

Wilkins, G.W., and Hoffman, E.L. The Use of Cognates in Testing Pronunciation. Language Learning, Vol. 14, 1964, 39-43.

English-Swedish Cognate Bibliography

Ekblom, E. Skenbar och verklig betydelse i engelskan, Engelsk ordförtechkning med exempel. Stockholm, 1932.

Ernolv, C. False friends--förrädiska ord. Modern Sprak, Vol. 52, 1958, 347-368.

Dravidian Cognate Bibliography

Sivaramamurty, N., & Subramoniam, V.I. Telugu: An Intensive Course. Department of Linguistics, University of Kerala, 1971.

Andrewskutty, A. Malayalam: an intensive course. Method by V. I. Subramoniam, Trivandrum, Dravidian Linguistic Association, 1971.

French-Italian Cognate Bibliography

Debyser, F. Comparaison et interférences lexicales (français-italien). Le Français dans le Monde, Nos. 78-85, juin 1971, 51-57.

PART IV

TRANSFER OF SIMILARITIES

Transfer of Commonalities Between Related Languages

The ease with which a learner masters a second language may depend on his ability to see resemblances, and thus to readily classify the new and strange materials. Similarities between languages should be pointed out explicitly to students. It has been noted by various writers (Limper, 1932; Johnston, 1939; Stephens, 1960) that transfer of common elements from one language to another may not automatically occur in second language learning. A possible explanation of this phenomenon could be that the ability to transfer is related to the individual's level of cognitive development. That is, competence in one language may influence the abilty to transfer applicable elements to a second. For French language acquisition by an English speaker, cognate study requires that the learner know the cognate word in his first language and be able to perceive the similarities between the two language systems. Thus, the amount of transfer is not only dependent upon previously acquired knowledge but also upon the quality and flexibility of an individual's cognitive structure (Klausmeier, 1969). By circumstance, the learner's exposure to the second language normally is limited. From a relatively small number of lexical items, the learner cannot be expected to know _a priori_ that the English and French languages share approximately 11,000 words which may be defined as cognates. Stephens (1960), who investigated transfer of learning, claimed that the amount of transfer induced could be increased by bringing out the feature to be transferred.

Hammer (1975) and Limper (1932) found that the possible utility of English-French cognates appeared to depend on a relatively large English vocabulary knowledge of the individual. It is difficult to assess whether all of the approximately 11,000 cognates of the Hammer and Monod (1976) list are familiar to an English speaking person, whether he is a secondary student or an educated adult. The possible utility of cognates as a vocabulary acquisition device may be large or small, since all the 10,993 English-French cognates may or may not be part of the learner's vocabulary. Yet words like "train" and "table" may be useful already to an English-speaking elementary pupil learning French.

Some arguments in favor of using cognates as a vocabulary acquisition device are:

1. Since the ratio of cognates to deceptive cognates is approximately 11,000 to about 950, the memory effort required by students to learn vocabularies could be greatly reduced by cognate study.

2. The acquisition of meaning is a gradual process consisting of progressive discrimination. This is true in the learning of the native language as well as a second one; it is never complete nor is it a simple process. Second language students of French may benefit from cognates and partial cognates because not all word meanings are learned at the same time.

3. Word-ending regularities like the equivalence of the French "-té" and the English "-ty" in words such as "beauté - beauty" can be easily learned by students if the spelling and meaning of the English and French cognates are otherwise the same. Chamberlin observed that:

> The amount of time required at first to master the principles (or rules about the corresponding English-French cognate endings) grows relatively less, in proportion as the number of cases increased to which it applies, until the time may be practically disregarded (Chamberlin, 1905: 316).

4. The acquisition of meaning may be enhanced by knowledge of key prefixes, roots and suffixes. The Greek and Latin suffixes which Jean Dubois (1962) listed in his <u>Etude sur la Dérivation Suffixale en Français moderne et contemporain</u> are generally as applicable to English words as to French words. For example:

<u>Prefix</u>	<u>Meaning</u>	<u>Example words</u>	
		English	French
a-, an-	(not, without)	apathy	apathie
		atheism	athéisme
bene-	(well,good)	benefit	bénédiction
<u>Root</u>	<u>Meaning</u>	<u>Example words</u>	
		English	French
magna	(great)	magnitude	magnitude
		magnificent	magnifique
med	(middle)	medium	médium
		mediocre	médiocre
<u>Suffix</u>	<u>Meaning</u>	<u>Example words</u>	
		English	French

-or, -er	(one who)	actor	acteur
		employer	employeur
-ism	(belief in)	communism	communisme
		journalism	journalisme

5. Cognate learning can aid vocabulary acquisition by enriching the vocabulary in the second language and by complementing the vocabulary of the mother tongue.

6. By using cognates, reading in the second language may be facilitated because the time spent looking up unknown words in the dictionary could be reduced. Thus, the student is brought into contact with the target language on a broader scale. This in turn may help him to develop a Sprachgefühl or sensitivity to lexical appropriateness as well as to structural forms. Thus, with cognates, the recognition and acquisition of a reading vocabulary may be facilitated.

Since English-French cognates share the semantic, lexical and graphemic realms in the two languages, cognates should prove to be of greatest utility in facilitating reading, once the recognition of these cognates and the familiarity of meaning is taken into consideration.

The oral recognition of cognates is complicated by differences in the consonantal and vocalic systems of the English and French languages as well as from differences in stress, rhythm and intonation, Mackey writes:

> . . .il nous faudra distinguer dans la compréhension d'un mot, la forme orale de la forme écrite. Pour la compréhension de la parole, les mots qui ont une même orthographe, pour être semblables, ne nous sont pas d'un grande secours. Des mots comme nation, qui s'écrivent de la même façon en anglais et en français, ne se prononcent pas de la même façon dans la langue parlée: en anglais /neiʃn/ et en français /nasjɒ/ (Mackey, 1972: 136).

A comparison of the consonantal and vocalic systems of English and French, presented by Pierre Delattre, reveals that an American learning French ". . . has to learn only three really new consonants, the /ɲ/, /ɥ/ and /R/, (and nine new vowels): /y/, /ø/, /oe/, the two low "a" sounds /ɑ/ and /a/, and four nasal vowels /ɛ̃/, /œ̃/, /ɑ̃/ /ɔ̃/" (Delattre, 1965: 82).

An Anglophone will probably experience the greatest difficulty in oral comprehension with those cognates which contain one or more of the 12 unfamiliar phonemes or the pure French vowel sounds. Phoenetic training will likely be necessary to facilitate the oral recognition of cognates.

Possible negative transfer due to the use of cognates may exist in the active language skills.

a) There may be a danger of making up words, since recall rather than recognition of cognates is a criterion in speaking and writing.

b) A greater amount of phonetic instruction could be required for the use of English-French cognates in speaking to counteract the habit of pronouncing the cognate in the dominant language.

c) Interference in spelling ability in the two languages may occur for single letter difference of cognates, for example, "mentionner" = to mention, if the pronunciation does not provide a spelling clue, as for example in "avantage" = advantage, or "oncle" = uncle.

Questions

1) Can you list additional arguments in favor of utilizing cognates in second language teaching?
2) Could you rank order the arguments listed in the order of most important to least important? Justify your rank order.
3) Please indicate the order of important English-French cognates could be of help to the second language learner in writing, listening, reading and speaking.
4) If you can, please list additional sources of negative tranfer due to the use of cognates.

References

Chamberlin. W.A. The Comparative Study of Words in Foreign Languages. _The School Review_, Vol. XIII, 1905, 315-323.

Delattre, P. _Comparing the Phonetic Features of English, French, German and Spanish: An Interim Report_. Julius Groos Verlag, Heidelberg, 1965.

Dubois, J. _Etude sur la dérivation suffixale en français moderne et contemporain_. Larousse, Paris, 1962.

Hammer, P., & Monod, M.J. _English-French Cognate Dictionary_. The University of Alberta, Edmonton, 1976.

Johnston, M.C. _Cognate Relationship Between English and Spanish Vocabularies as a Basis for Instruction_. Ph.D. Thesis, The University of Texas at Austin, 1939.

Klausmeier, H.J. Transfer of Learning. In _Encyclopedia of Educational Research_. Fourth Edition, Editor Robert L. Ebel & Victor H. Noll, The Macmillan Company, London, 1969. 1483-1493.

Limper, L.R. Student Knowledge of Some French-English Cognates. *The French Review*, Vol. VI, 1932-33, 37-49.

Mackey, W.F. *Principes de didactique analytique*, traduite et mise à jour par Lorne Laforge, Librairie Marcel Didier, France, 1972.

Stephens, J.M. Transfer of Learning. In C.W. Harris & M.R. Liba (eds.) *Encyclopedia of Educational Research*, Macmillan, New York, 1960, 1535-1543.

Oral Recognition of English-French Cognates

To facilitate the oral recognition of cognates it may be helpful to study the French alphabet at the level of sound-letter correspondence. The study of the French alphabet would give the learner the opportunity 1) to establish the auditory - visual correspondence, i.e., hear the sound and see the letter corresponding to it and 2) as a modification, to produce the sound of the letter when he sees it. Additional phonetic information to be given to the learner include the following: 1) the French phonetic system contains no dipthongs, that is, vowel slurs, 2) in French there are only three consonants which do not exist as such in English, the /ɲ/, /ɥ/ and /R/, 3) nine new vowel sounds must be mastered, the /y/, /ø/, /oe/, the two low "a" sounds /ɑ/ and /a/ and four nasal vowels /ɛ̃/, /œ̃/, /ɑ̃/, /õ/, and 4) the French "h" is never pronounced and "y" very often has the phoneme sound of an "i".

In addition, the French vocalic system is reviewed. The lesson objective for the study of the French vocalic system is:

1. L'étudiant étudie d'abord les sons des voyelles.
2. On lui donne les règles correspondant à l'usage de ces voyelles (son) ainsi que de leurs transcriptions graphiques afin qu'il sache comment écrire ce qu'il sait dire et comment prononcer ce qu'il lit.
3. L'étudiant est amené à appliquer les règles à la prononciation des congénères.

Les Voyelles

<u>La voyelle écrite "i"</u>

Le "i" n'a qu'un seul son représenté par le symbole /i/.

Quelques graphies du son "i" sont:

i = ici
ï = (trêma] laïque (lay, secular)
î = (accent circonflexe) île (island, isle)
-il = baril (keg, cask)
-id = nid (nest)
-it = habit (dress, costume, outfit)
-ie = magie (magic)

Les voyelles écrites "e", "é, "è", "ê"

1. Le "e" muet /ə/ en général est prononcé après deux ou trois consonnes différentes et articulées. ex. justement, mercredi, etc.
2. Le "é" est fermé /e/ lorsqu'il est surmonté d'un accent aigu. ex. difficulté, idée, été.
3. a) Le "è" et "ê" sont ouverts /ɛ/ quand ils sont surmonté d'un accent grave ou d'un accent circonflexe. ex. père, tête, progrès.

   b) On entend le même son /ɛ/ dans la "-et", ex. objet, effet, etc., dans toutes les terminaisons en "er", ex. cancer, univers, etc. quand le "r" est sonore, ainsi que si le "e" se trouve devant "x": examen, express, complexe, texte, etc.

La voyelle écrite "a"

Nous distinguons deux sortes de sons "a":

1. Le "a" /a/ est antérieur sans accent. ex. ami, avocat, etc. ou surmonté d'un accent grave. ex. voilà, ça et là, déjà, il est là etc.
2. Le "a" /ɑ/ est postérieur a) quand il est surmonté d'un accent circonflexe, ex. mâle, pâle, infâme, etc. b) dans les terminaisons "-ation, -asion, -assion" ex. végétation, fondation, invasion, occasion, évasion, persuasion, compassion, passion, etc. et c) dans la terminaison "-as" (s sonore), ex. hélas, atlas, etc.

La voyelle écrite "o"

1. a) Le "o" ouvert /ɔ / est toujours sans accent, ex. objet, occasion, globe, encore, etc. (l'hôpital est la seule exception).

   b) Les terminaisons en "-um" font entendre un "o" ouvert, ex. pensum, radium, harmonium, opium, aqarium, album, maximum, etc.
2. a) Le "o" /o/ surmonté d'un accent circonflexe est toujours fermé, ex. côté, (side), nôtre, etc.

   b) Le "o" est fermé quand il s'écrit "au, eaux, aux" ex. travaux, journaux, aussi, beaux, etc.

   c) Le "o" à la fin des mots est toujours fermé qu'il soit ou non suivi d'une consonne muette, ex. zéro, vos, galop, etc.

   d) Le "o" est fermé dans la terminaison "-otion", ex. émotion, dévotion, motion, etc.

La voyelle écrite "u"

La voyelle "u" n'a qu'un seul son /y/. Le "u" avec ou sans accent se prononce toujours /y/, ex. tu, le but (goal), la bûche (log), etc.

L'ensemble écrit des voyelles "ou"

La voyelle "ou" /u/ n'a qu'un seul son. Le "ou" avec ou sans accent se prononce toujours /u/, ex. tout, où, aujourd'hui, août, etc.

L'ensemble écrit des voyelles "eu"

L'ensemble écrit des voyelles "eu" a deux sons possibles:

1. Le "eu" /ø/ est fermé à la fin des mots, quelle que soit la façon dont il est écrit, ex. Dieu (God), milieu, jeu, etc.

   b) Le "eu" est fermé au commencement des mots, ex. Eugène, euphorie, européen, etc.
2. Le "eu" /oe/ est ouvert devant le "r", ex. beurre, heure, coeur, etc.

Les voyelles nasales orales

Les voyelles nasales ont une résonnance nasale. C'est pour cela qu'on les appelle voyelles nasales. Il y a quatre voyelles nasales orales.

Les ensembles écrits correspondant à la voyelle nasale "in"

L'ensemble écrit "in" correspond à la voyelle orale /ɛ̃/. Lorsque le "i, ie ou y" est suivi de "m" ou "n," vous le prononcez /ɛ̃/ nasal. ex. intérieur, instant, simplicité, impression, académicien, rien, chien, syntaxe, nymphe, Olympe, symbole. L'ensemble "en" se prononce "in" dans les mots d'origine étrangère ou savante. ex. examen, pentagone, etc.

Les ensembles écrits correspondant à la voyelle nasale "an"

L'ensemble écrit "an" correspond à la voyelle orale /ɑ̃/. Lorsque le "a" est suivi de "m" ou "n," il se prononce /ɑ̃/ nasal. ex. océan, danse, volcan, etc. "En" suivi ou non d'une consonne se prononce en général "an", ex. en, centre, offense, agence, encore, etc.

Les ensembles écrits correspondant à la voyelle nasale "on"

L'ensemble écrit "on" correspond à la voyelle orale /ɔ/. Lorsque le "o" est suivi de "m" ou "n," vous le prononcez /ɔ/ nasal, ex. concert, oncle, pardon, surnom, prénom, complet, etc.

Les ensembles écrits correspondant à la voyelle nasale "un"

L'ensemble écrit "un" correspond à la voyelle orale /œ/. Lorsque le "u" est suivi de "m" ou "n," il se prononce /œ̃/ nasal, ex. lundi, brun, humble, etc. (For reference see Armande Lebrun. La Phonétique rendue facile, Edition de Rodage, Montréal, 1966).

The phonetic information, as presented, is specifically geared to the phonetic differences of English-French cognate words. Mastery of this material could be regarded as the first step towards oral comprehension of natural speech. Phonetic training should be extended to include sentences incorporating French rhythm, intonation and pitch and longer oral excerpts.

Design of an English-French Cognate Unit

An English-French cognate unit was designed to provide a systematic exposition of cognates, tying various research findings together in an orderly fashion.

Since it is pedagogically unsound to assume that the learner knows the teaching material, the cognate unit consists of components probably learned previously, as, for example, some characteristics of the parts of speech, the English-French cognate word meaning in English, some meanings of suffixes, using context clues to infer unfamiliar words, and types of sentence construction. Should these elements of commonality not be known in English, the student can learn them in his second language study and transfer could occur on the basis of the underlying principles of word formation, vocabulary acquisition devices and syntax.

The concepts to be taught and the order in which the material was presented in the English-French cognate unit were carefully arranged. Since the English-French cognate unit was designed to foster learning of vocabulary and syntax to be used in unfamiliar reading material, the objectives of reading skill development were pursued using three strategies for vocabulary acquisition: 1) the use of cognates, 2) the use of word part analysis with emphasis on a) the meaning of suffixes and b) the morphological characteristics of suffixes with respect to cognates and 3) the use of context clues. The syntactic component of the English-French cognate unit was structured inductively. It begins with a review of some characteristics of the parts of speech, proceeds with possible combinations of the parts of speech in sentences, and concludes with the semantic component of syntax, i.e., how a change in syntactic structure may be related to a change in semantic structure. Essentially, then, the English-French cognate unit deals primarily with lexical items (words) and syntactic structures wherein the lexical items are placed.

The core of the English-French cognate unit centers on the similarity of the English and French languages with respect to vocabulary (cognates) and syntax. Knowledge of word formation is applicable to both languages. Included in the cognate unit is a list of the meanings of the suffixes contained in the cognate word-ending regularities and their morphological characteristics. In both English and French the suffix may change the part of speech of words, for example:

French	English
nationalisme (noun)	nationalism
nationaliser (verb)	to nationalize
national (adjective)	national
nationalement (adverb)	nationally
rigidité (noun)	rigidity
rigidifier (verb)	to rigidify, to make rigid
rigide (adjective)	rigid
rigidement (adverb)	rigidly

Using context clues to guess the meanings of unfamiliar words is helpful in both English and French reading.

The similarity of English and French syntax with respect to types of sentence construction and word order is emphasized. The four basic types of sentence constructions, namely, statement, question, command and exclamation, are reviewed. Although there is a peculiarity of pronominal order in French, Greenberg (1966), who investigated some universals of grammar with particular reference to the order of meaningful elements, notes that "in declarative sentences with nominal subject and object, the dominant order is almost always one in which the subject precedes the object" (Greenberg, 1966: 110).

The English-French cognate unit consists of seven lessons. The first lesson presents the essence of English-French cognates and their characteristics. Lessons two to six consist of the following: 1) the grammar section for learning some characteristics of the parts of speech, 2) the English-French cognate word-ending regularities for memorizing them, and 3) the French excerpts for practising recognition of cognates. Lesson seven shows how the parts of speech previously studied are arranged in sentences.

It should be pointed out to the learner that the information provided is applicable with reference to English-French cognates as they are defined in the English-French cognate unit. However, cognates represent only a fraction of French second language study. The differences between the two languages must also be studied. The learner must be prepared to modify his knowledge about the second language in accordance with advanced language study. For example, the "-eur" suffix may indicate a noun or adjective in

French. When the "-eur" ending is used as an adjective in French it is no longer a cognate with English.

The cognate unit is self-contained in the sense tha all questions in the unit may be answered from the teaching material included in the lessons. The questions are intended to teach the content of the unit and deal primarily with the information about English-French cognates and the recognition of cognates in the selected French excerpts. The English-French cognate unit contains specific factual information, which can be applied, analyzed and synthesized in responding to the questions which conclude each lesson.

Questioning by the teacher, either prior to or following the reading of an assignment, has been regarded as the most common and effective technique in the guidance of reading behavior (Weintraub, 1969). However, Herber and Nelson (1975) suggested that questions which require the use of the reading skills necessary for answering the questions do not really teach the student these skills. They proposed a simulation strategy in which the instructor writes the answers to his own questions and asks the student to determine if the answer can be supported by evidence from the reading text. The questions in French, on the French excerpts in each lesson, were designed to be used as Herber and Nelson (1975) suggested.

The cognate unit may be further explained as a guided approach to discovery learning. The student following the English-French cognate unit is required to respond in writing, or to restate in some other form, the rules, principles or steps necessary for the solution of learned concepts in the cognate unit. Guidance and progression is thus built into the structure of the unit. This approach was studied by Gagné and Brown (1961), who examined factors in the programming of conceptual learning. They concluded that "guided discovery was found to be more effective than the discovery method or the rule and example method" (p.319).

Following initial construction, subject matter consultants reviewed the organization and instructional material included in the English-French cognate unit. Two French professors in the Department of Romance Languages at the University of Alberta examined the French material for its accuracy and correctness, and two professors of the Department of Secondary Education in modern language instruction and teaching secondary English verified the English material included in the cognate unit.

Questions

1. List as many vocabulary acquisition devices as you know.
2. What are the basic sentence constructions? Please list them.
3. According to the description of the design of the English-French cognate unit, is the cognate unit structured inductively or deductively?
4. How would you define guided discovery learning?

References

Finstein, M.W., & Thomas, E. Reading Center Techniques for Second Language Reading Skills. The French Review, Vol. 41, 1967-1968, 377-382.

Gagné, R.M., & Brown, L.T. Some Factors in the Programming of Conceptual Learning. Journal of Experimental Psychology, Vol. 62, 1961, 313-321.

Greenberg, J.H. (ed.). Universals of Language. Second Edition, The M.I.T. Press, Massachusetts, 1966.

Herber, H.L., & Nelson, J.B. Questioning is Not the Answer. Journal of Reading, Vol. 18, No. 7, April 1975, 512-517.

Weintraub, S. The Question as an Aid in Reading. The Reading Teacher, Vol. 22, No. 8, May 1969, 751, 753, 755.

Objectives of the Teaching Material in the Cognate Unit

The French Excerpts

It is dangerous for the student to think that there exists only one "correct" interpretation of a word; polysemy of words is the rule rather than the exception. What can be named (things, characteristics, events, conditions, relations, etc.) is infinite whereas the number of words is limited. Thus, the same word will express different meanings in different contexts. Darmesteter wrote that ". . . words by themselves are but uncertain guides, and need the setting of circumstances which, like the key in music, determines the value of the signs" (Bréal, 1964: 287). To understand words means to infer or guess their meaning from a context. For these reasons short French excerpts were used in the Enlgish-French cognate unit. They provide a context learning situation for vocabulary acquisition.

Correct usage and delicate nuances can come only from a thorough knowledge of the meaning of words. It may be quite difficult to explain the semantic difference between the French and English word "suggestion" to the second language learner who may be unaccustomed to close vocabulary analysis. Reading authentic French material can provide the linguistic context necessary to learn the denotative and connotative aspect of words and to acquire the finer shades in meaning.

Cognate Word-ending Regularities

English-French cognates of high frequency in French, as identified by Savard and Richards' (1970) "indices d'utilité du vocabulaire fondamental français" are employed as example words illustrating cognate word-ending regularities. They are provided to aid the learner in recognizing and memorizing word-ending regularities.

Grammar Instruction

Certain technical grammatical notions were included in the English-French cognate unit. Reasons for the inclusion of this non-cognate concept approach were several:

1) It was found in a previous study of cognates (Hammer, 1975) that students were unable to distinguish between parts of speech, and thus could

not meaningfully interpret cognates in the French excerpts. Vygotsky's (1962: 100-101) studies showed that the study of grammar is of paramount importance for the conscious control of language operations.

2) Shawl (1969) found that students who were given explicit statements about syntactic composition and interrelationships performed noticeably better (p 0.01) in reading than students who did not receive these statements.

3) Chastain and Woerdehoff (1968) also found a significant advantage in reading ability favoring a group receiving an explanation in English of grammatical principles.

4) The success of second language learning may depend on the individual's sensitivity to the functions and arrangements of words in a variety of contexts. Carroll and Sapon (1959) identified this ability to handle "grammar" as an important variable in language aptitude. It is assumed that this ability can be taught.

5) The grammar included in this cognate unit is basic and practical rather than exhaustive, and the learner is given opportunity to apply his grammatical knowledge to a variety of French excerpts.

The Use of Two Languages

The cognate unit was written in both English and French. This procedure was selected on the following grounds.

1) Although the teacher may try to increase the relevance of the second language through a variety of creative language experiences, second language learning in the classroom is artificial. Lambert *et al* (1963) found that those students who use both their languages in cognitively demanding situations perform better than those who do not.

2) Providing some grammatical instruction in French gives the learner an additional opportunity to practice cognate recognition and comprehension.

3) Switching from one language to the other may result in a greater degree of cognitive flexibility (Rogers, 1976; Bain, 1975; Jakobovits, 1969). Jakobovits listed "mental flexibility, a superiority in concept formation, and a more diversified set of mental abilities" as a possible result of bilinguality (Jakobovits, 1969: 82-83).

The English-French cognate unit, based on the similarities of the English and French languages, aims at producing a level of proficiency in reading French. Further, it is designed to produce this efficiency in a minimum of time. If the learner relies on his English knowledge to help him acquire French as a second language, the rate of learning should be accelerated. However, the extent to which this objective can be achieved will depend to some extent on the characteristics of the individual learner, the teacher, the learning context, and the tested validity of the cognate approach.

Questions

1. What purpose(s) do the French excerpts serve?
2. Why are the cognate word-ending regularities included?
3. Why is it important to teach grammar?
4. What arguments can you give in favor of and against the use of two languages?

References

Bain, B. Bilingualism and Cognition: Toward an Integration of Piaget and Vygotsky: Bilingual Considerations. _Linguistics_, Mouton Publishers, 1975, 5-20.

Bréal, M. _Semantics: Studies in the Science of Meaning_. Translated by Mrs. H. Cust, Dover Publications, Inc. New York, 1900/1964.

Carroll, J.B., & Sapon, S.M. _Modern Languages Aptitude Test_. The Psychological Corporation, New York, 1959.

Chastain, K., & Woerdehoff, F.J. A Methodological Study Comparing the Audio-Lingual Habit Theory and the Cognitive-Code Learning Theory. _Modern Language Journal_, Vol. LII, 1968, 268-279.

Hammer, P. _The Role of English-French Cognates in Listening and Reading Comprehension in the Learning of French as a Second Language_, M. Ed. Thesis, The University of Alberta, Edmonton, 1975.

Jakobovits, L.A. Second Language Learning and Transfer Theory: A Theoretical Assessment. _Language Learning_, Vol. 19, 1969, 55-86.

Lambert, W.E., Gardner, R.C., Barik, H.C., & Tunstall, K. Attitudinal and Cognitive Aspects of Intensive Study of a Second Language. _Journal of Abnormal and Social Psychology_. Vol. LXVII, 1963, 358-368.

Rogers, M. _Early Bilingual Immersion: Some Effects_, M. Ed. Thesis, The University of Alberta, Edmonton, 1976.

Savard, J.G., & Richards, J. _Les indices d'utilité du vocabulaire fondamental français_. Les Presses de L'Université Laval, Québec, 1970.

Shawl, J.R.A. Definition of One Level of Achievement in the Reading and Writing of Spanish. Final Report. Washington, D.C., Office of Education, U.S. Bureau of Research, 1969.

Vygotsky, L.S. Thought and Language. The M.I.T. Press. Cambridge, published posthumously in 1934/1962.

Teaching Suggestions for the English-French Cognate Unit

The English-French cognate unit may serve as a self-instructional unit for senior high school students or as teaching material for individualized instruction. However, the self-instructional quality of the English-French cognate unit allows for modifications for different classroom situations and presentation styles.

The ten example words illustrating the cognate word-ending regularities in the English-French cognate unit could lend themselves to phonetic exercises. The necessary phonetic instruction to facilitate the oral recognition of cognates was not included in the cognate unit, because only if the learner knows the sounds associated with the international phonetic symbols would a written phonetic lesson be of any help to him or her. However the teacher could explain a few phonetic rules, as for example, é is pronounced /e/, u as /y/, ou as /u/, rules for nasalization, etc. With these phonetic rules the student could try to pronounce the cognates in French.

Another alternative to enliven the study of the cognate word-ending regularities could be through a game of definition. One student would read the definition while the others try to guess the cognate. If no one finds the answer, say after thirty seconds, the cognate word is supplied. If a student guesses the appropriate cognate he or she may read the next definition. The benefit of such an exercise would be that the student who reads the definition has to speak up and the others have to listen and try to understand French without the help of the written word. Allowance has to be made, if the cognates are used in such a way, that the definitions of the cognate words were not expressly written for the purpose of guessing the word.

Lesson one, definition of cognates and their characteristics, explains the essential nature of cognates. This information was extracted from a detailed and systematic comparison of the English and French vocabularies. Sixteen cognate word-ending regularities account for 5,613 words in the cognate dictionary (Hammer & Monod, 1976). The endings are worth memorizing. Everything else in the cognate unit can be modified to suit the teacher and students. For example, if the excerpts to practice the recognition of cognates do not interest the students, other selections of genuine French texts can be chosen. Similarly, different example words illustrating the cognate word-ending regularities can be selected from the English-French cognate dictionary (Hammer & Monod, 1976).

The presentation of the articles, pronouns, prepositions and conjunctions in French should be explained if the unit is used at the secondary school level. Grade ten students in their fourth year of French second language study may experience difficulty with the parts of speech presented in French. For example, it could be explained that in French the three forms for the definite article, i.e., singular and plural, masculine and feminine, and the contracted article l' which is used irrespective of gender, correspond to the English "the".

The questions at the end of each lesson are based upon the material included in the lesson. Questions like "how many words does a particular cognate word-ending apply to?" should highlight the extent of applicability to the given word-ending regularity. Questions on the content of the excerpts are used to verify comprehension. If a student works conscientiously through a lesson, the questions at the end of each lesson could be done as a quiz.

A separate answer key for each lesson could be prepared if the cognate unit is used in individualized instruction or as a self-instructional unit. In this way the student can try to answer the questions at first by himself. After completion of this task, the teacher could give the student the answer key for the particular lesson for which the student answered the questions.

The amount of time spent per lesson could vary, depending upon the cognitive ability and the interest generated in the study of cognates. For example, if a French excerpt is read out loud in class, unfamiliar words and/or sentence constructions are explained and questions are posed to verify comprehension. This exercise could last a forty minute class period. The presentation and explanation of the parts of speech presented in French could also take a class period of forty minutes. Students could read out loud the material presented, for example, on the conjunction, thereby practicing their French pronunciation; translation and some explanations may be needed for comprehension. If the example words in the word-ending regularities are used for pronunciation drills and/or a game of definition, a forty-minute class period could be devoted to this exercise. Depending upon how the lesson is presented, a lesson in the English-French cognate unit could take more time than one forty-minute class period.

It may be helpful if a teacher points out to the students how to study cognates. The student may indiscriminately place the same importance and emphasis on all the material included in the cognate unit without distinguishing that only the cognate word-ending regularities need to be memorized if the familiarity of meaning and the correct identification of the part of speech of the cognate poses no problem. The ten example words for each of the cognate word-ending regularities should help in memorizing them and the French excerpts in practicing cognate recognition. The teacher would be well-advised to heed the precept of Claparède (1916: 125) ". . .(vous) n'apprenez rien à l'enfant, . . .avant de lui en avoir préalablement fait sentir le besoin. . ."

Questions

1. What arguments could you think of in favor of and against the answer key in a student's manual?
2. List as many presentation styles for the cognate unit you can think of.
3. What is essential to know about cognates?
4. How much time would you as a teacher allow for cognate study? Justify your answer.

References

Claparède, E. Psychologie de l'enfant et pédagogie expérimentale. Septième édition, Librairie Kundig, Genève, 1916.

Hammer, P., & Monod, M.J. English-French Cognate Dictionary. The University of Alberta, Edmonton, 1976.

English-French Cognate Unit

"The shock of difference is as strong as that of familiarity"
(Steiner, 1975: 379).

In the pursuit of the 'Canadian Dream'

Lesson One

The objective of the lesson is to acquaint you with a comparison of the English and French vocabulary systems, the definition of cognates and the most frequent deceptive cognates contained in a French frequency word count, Le Français Fondamental, Premier Degré.

Comparison of the English and French Vocabulary Systems

The comparison of the two vocabulary systems of the English and French languages is based upon the similarities and differences between them. We will find seven word classifications (Lado, 1960).

1. There are words that are similar or identical in spelling and in meaning. For example, the word "piano" refers to the same musical instrument in both English and French. If these words share their etymological origin they are called cognates.

2. There are words which have the same spelling in the two languages but different meanings. For example the English word "coin" refers to money but the French word "coin" means corner. If these words share an etymological origin but have acquired different meanings in the two languages, they are called deceptive cognates.

3. Then there are words which are similar in meaning but are spelled differently in the two languages. For example "tree" in English is "arbre" in French.

4. There are words which have no equivalent meaning in the other language. For example "le concierge" in French has no exact counterpart in English.

5. There are words which are different in their type of construction. For example, for a French person studying English as a second language the two-word verbs may be difficult to learn. e.g., to call up = to telephone, to call on = to visit.

6. A special difficulty group is represented by the words that are harmless in connotation in the native language but offensive or taboo in the second language or vice versa. For example, the French word "tabernacle" is not used as a swear word in English.

7. Finally some words are used and understood only within a particular geographical region. Dialects fall into this category.

Definition of Cognates and Their Characteristics

The word "cognate" is derived from the Latin _cognatus_, meaning "born together, kindred, related, from the same stock". Applied to words, it refers to those having the same root or some derivation in common or to words that are similar or identical in spelling and meaning in two or more languages regardless of origin. The term cognate is also loosely applied to words borrowed in two or more languages from the same source. For example, English and French both adopted the word "malaria" from the Italian language. If the two words have the same origin but are now so different that speakers of the two languages do not identify them as similar, they are not considered cognates. The term _similar_ is restricted here to include items that have the "same" meaning in both languages in ordinary use. _Similar in form_ refers either to a change of one letter in the spelling of the French and English word, for example, oncle - uncle, avantage - advantage, or to the following regularities, among others, _if the spelling of the English and French words is otherwise the same_:

Nouns

1.	French -té (542)	=	English -ty
	qualité		quality
2.	French -ie (533)	=	English -y
	industrie		industry
3.	French -re (339)	=	English -er (or) -re
	mètre		meter
	centre		center
	agriculture		agriculture
4.	French -isme (302)	=	English -ism
	communisme		communism
5.	French -nce (274)	=	English -nce (or) -ncy
	fréquence		frequence, frequency
6.	French -iste (259)	=	English -ist
	journaliste		journalist
7.	French -eur (160)	=	English -or (or) -er
	acteur		actor

	employeur		employer
8.	French -cien (10)	=	English -cian
	électricien		electrician
9.	French -ion (1,176)	=	English -ion
	omission		omission
	aviation		aviation
	Verbs		
10.	French -er (829)	=	English: drop -er (or) -r
	confesser		to confess
	commencer		to commence
11.	French -ier (107)	=	English -y
	varier		to vary
	Adjectives		
12.	French -ique (605)	=	English -ic
	classique		classic
13.	French -if, ive (196)	=	English -ive
	collectif		collective
14.	French -eux, euse (161)	=	English -ous
	curieux		curious
15.	French -é (104)	=	English -ed
	sacré		sacred
16.	French -tiel, elle (16)	=	English -tial
	confidentiel		confidential

The numbers in parenthesis indicate the frequency of the cognates within each word-ending similarity class. For example, there are 542 cognates which have the French "-té" and English "-ty" ending. The cognates with these sixteen word-ending regularities account for 5,613 words in the cognate list. These cognate word-ending regularities are easily recognized, and there are almost no spelling exceptions.

The following cognate regularities may also be useful:

	Nouns		
17.	French -tie	=	English -cy
	diplomatie		dimplomacy

18.	French -et effet	= English -ect effect
19.	French -(^) forêt	= English: replace with "s" forest
20.	French -aire militaire	= English -ary military
21.	French -ès progrès	= English -ess progress
22.	French -oire histoire	= English -ory history
23.	French -ai aigle	= English -ea eagle
	Verbs	
24.	French -iser organiser	= English -ize (or) -ise to organize
25.	French -er humilier	= English -ate to humiliate
26.	French -quer indiquer	= English -cate to indicate
27.	French -ir finir	= English -ish to finish
	Adjectives	
28.	French: initial é étrange	= English: initial s strange
	Adverbs	
29.	French -ment certainment	= English -ly certainly

French roots that are spelled differently from the English roots have not been considered in the cognate count, because they may offer difficulty for recognition. For example,

accoutumer = to accustom, to habituate (à, to).

affliger - to afflict, to distress, to grieve.

However, with practice, these cognates will be recognized.

Partial Cognates

Most words have more than one meaning, depending on the context, and not all meanings necessarily coincide for a given cognate in the two languages. Some word pairs coincide in a few meanings, vary in many, and some coincide in many and vary in few. For example, "cascade" refers to a water-fall in both English and French, but in French it can also have the meanings of "ce qui se produit par saccades, par rebondissements successifs".

Deceptive Cognates

Deceptive cognates are words which are similar or identical in spelling in English and French but having a different meaning in the two languages. The term deceptive cognate does not refer exclusively to the origin of the words because different meanings may be observed in words sharing their origin or having similar spelling. For example, the word "decade" in English and French share the same Latin origin "decas, -adis", however in French the main meaning refers to ten days and in English to ten years. "Pain" meaning "bread" in French is derived from the Latin word "panis" whereas the English word "pain" developed from the Latin "poena" meaning penalty, punishment, pain. There are approximately 950 deceptive cognates for English and French (Seward, 1947).

Examples of Deceptive Cognates

<u>Verbs</u>

attendre	"to wait, to expect", <u>not</u> "to attend" (assister à) nor "to attend to" (s'occuper de)
chanter	"to sing", <u>not</u> "to chant" (psalmodier).
défendre de	"to forbid", <u>not</u> "to defend."
demander	"to request", <u>not</u> "to demand." (exiger)
partir	"to depart, to go off (a gun)", <u>not</u> "to part" (se séparer, se quitter). To part with = se débarrasser de.
regarder	"to look at, to concern", <u>not</u> the usual sense of "to regard" (considérer).
rester	"to remain", <u>not</u> "to rest, repose, rest upon" (reposer, appuyer sur).

retourner — "to return - go back", <u>not</u> "to return - come back" (revenir, rentrer).

sortir — "to come out, go out, to come from, to bring out", <u>not</u> "to sort" (trier).

travailler — "to work, to worry, agitate", <u>not</u> "to travail" (souffrir, peiner) nor "to travel" (voyager).

vendre — "to sell, to be bribed" (il s'est vendu), <u>not</u> "to vend" (colporter).

<u>Nouns</u>

actualité — "an event or topic of the present", generally <u>not</u> English "actuality" (réalité)

l'allée — "the garden path, lane, aisle", <u>not</u> "the alley" (la ruelle).

appareil — "preparations for display, equipment, apparatus (telephone, airplane, stove, denture)", <u>not</u> "apparel" (costume, vêtement).

armoire — "wardrobe, closet", <u>not</u> "an armory" (arsenal, salle d'armes).

barbe — "a beard", <u>not</u> "a barb" (la dent d'une flèche).

bonhomme — in spite of its apparent meaning, it means "old fellow, old cuss, etc.

boxe — "boxing, pugilism", <u>not</u> "a box" (une boîte).

bureau — "a desk", <u>not</u> "a bureau" (un chiffonnier, une commode).

cabine — "a cabin (on board of ship)", <u>not</u> "a cabin" (on land), (une cabane).

cave — "cellar, wine cellar", <u>not</u> "cave" (caverne).

chance — "luck, possibility, risk", <u>not</u> often "an opportunity" (une occasion).

citron — "a lemon", <u>not</u> "a citron" (un cédrat, une sorte de pastèque).

course — "running, a race, an errand, a trip", <u>not</u> "a course" (un cours, un service, un plat).

dent — "the tooth, the cog, the scallop (of an edge)", <u>not</u> "a dent" (une entaille).

enfant — "a child", <u>not</u> "an infant" (un bébé).

étage — "a story, floor (of a building)", <u>not</u> "a stage" (in a theater: une scène).

fête — "the festival", <u>not</u> "the feast" (le banquet, le festin).

gardien — "a guard, keeper", <u>not</u> (a legal) guardian (of children), (un tuteur).

habit — "a swallow tail, dress coat, attire, clothing (les habits)", <u>not</u> "a habit" (clothing) (habit de cheval, habit de nonne) nor "the habit" - custom (l'habitude).

patron — "the boss, the captain (of a ship)", <u>not</u> "the patron" (except for "le saint patron"), (le client).

place — "a public square, market, a seat", <u>not</u> English "place" (endroit).

prune — "a plum", <u>not</u> "a prune" (pruneau).

raisin — "a grape", <u>not</u> "a raisin" (un raisin sec).

station — "a stopping place", <u>not</u> English "railway station" (une gare).

tarte — "a pie (of fruit or custard, generally open-faced)", <u>not</u> "a tart" (une petite pâtisserie aux fruits).

voyage — "trip, travel", <u>not</u> "a voyage" (voyage par mer).

<u>Adjectives</u>

ancien (before a noun) "former", <u>not</u> "ancient" (this sense if adjective follows)

content — "glad, happy", <u>not</u> English "content" (satisfait, contenté).

gentil — "nice, Gentile", <u>not</u> English "gentle" (doux) nor "genteel" (distingué).

It should be noted that not all meanings of a deceptive cognate must necessarily be deceptive. Like partial cognates, one meaning of the English-French cognate may be deceptive in a given context but permissible and correct in another one. For example, the French verb "défendre" may be used in the sense of "to forbid" and in the sense of "to defend" (or protect). Thus, you could use it correctly or incorrectly depending on the context. Some cognates listed as deceptive may never be a deceptive cognate for you, because it depends on the context in which you learn the word. Thus, you may never have confused "le coin" meaning corner in English with "the coin" meaning "la pièce, la monnaie" in French.

Any possible confusion you experience with deceptive cognates may depend on how much French knowledge you have already acquired prior to using or studying with cognates and to what extent you read English into French. It may be possible that, for example, you mistake the French word "an", meaning "year" in English, for the indefinite article "an" in English. If no other word is recognized and the context of the reading passage is not known, this confusion could probably arise. To keep this type of mistake to a minimum, learning French with cognates requires constant alertness and cognitive flexibility to expand, narrow or qualify the meanings of English-French cognates in accordance with all possible morphological, syntactical and contextual clues to decode a French reading passage.

The possible utility you can derive from cognate study depends essentially on your ability to recognize cognates and know their meaning in English. It is assumed that your ability to ignore small differences in the spelling of English and French and to see "abuse" in "abus", "act" in "acte" and "achieve" in "achever" may be enhanced with practice.

How to study with English-French cognates depends on whether or not you can determine in advance which cognates you already know. With the information on English-French cognates as presented in "Definition of Cognates and Their Characteristics" (earlier in this lesson) you could do the following:

1) You could read the English-French Cognate Dictionary (1976) and study these cognates like a word list.

2) You could focus your attention on the deceptive cognates and study Seward's dictionary of French Deceptive Cognates (1947).

3) You could learn the cognate word-ending regularities and plunge into reading French. You know that the ratio of cognates to deceptive cognates is approximately eleven to one.

To facilitate the third suggestion, studying cognates in reading selections, the following lessons concentrate on vocabulary development techniques and an analysis of sentence constructions.

Questions

1) Should you find any more cognate regularities, please list them.
2) What are the meanings of the following words: linguistic interference, phonetics, morphology, context, cognition, lexicon, semantics, syntax?
3) Write in your own words a short definition of cognates, partial cognates and deceptive cognates.

Lesson Two
Recognition of Written Cognates

Cognates should prove useful in facilitating reading once the recognition of them and familiarity with their meaning are taken into consideration. In order to facilitate the recognition of English-French cognates in reading, you learn:

1. The word-ending regularities of the English-French cognates (see "Definition of Cognates and Their Characteristics," Lesson One);
2. Some characteristics of the French nouns, articles, pronouns, verbs and auxiliaries, adjectives, adverbs, prepositions and conjunctions;
3. How to use context clues in word recognition and comprehension;
4. How to recognize the main elements of the sentence;
5. How to understand sentence structure;

In this lesson you will learn some formulate rules about French noun characteristics, i.e., gender - masculine or feminine, number - singular or plural; you will also (1) study the first four word ending regularities of nouns: the "-té, -ie, -ance (or) - ence, and -iste", (2) practice the recognition and pronunciation of cognates with the French excerpt "La Renaissance italienne", and answer the questions at the end of the lesson.

Nouns

1. Nouns are words like "électricité, comédie, tracteur" which usually name a person, place or thing.
2. Nouns are preceded by articles ("le, la, l', les, un, une, de la, du, de l', des"), and/or adjectives.
3. Nouns usually form the plural by adding an "s".

Cognate Word-ending Regularities

1. French -té = English -ty (nouns)

1. admissibilité = fait d'être admissible
2. beauté = caractère de ce qui est beau
3. calamité = grande infortune ou malheur, catastrophe
4. captivité = état de celui qui est captif
5. collectivité = ensemble d'individus groupés naturellement ou pour atteindre un but

6. curiosité = désir de savoir les secrets d'autrui
7. diversité = caractère, état de ce qui est divers
8. électricité = une des formes de l'énergie
9. éternité = durée qui n'a ni commencement ni fin
10. extrémité = la partie extrême, qui termine une chose

All 542 English-French cognate nouns ending in "-té" are feminine.

2. French -ie = English -y (nouns)

1. catégorie = comment on range des objets
2. comédie = le genre comique
3. économie = art de bien administrer un état
4. épilepsie = maladie nerveuse caractérisée par de brusques attaques convulsives avec perte de connaissance
5. géologie = l'étude de la structure et de l'évolution de l'écorce terrestre
6. géométrie - une branche des mathématiques
7. ironie = manière de se moquer (de qqn. ou de qqch.) en disant le contraire de ce qu'on veut faire entendre
8. philosophie = les recherches sur la connaissance
9. théorie = ensemble d'idées, de concepts abstraits, plus ou moins organisées, appliqué à un domaine particulier
10. pharmacie = science des remèdes et des médicaments

The English-French cognate word-ending "-ie" is most often feminine.

3. French - nce = English - nce (or) -ncy (nouns)

1. fréquence = caractère de ce qui arrive plusieurs fois
2. assurance = confiance en soi-même
3. indécence = caractère de ce qui est indécent
4. inélégance = manque d'élégance
5. pertinence = caractère de ce qui est pertinent
6. science = activité scientifique
7. régence = gouvernement d'une monarchie par un régent
8. transparence = phénomène par lequel les rayons lumineux visibles sont perçus à travers certaines substances
9. distance = longueur minimum qui sépare une chose d'une autre

10. importance = caractère de ce qui est important

All 274 English-French cognate words with the "-nce" ending are feminine words.

4. French -iste = English -ist (nouns)

1. artiste = créateur d'une oeuvre d'art
2. loyaliste = qui a des sentiments de loyalisme
3. humaniste = homme qui a une connaissance approfondie des langues et des littératures grecques, latines
4. journaliste = personne qui collabore à la rédaction d'un journal
5. linguiste = spécialiste en linguistique, science de la langue
6. météorologiste = personne qui s'occupe de l'étude scientifique des phénomènes atmosphériques
7. touriste = personne qui se déplace, voyage pour son plaisir
8. impérialiste = homme qui est favorable à la politique d'expansion nationale
9. spécialiste = personne qui a des connaissances approfondies dans un domaine déterminé et restreint
10. socialiste = personne qui fait profession de socialisme

The "-iste" ending may be feminine or masculine.

La Renaissance italienne

Au XVe siècle, la riche famille des Médicis règne sur la ville de Florence en Italie. Elle se fait la protectrice des peintres et des sculpteurs désireux de retrouver l'harmonie et la magnificence de l'art gréco-romain. La cité rivalise de splendeur par ses palais, ses églises, ses monuments et ses fêtes, avec Venise, Rome, etc. Tous les "humanistes", ces hommes à la culture universelle, se passionnent alors pour la botanique, la zoologie, l'anatomie, la géologie, l'astrologie, la navigation, et surtout l'étude des textes anciens pour retrouver les premières sources d'inspiration. On appelle cette période la "Renaissance".
(<u>Vidéo-Presse</u>, Vol. IV, Numéro 4, décembre 1974, p. 38.)

Questions

1) State the rules for the four cognate word-ending regularities in this lesson.
2) To how many English-French cognates does the "-té" ending apply?
3) How might you remember whether the "-iste" cognate word-ending regularity is masculine or feminine?
4) Do you notice something about the French definition given of the cognate words? Yes, or no? Please specify.
5) Write out the words you think are English-French cognates in the excerpt "La Renaissance italienne".
6) How many did you find?
7) Did you recognize "famille, règne, ville, peintres, palais, rivalise, fêtes"? Write down the English equivalent of these words.
8) Try to answer the following French questions on the content of the excerpt:
   a) Quel est le siècle de la Renaissance italienne?
   b) Qui a protégé les peintres et les sculpteurs?
   c) Que signifie l'expression "les humanistes"?
   d) Quelle ville rivalise de splendeur avec Venise et Rome?
   e) Où les humanistes cherchaient-ils leur inspiration?
   f) Comment était la famille des Médicis?
9) What part of speech is "la protectrice"? List all the possible reasons for your choice.
10) What parts of speech may precede a noun?
11) How do you generally form the plural of French nouns?

Lesson Three

The semantic value of the suffixes contained in the word-ending regularities are explained as well as their morphological characteristics. The remaining four word-ending regularities of French-English cognate nouns: the "-eur, -isme, -cien, and -re" are to be studied as in lesson two. Some characteristics of articles and pronouns are reviewed. Recognition of cognates is practiced with the excerpt on "la Pollution" taken from <u>Vidéo-Press</u>. You should review the French noun characteristics in lesson two before doing this lesson.

Suffixes

A suffix is an ending which is added to a word root in order to form a new word. Suffixes are also often used to change a word from one part of speech to another, e.g., calme = adj., calmement = adv.

Les suffixes "-té, -ie, -ence (ou) -ance, et -re" forment de nombreux substantifs. ex. beauté, comédie, fréquence, mètre.

Les suffixes "-isme, -iste" forment des substantifs indiquant: la doctrine ou la profession: socialisme, journalisme; la personne qui la pratique: socialiste, journaliste.

Les suffixes "-eur, -cien" forment de nombreux substantifs (personne qui fait quelque chose (qqch.), ex. docteur, mécanicien.

Le suffixe "-ique" forme des adjectifs ex. ironique, ou des substantifs, ex. fabrique.

Les suffixes "-eux, euse; -if, ive; -tiel, tielle; -é, ée" forment de nombreux adjectifs. ex. ambitieux, érosif, substantiel, exilé.

Le suffixe "-ment" forme de nombreux adverbes. ex. certainement.

Suffixes généraux issus d'éléments grecs et latins

suffixe	sens	mot examplaire
-cratie n.f.	pouvoir politique ou social	démocratie.
-graphe n.m.	personne qui enregistre	lexicographe,
	appareil enregistreur	phonographe.
-graphie n.f.	mode d'enregistrement	sténographie.
-logie n.f.	science	bactériologie, psychologie.

-logue	m.et f. spécialiste scientifique	géologue,
-logiste	" "	psysiologiste.
-mètre	n.m. qui mesure	baromètre, thermomètre.
-métrie	n.f. mesure	psychométrie.
-phile	m.et f. qui aime, qul a de l'affinité pour	francophile.
-philie	n.f. affinité pour, attachement	anglophilie.
-phone	m.et f. qui parle, qui est enregistré ou enregistre	téléphone, francophone.
-phonie	n.f. transmission de sons	radiophonie.
-scope	m.et f. qui examine	téléscope, stéthoscope.

n. Øf. = nom féminin; n.m. = nom masculin

Cognate Word-ending Regularities

5. French =eur = English -or (or) -er (nouns)

1. constructeur = celui qui construit quelque chose (qqch.)
2. décorateur = personne qui fait des travaux de décoration
3. docteur = personne qui possède le titre de docteur en médecine
4. évaporateur = apparell employé à la compression où se produit l'évaporation
5. exploiteur = personne qui tire un profit abusif d'une situation ou d'une personne
6. gladiateur = homme qui combattait dans les jeux du cirque, à Rome
7. imitateur = personne qui imite les gestes, le comportement d'autrui
8. imposteur = celui qui abuse de la confiance, de la crédulité d'autrui par ses discours mensongers, dans le dessein d'en tirer profit
9. narrateur = personne qui raconte
10. tracteur - véhicule automobile

The "-eur" ending may be feminine or masculine. The feminine ending for the nouns in "-eur" when they refer to a person generally is "-rice," e.g., acteur - actrice.

6. French -isme = English -ism (nouns)

1. existentialisme = doctrine philosophique de l'existence individuelle
2. dogmatisme = caractère des croyances (religieuses, philosophiques) que s'appuient sur des dogmes
3. égotisme = culte du moi, poursuite trop exclusive de son développement personnel
4. humanisme = formation de l'esprit humain par la culture littéraire ou scientifique
5. hypnotisme = ensemble des phénomènes qui constituent le sommeil artificiel.
6. individualisme = attitude d'esprit, état de fait favorisant l'initiative et la réflexion individuelle, le goût de l'indépendance
7. matérialisme = état d'esprit caractérisé par la recherche des jouissances et des biens matériels
8. militarisme = prépondérance de l'armée, de l'élément militaire dans la vie d'une société
9. tourisme = le fait de voyager
10. socialisme = une doctrine de l'organisation sociale

the "=isme" noun ending is always masculine.

7. French - cien = English - cian (nouns)

1. électricien = technicien ou ouvrier spécialisé dans le matériel et les installations électriques
2. magicien = personne qui pratique la magie
3. métaphysicien = personne qui s'occupe de réflexions abstraites
4. opticien = celui qui connaît l'optique
5. patricien = personne qui appartenait à la classe supérieure des citoyens romains, aristocrate
6. phonétician = linguiste spécialisé dans la phonétique
7. politicien = personne qui exerce une action politique dans le gouvernement ou dans l'opposition
8. tacticien = celui qui est spécialiseé dans l'emploi des moyens de combat, dans l'exécution des plans stratégiques

9. technicien = personne qui possède, connaît une technique particulière
10. muscien = personne qui connaît l'art de la musique

The '-cien" is a masculine ending.

8. French -re = English -er (nouns)

1. baromètre = instrument qui sert à mesuer la pression atmosphérique
2. hexamètre = qui a six pieds ou six mesures, ex. un vers hexamètre
3. kilomètre = unité pratique de distance qni vaut mille mètres (km)
4. lettre (f) = écrit que l'on adresse à qqn. pour lui communiquer qqch.
5. millimètre = de milli- et mètre; millième partie du mètre
6. ministre = homme d'Etat placé à la tête d'un département ministériel
7. monstre = être, animal fantastique et terrible (des légendes, mythologies)
8. novembre = onzième mois de l'année
9. septembre = neuvième mois de l'année
10. thermomètre = instrument destiné à mesurer des températures

The "-re" ending may be feminine or masculine.

Vocabulary Development

We communicate in a variety of ways but mainly we communicate verbally. Words are not things but symbols that stand for things. Words are independent units of speech and writing. What a person speaks, hears, reads, writes, and often what he visualizes and observes--the whole sensorium of man--is expressed in words. Thus, your study habits should include analyzing, observing, investigating, and interrelating systematically word parts (roots, prefixes and suffixes) so as to increase your knowledge of vocabulary.

L'article défini et indéfini

	L'article défini		L'article indéfini	
	Genre		Genre	
	Masculin	Féminin	Masculin	Féminin
singulier	le (l')	la (l')	un	une
pluriel	les	les	des	des

1. On distingue deux espèces d'articles: l'article défini et l'article indéfini. L'article défini est celui qui se met devant un nom pris dans un sens complètement déterminé; il individualise l'être ou l'objet nommeé. Par exemple, donnez-moi <u>la</u> clef (c'est-à-dire la clef que l'on sait). L'article indéfini n'individualise pas l'être ou l'objet nommé. Par exemple, donnez-moi <u>une</u> pomme (c'est-à-dire n'importe laquelle].
2. L'article est un mot que l'on place devant le nom.
3. Il sert aussi à indiquer le genre et le nombre du nom qu'il précède.

Le Pronom

1. Le pronom est un mot qui souvent représente un nom, une idée ou une proposition exprimés avant ou aprés lui.
2. Pronoms Personnels

SUJET	OBJET DIRECT	OBJET INDIRECT	POSSESSIF	
je	me	me	le mien	les miens
			la mienne	les miennes
tu	te	te	le tien	les tiens
			la tienne	les tiennes
il, elle	le, la	lui	le sien	les siens
			la sienne	les siennes
nous	nous	nous	le nôtre	les nôtres
			la nôtre	les nôtres
vous	vous	vous	le vôtre	les vôtres
			la vôtre	les vôtres
ils, elles	les	leur	le leur	les leurs
			la leur	les leurs

3. Les pronoms dits "indéfinis" sont "quelqu'un, quelque chose, chacun, quiconque, on, etc."

La Pollution

Comment l'air se pollue:

Le plus grand responsable de la pollution de l'air est certainement le tuyau d'échappement de l'automobile. Et nous sommes loin de faire des efforts pour éliminer cet ennemi. Que de déplacements nous pourrions effectuer sans avoir recours à l'automobile: Nos moindres déplacements requièrent un véhicule. Afin de diminuer l'effet néfaste de l'oxyde de carbone, le Gouvernement oblige les fabricants d'automobiles à installer des systèmes anti-pollution sur tous les nouveaux véhicules. Informe - toi auprès de plusieurs garagiste pour savoir si les dispositifs anti-pollution ont une influence sur le coût de l'essence et sur le rendement de l'automobile.

Dans les usines, on dépense tous les ans des milliers de dollars pour dimineur la pollution de l'air. Le Gouvernement se montre assez sévère envers les fabricants d'automobiles. Et toi, que feras-tu? Il n'est plus possible de rester indifférent. Tu dois faire ta propre campagne en vue d'une plus grande utilisation de la bicyclette.
(Vidéo-Presse, Vol. III, Numéro 7, mars 1974, p. 53.)

Questions

1) State the rules for the four cognate word-ending regularities in this lesson.
2) What does the "-isme" suffix mean?
3) What part of speech is indicated with the "-eur" ending?
4) What does the suffix ending "-eur" mean?
5) To how many English-French cognates do the "isme", the "-ie" and "-re" endings apply?
6) There are 28 English-French cognates, not counting the same word twice, in the excerpt "la Pollution". Can you find them? Please list them.
7) Did you guess the meaning of "les fabricants," "le coût," "bicyclette?" Write down the English meaning for these words.
8) Did you beware of "rester" and "millier"? What is the meaning of these words?
9) Try to answer the following French questions on the content of the excerpt:
   a) Qu'est-ce qui est responsable de la pollution de l'air?
   b) Qu'est-ce qu'on fait pour diminuer l'effet de l'oxyde de carbone?

c) De quels moyens de transport pourrait-on se servir pour diminuer la pollution de l'air?
d) Est-ce que le système anti-pollution augmente le coût de l'essence?
e) Qui oblige les fabricants d'automobiles à installer des systèmes anti-pollution?
f) Y a-t-il d'autres sources de pollution?

10) What part of speech is "véhicules" in "tous les nouveaux véhicules"? List all the possible reasons for your choice.
11) What part of speech is "ennemi"? List the reason(s) for your choice.
12) What part of speech does the personal pronoun replace?
13) What part of speech indicates the gender of nouns?
14) Define the indefinite article.
15) What is the English definite article? Give an example. What is the English indefinite article? Give an example.

Lesson Four

Study some of the characteristics of the French verb and auxiliaries. In addition, study the following cognate word-ending regularities: "-er and -ier" in the same way as in Lesson Two. Practice the recognition of cognates with the excerpt "L'Empire Inca" taken from Vidéo-Presse.

Verbs

1. Verbs are words like "examiner, dénier, citer" that express an action or a state of being.
2. Verbs can show a change in tense by a change in sound and spelling; e.g., you can form the present indicative of the verb "parler," "je parle;" the imperfect "je parlais"; the future "je parlerai"; and the present conditional "je parlerais."
3. Verbs may be preceded by nouns, personal pronouns or direct and indirect objects, (e.g., "je, tu, il, elle, nous, vous, ils, elles, le, la, lui, leur, etc.").
4. Verbs that join two nouns that refer to the same person or thing, or a noun and an adjective that refer to the same person or thing, are called linking verbs or copulas. Common linking verbs (copulas) are "être, sembler, paraître, avoir l'air, devenir, etc."

Auxiliaries

1. The most frequent auxiliary verbs are "avoir" and "être." For example, "j'ai chanté, je suis venu, etc."
2. Auxiliaries always pattern with (appear next to) verbs in statements and can be thought of as "helping" verbs.
3. If there are two or more verbs that can stand together (i.e., be placed side by side without changing the general meaning), the last one is the main verb and the others are auxiliaries, e.g., "Pierre a fait son devoir."
4. Other common auxiliaries are: "aller, devoir, faillir, manquer de, faire, laisser, pouvoir, venir de, vouloir, se mettre à, etc."

At this point you would be well advised to study carefully the conjugation of the verbs listed for your convenience in Appendix A.

Cognate Word-ending Regularities

9. French -er = English drop -er (or) -r (verbs)

1. citer = rapporter un texte pour démontrer ce que l'on avance
2. confirmer = affirmer l'exactitude, l'existence de qqch.
3. dater = mettre la date sur (un écrit, un acte)
4. déplorer = beaucoup regretter
5. déclarer = faire connaître (un sentiment, une volonté, une vérité) d'une façon expresse
6. destiner = fixer d'avance, assigner, réserver
7. détecter = révéler l'existence de (un corps, un phénomène caché)
8. discipliner = accoutumer à la discipline, donner le sens de l'ordre, du devoir
9. disputer = ne pas vouloir accorder qqch. à qqn.
10. examiner = considérer avec attention

The "-er" verbs in this list form their present tense by adding to the stem (---) the following endings:

je --- e	nous --- ons
tu --- es	vous --- ez
il --- e	ils --- ent

10. French - ier = English -y (verbs)

1. défier = inviter à venir se mesurer comme adversaire
2. dénier = refuser de reconnaître comme vrai (un fait)
3. glorifier = honorer qqn., qqch. en proclamant ses mérites, sa gloire
4. horrifier = remplir d'horreur
5. identifier = reconnaître
6. modifier = changer (une chose) sans en altérer la nature
7. simplifier = rendre plus simple, moins complexe
8. terrifier = frapper de terreur, d'une vive crainte
9. unifier = faire de (plusieurs éléments) une seule et même chose
10. purifier = rendre pur, débarrasser de la corruption

L'Empire Inca

A l'origine, une humble peuplade indienne installée sur les bords de l'océan Pacifique avait entrepris la conquête des territoires avoisinants. Au lieu, cependant, d'anéantir complètement les vaincus, elle les intégrait à sa propre société et faisait corps avec eux. Un réseau efficace de communications et de voies commerciales était établi aussi rapidement que possible, de façon à accélérer toutes espèces d'échanges. L'usage des terres était concédé à diverses classes sociales.

La succession royale, chez les Incas, ne se faisait pas automatiquement, comme chez les monarques européens de l'époque. Non seulement l'aîné, mais tous les fils de l'empereur possédaient un statut égal, celui de descendant du Dieu-Soleil.

(*Vidéo-Presse*, Vol. III, no. 7, mars 1974, page 8.)

Questions

1. State the rules for the cognate word-ending regularities in this lesson.
2. What part of speech does the "-cien" word-ending signal?
3. To how many English-French cognates do "-ion," "-nce, "-iste," "-eur" and "-cien" apply?
4. How many English-French cognates are in the excerpt "L'Empire Inca"? Please list them.
5. Did you recognize the meaning of "peuplade, bords, établi, échanges, espèces, époque"? Write down the English equivalent for these words.
6. Did you think of "propre" as meaning "own"?
7. Did you beware of "corps"? In what sense is it used in this excerpt?
8. Try to answer the following French questions on the content of the excerpt:
   a) Où vivait la peuplade indienne au début?
   b) Qu'est-ce que les Incas faisaient des vaincus?
   c) A qui appartenait la terre?
   d) Pourquoi les voies de communication étaient-elles importantes?
   e) Qui avait le droit à la succession du trône?
   f) Quelle était la differnce entre les lois de succession en Europe et dans l'empire Inca de la même époque?
9. What part of speech is the word "intégrait"? List all the possible reasons for your choice.
10. How many simple and compound tenses are there in French? Hint: look in Appendix A.
11. What part of speech is "avait" in the first sentence of the excerpt "L'Empire Inca"?

Lesson Five

Review the characteristics of the French adjective. Study the following cognate word-ending regularities: "-ique, -if, -eux, -tiel, -é" in the same way as in Lesson Two. Practice the recognition of cognates with the excerpt "Les Dinosaures" taken from Vidéo-Presse.

Adjectives

1. Adjectives are words like "dramatique, furieux, défensif" that describe or qualify nouns.
2. Adjectives agree in number and gender with the noun they modify. e.g., "un plan secret -- une décision secrète; les hommes intelligents -- les femmes intelligentes."
3. Descriptive adjectives follow the noun.
4. Adjectives can be changed to comparative and superlative forms.
5. Adjectives are words that will fill the blank in the test sentence:

   The (any suitable noun) is/are very ---.

Cognate Word-ending Regularities

11. French -ique = English -ic (adj. +/or nouns)

1. arithmétique adj., f = relatif à l'arithmétique
2. clinique adj., f = méthode qui consiste à faire un diagnostic par l'observation
3. comique adj., m = qui appartient à la comédie
4. dramatique adj., f = le genre dramatique; très grave et dangereux
5. économique adj., m - qui réduit les frais
6. électronique adj., f = propre ou relatif à l'électron
7. électrique adj. = propre ou relatif à l'électricité
8. gothique adj., f = l'art du moyen âge en Europe du XIIe au XVIe siècle
9. historique adj., m = qui se rapporte à l'histoire
10. humoristique adj. = qui s'expime avec humour

The French "-ique" ending can be an adjective or noun ending. The French adjective generally forms the plural by adding an "s." Feminine and masculine.

12. French -if = English -ive (adjectives)

1. décisif = qui décide, qui conduit à un résultat définitif
2. défensive = qui est fait pour la défense

3. définitif = qui est fixé de manière qu'il n'y ait plus à revenir sur la chose
4. digestif = qui contribue à la digestion
5. diminutif = qui donne, ajoute une idée de petitesse
6. duplicatif = qui double une quantité, un volume
7. érosif = qui produit l'érosion
8. excessif = qui dépasse la mesure souhaitable ou permise
9. expressif = qui a beaucoup d'expression
10. expulsif = qui fait sortir avec violence

Adjectives ending in "f" change "f" into "ve" to form the feminine form of the adjective, e.g., décisif, décisive

13. French -eux = English -ous (adjectives)

1. dangereux = qui constitue un danger
2. délicieux = qui est extrêmement agréable
3. fabuleux = invraisemblable quoique réel, qui appartient à la fable, au merveilleux
4. furieux = qui est animé, excité par une passion folle, sans frein
5. harmonieux = agréable à l'oreille (en parlant d'un son, d'une combinaison de sons)
6. lumineux = qui émet ou réfléchit la lumière
7. malicieux = qui a de la malice
8. mélodieux = agréable à l'oreille
9. miraculeux = qui est le résultat d'un miracle
10. mystérieux = qui est incompréhensible ou inconnu

Adjective endings in "x" change "x" into "se" to form the feminine, e.g., courageux, courageuse

14. French - tiel = English -tial (adjectives)

1. différentiel = relatif aux différences ou aux variations
2. substantiel = qui a de la substance
3. pénitentiel = relatif à la pénitence
4. pestilentiel = qui tient de la peste
5. préférentiel = qui établit une préférence
6. présidentiel = relatif au président, à la présidence
7. providential = qui se rapporte à la providence
8. résidentiel = propre à l'habitation, à la résidence

9. substantiel = qui appartient à la substance
10. torrentiel = qui caractérise les torrents

Adjectives in "el" double the final consonant before adding "e" to form the feminine, e.t., résidentiel, résidentielle

15. French -é = English -ed (adjectives)

1. condensé = qui contient beaucoup de matière sous un petit volume
2. déterminé = qui a été précisé, défini
3. discipliné = qui observe la discipline
4. excité = qui a une activité mentale, psychique très vive
5. exilé = qui est en exil
6. exposé = qui est mis en vue
7. incliné = enclin, porté (à)
8. inspiré = animé par l'inspiration, souffle divin ou créateur
9. persuadé = qui est amené à croire, à penser, à vouloir
10. qualifié = qui satisfait aux conditions requises

To form the feminine form of a French past participle you add another "e", e.g., condensé, condensée.

Les Dinosaures

Les lézards terribles du Canada :

Le Canada passe pour un pays jeune et peu peuplé. En fait, la plus grande partie de son immense territoire se classe parmi les plus vieilles terres émergées du monde.

Notre pays compta jadis une population si nombreause et si terrible que les Canadiens du XXe siècle s'enfuiraient à toutes jambes s'il leur était donné de voir un seul de ses "anciens Canadiens." Mais rassurez-vous: il y a bien peu de chances de croiser, sur l'autoroute Québec-Montréal, . . . un dinosaure : Cet étrange animal --- dinosaure veut dire, en grec, lézard terrible --- vivait il y a plus de 60 millions d'années, bien avant que l'homme n'apparaisse sur notre plantête!

Des dinosaures ont été découverts dans diverses parties du monde, mais c'est en Alberta qu'on a retrouvé le plus grand nombre et la plus grande variété de spécimens de la période du crétacé supérieur: plus de 65 espèces différentes!

Vidéo-Presse , vol. I, Numéro 7, avril 1970, pp. 7-8)

Questions

1 State the rules for the cognate word-ending regularities in this lesson.
2. What do the suffixes "-phone," "-phile," "-logie" and "-mètre" mean?
3. To how many English-French cognates do the "-é," "-eux" and "-tiel" word-ending regularities apply?
4. Write three examples of cognate words where the suffix affects the part of speech of words but not necessarily the essential meaning.
5. How many English-French cognates did you identify in the excerpt? Please list them.
6. Did you recognize or guess the meaning of the following words: "fait, découverts, nombre, nombreuse, rassurez, autoroute, grec, peuplé, espèces"? Write down the English equivalent for these words.
7. What is the meaning of "partie," "anciens" and "chances" in this excerpt?
8. Try to answer the following French questions on the content of the excerpt:
   1) Le Canada est-il une nation jeune ou âgée?
   b) Où a-t-on trouvé le plus grand nombre et la plus grande variété de dinosaures?
   c) Que ferais-tu si tu rencontrais un dinosaure?
   d) Que veut dire dinosaure en grec?
   e) Combien de spécimens de dinosaures a-t-on identifiés en Alberta?
   f) D'après cet extrait, qui sont les "anciens Canadiens"?
9. Identify the parts of speech of the following words: a) peuplé, b) passe, c) territoire and d) émergées. List all the characteristics applicable to these words.
10. With what part of speech does the French adjective agree in number and gender?
11. How would you form the plural of the French adjective?
12) How would you verify whether a word is an adjective?

Lesson Six

Review some characteristics of the adverbs, prepositions and conjunctions. Study the "-ment" cognate word-ending regularity in the same way as in Lesson Two. Learn how to use context clues, and practice cognate recognition with the excerpt "L'Avenir de l'Amérique Centrale."

Adverbs

1. Adverbs are words like "certainement, simplement, immédiatement" that modify verbs, adjectives or other adverbs.
2. Words that end in -ment (and are neither nouns nor verbs) are adverbs.
3. Adverbs modify verbs, adjectives or other adverbs. e.g., Nous allons quelquefois au théâtre. (modifie le verbe "aller")
   Madame Curie était une femme vraiment géniale. (modifie l'adjectif "géniale")
   Nous allons très rarement au cinéma. (modifie l'adverbe "rarement")
4. There are no absolute rules concerning the position of an adverb in a sentence. Generally speaking, the adverb which modifies a verb is placed directly after the verb. e.g., La rivière coulait lentement sous le pont.
5. Adverbs may frequently be moved to new positions in the sentence without changing the general meaning of the sentence. e.g.,
   Maintenant je comprends votre inquiétude.
   Je comprends maintenant votre inquiétude.
   Je comprends votre inquiétude maintenant.

La Préposition

1. La préposition est un mot invariable qui sert ordinairement à introduire un élément qu'il relie et subordonne, par tel ou tel rapport, à un autre élément de la phrase: ex.,
   habiter dans une chaumière (rapport de lieu)
   il régnait depuis deux ans (rapport de temps)
   le jardin de mon voisin (rapport d'appartenance)
   pêcher à la ligne (rapport de moyen)
   ingénieux par besoin (rapport de cause)

2. Liste des principales prépositions:

à	de	excepté	parmi	selon
après	depuis	hormis	passé	sous
attendu	derrière	hors	pendant	suivant
avant	dès	jusque(s)	plein	suppose
avec	devant	malgré	pour	sur
chez	durant	moyennant	près	touchant
concernant	en	nonobstant	proche	vers
contre	entre	outre	sans	voici
dans	envers	par	sauf	vu

Il faut observer que la présente liste comprend des mots qui n'appartiennent pas exclusivement à la catégorie des prépositions (Grevisse, 1975: 957).

3. Une locution prépositive est une réunion de mots équivalent à une préposition: à cause de, auprès de, d'après, jusqu'à, par delà, en dehors de, etc.

4. L'usage ordinaire demande que la préposition soit suivie immédiatement de son objet, qui forme souvent avec elle une unité sémantique.

La Conjonction

1. La conjonction est un mot invariable qui sert à joindre et à mettre en rapport, soit deux propositions, soit deux mots ou groupes de mots de même fonction dans une proposition. Ex.,

Je t'aiderai <u>puisque</u> tu m'aides aussi.
Je t'aiderai <u>quand</u> tu auras besoin d'aide.
Je t'aiderai <u>si</u> tu m'aides aussi.
Je t'aiderai <u>parce que</u> tu m'as aussi aidé
Je t'aiderai <u>à condition que</u> tu m'aides aussi.
Je t'aiderai <u>dès que</u> tu auras besoin d'aide.
Je t'aiderai <u>même si</u> tu ne m'as pas aidé.
Je t'aiderai <u>malgré que</u> tu ne m'aies pas aidé.
Je t'aiderai <u>pourvu que</u> tu m'aides.
Je t'aiderai <u>attendu que</u> tu en as besoin.

ex., deux mots de même fonction: Paul <u>et</u> Pierre, automatiquement <u>et</u> immédiatement, jeune <u>et</u> beau, dormir <u>et</u> rêver

2. On distingue deux catégories de conjonctions: les conjonctions de

coordination et les conjonctions de subordination.

3. Les conjonctions de coordination servent à joindre, soit deux propositions de même nature, soit deux parties semblables d'une même proposition. Ces conjonctions peuvent donc unir des mots, des groupes de mots, ou des propositions.

4. Les principaux rapports indiqués par les conjonctions (et locutions conjonctives) de coordination sont:

a) union, liaison: et, comme, puis, ensuite, etc.

b) cause: car, en effet, etc.

c) conséquence: donc, par conséquent, par suite, etc.

d) transition: or, etc.

e) opposition, restriction: mais, au contraire, néanmoins, par contre, etc.,

f) alternative: ou, soit . . . soit, etc.

g) explication: à savoir, c'est-à-dire, etc.

5. Les conjonctions de subordination ou subjonctions servent à relier une proposition subordonnée à la proposition dont elle dépend. Ces subjonctions ne peuvent donc unir que des propositions.

6. Les principaux rapports indiqués par les conjonctions (et locutions conjonctives) de subordination sont:

a) cause: comme, parce que, puisque, attendu que, etc.,

b) but: à fin que, pour que, etc.

c) conséquence: que, de sorte que, de façon que, si bien que, etc.,

d) concession, opposition: bien que, quoique, malgré que, au lieu que, etc.

e) temps: quand, lorsque, avant que, dès que, jusqu'à ce que, etc.

(Grevisse, 1975: 1070-72)

En général, les conjonctions se placent avant les mots, les groupes de mots, les propositions quelles relient à d'autres mots ou à d'autres propositions. La conjonction et la préposition indiquent l'une et l'autre les rapports établis entre les éléments qu'elles unissent, mais la préposition lie les mots, tandis que la conjonction unit surtout des propositions.

Adverbs, prepositions and conjunctions are invariable words. There are no strict lines of separation between them. For example, in the following sentences:

Il ne l'a pas revu depuis. (adv.) since

Il ne l'a pas revu depuis deux jours. (prép.) since

Il ne l'a pas revue depuis qu'elle a déménagé en ville. (conjunction) since.

"Depuis" can serve as an adverb, prepostion, or conjunction.

Cognate Word-ending Regularities

16. French - ment = English -ly (adverbs)

1. certainement = d'une manière certaine
2. naturellement = conformément aux lois naturelles
3. rapidement = d'une manière rapide
4. complètement = d'une manière complète
5. automatiquement = d'une manière automatique
6. actuellement = dans les circonstances actuelles
7. extrêmement = d'une manière extrême
8. finalement = à la fin, pour finir
9. immédiatement = d'une manière immédiate
10. simplement = d'une manière simple, sans complication

Most French adverbs are formed by adding "-ment" to the feminine form of the corresponding adjective, e.g., calme, calmement.

Using Context Clues in Word Recognition

So far, you have become acquainted with the definition of cognates, including partial and deceptive cognates; ten example words for each of sixteen cognate word-ending regularities, some characteristics of French nouns, articles and pronouns, verbs and auxiliaries, adjectives, adverbs, prepositions and conjunctions; the suffixes of cognates which indicate parts of speech (like the noun suffixes "-isme, -cien," etc.) and some of the meanings of suffixes (like "-phone, -scope, -mètre," etc.). In order to practice and apply this knowledge, you have read different French excerpts.

The facilitation of French vocabulary acquisition by a knowledge of English-French cognates relates very closely to your vocabulary power in English. If you do not know the meaning of the French-English cognate in English, the word is of no help to you in understanding it in French.

One way of figuring out word meanings is the study and knowledge of suffixes, prefixes and root words, e.g., "tele" meaning far and "phone" meaning sound, thus "telephone" has the literal meaning of "far sound." But take care, most words have larger and more involved meanings than the sum of the parts would lead one to deduce.

Another strategy for figuring out meanings of unfamiliar words is the use of context clues. Linguistic context can provide clues to the meanings of unfamiliar words in the following ways:

1. through definition, e.g., To give the submarine the continual attention it needs, the officers and crew are divided into watches. A watch is a four-hour period of duty.
2. example, e.g., The boys were lying still, heads down, inert, like dead men except for their loud and broken gasps for air.
3. modifiers, e.g., Simultaneously the feminist movement, seeking to achieve for women as much equality with men as possible, was quick to capitalize on the behaviorist theories.
4. restatement, e.g., hypothesis, a sort of guess . . .
5. inference, which requires the reader to see relationships not explicitly stated, e.g., The practicing physician as a rule is completely unskilled in dietetics. His preliminary training encompasses little or nothing concerning the details of food prescription.

The attentive reader will observe the close parallel between unskilled and preliminary training. From this parallel he will infer that the second sentence is probably a modified restatement of the first. He will then conclude that dietetics has something to do with "details of food prescription." While he has by no means a full definition of dietetics, he has enough meaning to allow him to proceed.

Effective reading is really a thinking process and the extent to which context reveals meaning varies with the experience of the reader, but the following limitations of using context clues in word recognition should be mentioned:

1. If you guess the meaning of a word from its context, it may not always be a correct guess.
2. The context reveals only one meaning of a new word, not all its possible meanings.
3. The growth of vocabulary by context is a slow, developmental process.

You have been equipped to use word analysis and context clues to assist you in deciphering unfamiliar words. It is now up to you to make use of these aids to increase your English as well as French vocabularies.

L'Avenir de l'Amérique Centrale

L'Amérique Centrale n'a d'avenir que celui du Tiers monde. Même Costa Rica, véritable paradis au sein de cet isthme de misères, n'est pas capable d'un démarrage économique réel dans les conditions actuelles du marché international. Il faudrait que les nations développées révisent leur politique de prix et d'échange, qu'elles accordent des conditions plus favorables aux pays en voie de développement, qu'elles offrent des sommes plus avantageuses pour les produits de ces pays auxquels elles devraient vendre moins cher. Et n'allons pas croire que cet "il faudrait" correspond à un acte de charité, il équivaut bien au contraire à un acte de justice sociale, économique et humaine. Nous ne payons pas assez cher nos bananes et nous vendons trop cher nos tracteurs. Un travailleur agricole du Nicaragua doit travailler jusqu'à vingt fois plus longtemps qu'un travailleur canadien pour acheter le même produit . . . .
Quand l'admettrons-nous?
(Vidéo-Presse, Vol. III, Numéro 9, mai 1974, p. 41)

Questions

1. State the rule for the cognate word-ending in this lesson.
2. How many English-French cognates did you recognize in the reading? Please list them.
3. Did you guess the English equivalent for "isthme," "agricole," "échange," "prix," "sommes," "admettrons"?
4. What are the meanings of "vendre" and "travailler" in the excerpt?
5. Try to answer the following French questions on the content of the excerpt:
   a) Que veut dire "l'avenir de l'Amérique Centrale" en anglais?
   b) Quel est l'avenir de l'Amérique Centrale?
   c) Pourquoi est-ce que l'Amérique Centrale est pauvre?
   d) Comment les pays développés pourraient-ils aider les travailleurs du Nicaragua?
   e) Est-ce que nous admettons que nous exploitons les nations en voie de développement?
   f) Pour acheter le même produit, qui doit travailler plus longtemps?
6. Identify the parts of speech for each of the following words: "faudrait, démarrage, centrale" and list the reasons for your choice.
7. Note how the conjunctions in the sentences indicate relationships. Translate the ten conjunctions from the sentences "Je t'aiderai . . .."

8. Give an example of a preposition and a conjunction from the excerpt in this lesson.
9. What is the difference between a preposition and a conjunction?
10. State the context clue which has been used in the following examples:
    a) "dinosaure veut dire en grec, lézard terrible"
    b) "Tous les 'humanistes,' ces hommes à la culture universelle"

Lesson Seven

Syntax

The parts of speech you have studied (nouns, articles and pronouns, verbs and auxiliaries, adjectives, adverbs, prepositions and conjunctions) are the building blocks of sentences. A noun or pronoun may function as either the subject or the complement in a sentence. The noun complement may be used either as a direct object, an indirect object, a subjective complement (i.e., a complement which refers to the subject after a copular or linking verb), or as an object of a preposition in a prepositional phrase.

The verb is the essence of a sentence. It expresses either the action or being of the subject, the existence or state of the subject or the unity of the attribute with the subject. The general rule requires that the verb agree with the subject.

Understanding words in isolation is not enough for comprehension of continuous written discourse. Word order also carries meaning. The pattern of sentences is determined by the number and arrangement of certain essential parts of speech.

Table of Type of Sentence Construction
The parts of the sentence

Sentence Construction	Subject	Verb	Complement
Statements	Marie (verb)	arrive.	
	Elle (pronoun)	caresse (verb)	son chat. (direct object)
	Nous	indiquons	la route à ce voyageur. (direct/indirect obj.)
	Il est (copula)	gentil. (subjective complement)	
	Pierre devient (copula)	professeur. (subjective complement)	

Questions

1.	raising of the voice	Tu	aimes	la musique?
2.	inversion of subject and verb		Etes-vous heureux?	
3.	question words	Lequel	voulez-vous ?	
		Quand	pars-tu?	
		Quand	est-ce que tu pars ?	
		Qui	est venu ?	

Commands

Asseyez-vous !
Asseyez-vous, s'il vous plaît !
Veuillez-vous vous asseoir !

Exclamations

Que Lise	est	belle !
Comme il	fait	beau !

There are four basic types of sentences: 1) statement, 2) question, 3) command, and 4) exclamation, and each of these has its characteristic construction.

Types of Sentence

The number of possible types of sentences is limited. It is much easier to see the sentence patterns clearly in your reading if you bracket off: a) all articles, b) all auxiliaries, c) all nouns used as modifiers, d) all adverbs, e) all prepositional phrases, and f) all adjectives except those used as subjective complements.

The following basic arrangements of parts of speech in a statement are:

Subject	Verb	Complement
Noun or pronoun	Verb	
Noun or pronoun	Verb	Noun
Noun or pronoun	Verb	Noun, Noun
Noun or pronoun	Linking Verb	Adjective
Noun or pronoun	Linking Verb	Noun

1. In all statements the verb is preceded by the subject.
2. The subject-verb construction is the smallest statement sentence. For example, "Je danse. La neige tombe."
3. The complement follows the verb.
4. With a linking verb (copula) the adjective or noun following the verb refers to the subject. This is known as a subjective complement. For example, "Pierre est intelligent."

Another type of sentence construction is the interrogative sentence. The interrogative pronouns are:

Pour les personnes: Qui?

Pour les choses: Que?, Quoi?

Les Formes composées:

lequel?	laquelle?	lesquels?	lesquelles?
auquel?	à laquelle?	auxquels?	auxquelles?
duquel?	de laquelle?	desquels?	desquelles?

The interrogative adverbs are: quand? (when), oũ? (where), pourquoi? (why), and comment? (how).

Questions can be formed by

1. simply raising the intonation of a statement sentence,
2. inversion of the subject and the verb or auxiliary,
3. using interrogative pronouns and adverbs, or "est-ce que."

Any of the previously discussed statement sentences can be modified into a question by the above mentioned processes.

The command, also known as an imperative sentence, is characterized as follows:

1. The subject is omitted.

2. The verb is used as the imperative form (e.g., the second person singular or plural "parle -- parlez" or the first person plural "parlons."
3. The imperative may be softened with "please", or a polite paraphrase. Most people do not like to be ordered to do something. They prefer to be asked nicely.

Exclamations form a sentence pattern distinct from statements, questions or commands. Grevisse notes:

> Il y a, en effet, un rapport étroit entre l'expression grammaticale de la proposition et l'expressivité (tension émotionnelle quelconque). Plus on fait diminuer l'expressivité, plus la structure de la proposition tend vers la parfaite régularité selon les lois de l'analyse. Plus on fait croître l'expressivité, plus l'expression grammaticale se libère de la regularité: à la limite, cette expression grammaticale se réduit à la simple interjection. (Grevisse, 1975 : 136-137)

The exclamatory sentence pattern has the following characteristics:

1. Exclamations often start with "que" (what), "comme" (how) or sometimes "pourquoi" (why) as the initial word, e.g., "Que la vie est belle!"
2. An exclamation is terminated with an exclamation mark.

A simple sentence consists of a finite verb (a verb in a specific person and tense) and a subject (except for the imperative sentence construction when the subject is omitted). Any of the simple sentence constructions previously discussed may be connected by a coordinating conjunction, or placed side by side separated by a comma or semi-colon to form a compound sentence. If sentences are connected by a subordinate conjunction, the result is a complex sentence.

Questions

1. How many sentence types are there? Name them please.
2. Where do you usually find the subject in relation to the verb in a statement?
3. In what order and where do you place the direct and indirect object? Hint, look at the table.
4. Why is the command not used in the past tense?
5. With what part of speech does the verb agree in a sentence?

6a Which parts of speech are variable words?

6b Name the invariable parts of speech.

7. What is the characteristic of a command?
8. How can you identify a question in written material?
9. What is the difference between a compound and a complex sentence?

10a List an exclamatory sentence from the excerpt "les Dinosaures."

10b How did you decide that the sentence was exclamatory?
11a List a command from the excerpt "La Pollution."
11b What are the characteristics of a command?
12a From the same excerpt, "La Pollution," give an example of a question with subject-verb inversion.
12b From the excerpt "L'Avenir de l'Amérique Centrale," cite an example of a question with an interrogative adverb at the beginning of the sentence.
13a Find a subject-verb statement from the excerpt "La Renaissance italienne."
13b In the excerpt "L'Empire Inca," examine the first sentence and write down the subject - verb - direct object.
14. You may have become tired of and bored with reading the prepared excerpts in this cognate unit. Now it is your turn to prepare a French excerpt. You may follow the format of the excerpts presented in the previous lessons. Select an excerpt from any French reading material of interest to you, and about the same length as the excerpts you have read here. Check for cognates anf formulate questions and an answer key. Then pick a grammar point of particular difficulty for you, explain it with the aid of a grammar or textbook. Verify the comprehension of this point of grammar with questions and relate it to your excerpt. Should you have a better idea for the lesson format, try it. After having exchanged your lesson with your fellow students, hand it in to your instructor.

References

Bain, B. Bilingualism and Cognition: Toward an Integration of Piaget and Vygotsky: Bilingual Considerations. Linguistics, Mouton Publishers, 1975, 5-20.

Bréal, M. Semantics: Studies in the Science of Meaning. Translated by H. Cust, Dover Publications, Inc., New York, 1964.

Carroll, J.B. and Sapon, S.M. Modern Language Aptitude Test. The Psychological Corporation, New York, 1959.

Chamberlin, W.A. The Comparative Study of Words in Foreign Languages. The School Review, Vol. XIII, 1905, 315-325.

Chastain, K. and Woerdehoff, F.J.A. Methodological Study Comparing the Audio-Lingual Habit Theory and the Cognitive Code-Learning Theory. Modern Language Journal, Vol. LII, 1968, 268-278.

Chirol, L. Les "mots français" et le mythe de la France en anglais contemporain. Editions Klincksieck, Paris, 1973.

Claparède, E. Psychologie de l'enfant et pédagogie expérimentale. Septième édition, Librairie Kundig, Genève, 1916.

Dashwood-Jones, D. Patterns for Writing. W.J. Gage Limited, Toronto, 1966.

Dubois, J. Edude sur la dérivation suffixale en français modern et contemporain. Larousse, Paris, 1962.

Dubois, M.M. <u>Dictionnaire Moderne Français-Anglais</u>. Librairie Larousse, Paris, 1960.

Eddy, H.M. The French Element in English. <u>The Modern Languages Journal</u>, Vol. X, 1926, 271-280.

Eichler, J. <u>The Effects of Cognate Usage on Foreign Language Speaking Proficiency</u>. Ph.D. Thesis, University of Wyoming, 1972.

<u>Le Français Fondamental (Premier Degré)</u> Institut Pédagogique National, Ministère de l'Education Nationale, Direction de la Coopération, Paris, 1954.

Gagné, R.M. and Brown, L.T. Some Factors in the Programming of conceptual Learning. <u>Journal of Experimental Psychology</u>, Vol. 62, 1961, 313-321.

Gragg, D.B. The Contribution of High-School Latin, French, and Spanish to English Vocabulary. <u>Journal of Educational Psychology</u>, Vol. 53, November 1942, 615-622.

Grayson, C.J. The World of Mankind: Four Points of View. <u>Public Relations Journal</u>, Vol. 32, October 1976, 20-234.

Greenberg, J.H. (ed.). <u>Universals of Language</u>. Second Edition, The M.I.T. Press, Massachusetts, 1966.

Grevisse, M. <u>Le Bon Usage</u>. Dixième Edition, Editions J. Duculot, S.A. Gembloux, 1975.

Hammer, P. <u>The Role of English-French Cognates in Listening and Reading Comprehension in the Learning of French as a Second Language</u>. M.Ed. Thesis, University of Alberta, 1975.

Herber, H.L. annd Nelson, J.B. Questioning is Not the Answer. <u>Journal of Reading</u>, Vol. 18, No. 7, April 1975, 512-517.

Jakobovits, L.A. Second Language Learning and Transfer Theory: A Theoretical Assessment. <u>Language Learning</u>, Vol. 19, 1969, 55-86.

Johnston, M.C. <u>Cognate Relationship Between English and Spanish Vocabularies as a Basis for Instruction</u>, Ph.D. thesis, University of Texas at Austin, 1939.

Klausmeier, H.J. Transfer of Learning, in <u>Encyclopedia of Educational Research</u>. Fourth Edition, Editors Robert L. Ebel and Victor H. Noll, the Macmillan Company, London, 1969, 1483-1493.

Koessler, M., and Derocquigny, J. <u>Les Faux Amis</u>. Librairie Vuibert, Paris, 1946.

Lado, R. <u>Linguistics Across Cultures--Applied Linguistics for Language Teachers</u>. University of Michigan Press, Ann Arbor, 1960.

Lambert, W.E. Gardner, R.C., Barik, H.C., and Tunstall, K. Attitudinal and Cognitive Aspects of Intensive Study of a Second Language. Journal of Abnormal and Social Psychology. Vol. LXVII, 1963, 358-368.

Limper, L.H. Student Knowledge of Some French-English Cognates. The French Review, Vol. VI, 1932-33, 37-49.

Mackey, W.F. Le Vocabulaire disponible du français, Marcel Didier (Canada) Ltée., Montréal, 1971.

Robert P. Le Petit Robert, Dictionnaire de la langue française. Publ. Alain Rey, Paris, 1972.

Savard, J.-G. and Richards, J. Les indices d'utilité du vocabulaire fondamental français. Les Presses de l'Université Laval, Québec, 1970.

Seward, R.D. Dictionary of French Deceptive Cognates. Bates College, S.F. Vanni, New York, 1947.

Shawl, J.R.A Definition of One Level of Achievement in the Reading and Writing of Spanish. Final Report. Washington, D.C., Office of Education, U.S. Bureau of Research, 1969.

Steiner, G. After Babel. Oxford University Press, New York, 1975.

Stephens, J.M. Transfer of Learning. In C.W. Harris and M.R. Liba (eds.) Encyclopedia of Educational Research, Macmillan, New York, 1960, 1535-1543.

Thorndike, E.L. The Teacher's Word Book. Teacher's College, Columbia University, 1921.

Vander, Beke, G.E. The French Word Book. Macmillan Publishing Company, New York, 1929.

Vygotsky, L.S. Thought and Language. The M.I.T. Press, Cambridge, 1962.

Wadsworth, B.J. Piaget's Theory of Cognitive Development. David McKay Company, Inc., New York, 1971.

Webster, N. Webster's New International Dictionary of the English Language. Second Edition, unabridged, G. and C. Meriam Co., Springfield, 1955.

Weintraub, S. The Question as a Aid in Reading. The Reading Teacher, Vol. 22, No. 8, May 1969, 751, 753, 755.

West, M.P. Note on the Inferability of Cognates. High Points, Vol. 16, November 1934, 23-25.

APPENDIX A

The Conjugation of the Verb

Indicative of the "-er" Verbs

PRESENT	IMPERFECT	SIMPLE PAST	FUTURE
parle	parlais	parlai	parlerai
parles	parlais	parlas	parleras
parle	parlait	parla	parlera
parlons	parlions	parlâmes	parlerons
parlez	parliez	parlâtes	parlerez
parlent	parlaient	parlèrent	parleront

COMPOUND PAST	PLUPERFECT	PAST ANTERIOR	FUTURE PERFECT
ai parlé	avais parlé	eus parlé	aurai parlé
as parlé	avais parlé	eus parlé	auras parlé
a parlé	avait parlé	eut parlé	aura parlé
avons parlé	avions parlé	eûmes parlé	aurons parlé
avez parlé	aviez parlé	eûtes parlé	aurez parlé
ont parlé	avaient parlé	eurent parlé	auront parlé

CONDITIONAL	IMPERATIVE	SUBJUNCTIVE	
Pres Conditional		Present	Imperfect
parlerais		parle	parlasse
parlerais	parle	parles	parlasses
parlerait		parle	parlât
parlerions	parlons	parlions	parlassions
parleriez	parlez	parliez	parlassiez
parleraient		parlent	parlassent
Past Conditional		**Past**	**Pluperfect**
aurais parlé		aie parlé	eusse parlé
aurais parlé		aies parlé	eusses parlé
aurait parlé		ait parlé	eût parlé
aurions parlé		ayons parlé	eussions parlé
auriez parlé		ayez parlé	eussiez parlé
auraient parlé		aient parlé	eussent parlé

Indicative of the "-ir" Verbs

PRESENT	IMPERFECT	SIMPLE PAST	FUTURE
finis	finissais	finis	finirai
finis	finissais	finis	finiras
finit	finissait	finit	finira
finissons	finissions	finîmes	finirons
finissez	finissiez	finîtes	finirez
finissent	finissaient	finirent	finiront
COMPOUND PAST	**PLUPERFECT**	**PAST ANTERIOR**	**FUTURE PERFEC**
ai fini	avais fini	eus fini	aurai fini
as fini	avais fini	eus fini	auras fini
a fini	avait fini	eut fini	aura fini
avons fini	avions fini	eûmes fini	aurons fini
avez fini	aviez fini	eûtes fini	aurez fini
ont fini	avaient fini	eurent fini	auront fini
CONDITIONAL	**IMPERATIVE**	**SUBJECTIVE**	
Pres Conditional		**Present**	**Imperfect**
finirais		finisse	finisse
finirais	finis	finisses	finisses
finirait		finisse	finît
finirions	finissons	finissions	finissions
finiriez	finissez	finissiez	finissiez
finiraient		finissent	finissent
Past Conditional		**Past**	**Pluperfect**
aurais fini		aie fini	eusse fini
aurais fini		aies fini	eusses fini
aurait fini		ait fini	eût fini
aurions fini		ayons fini	eussions fini
auriez fini		ayez fini	eussiez fini
auraient fini		aient fini	eussent fini

Indicative of the "-re" Verbs

PRESENT	IMPERFECT	SIMPLE PAST	FUTURE
perds	perdais	perdis	perdrai
perds	perdais	perdis	perdras
perd	perdait	perdit	perdra
perdons	perdions	perdîmes	perdrons
perdez	perdiez	perdîtes	perdrez
perdent	perdaient	perdirent	perdront

COMPOUND PAST	PLUPERFECT	PAST ANTERIOR	FUTURE PERFECT
ai perdu	avais perdu	eus perdu	aurai perdu
as perdu	avais perdu	eus perdu	auras perdu
a perdu	avait perdu	eut perdu	aura perdu
avons perdu	avions perdu	eûmes perdu	aurons perdu
avez perdu	aviez perdu	eûtes perdu	aurez perdu
ont perdu	avaient perdu	eurent perdu	auront perdu

CONDITIONAL	IMPERATIVE	SUBJUNCTIVE	
Pres Conditional		Present	Imperfect
perdrais		perde	perdisse
perdrais	perds	perdes	perdisses
perdrait		perde	perdît
perdrions	perdons	perdions	perdissions
perdriez	perdez	perdiez	perdissiez
perdraient		perdent	perdissent
Past Conditional		Past	Pluperfect
aurais perdu		aie perdu	eusse perdu
aurais perdu		aies perdu	eusses perdu
aurait perdu		ait perdu	eût perdu
aurions perdu		ayons perdu	eussions perdu
auriez perdu		ayez perdu	eussiez perdu
auraient perdu		aient perdu	eussent perdu

Indicative of the "-oir" Verbs

PRESENT	IMPERFECT	SIMPLE PAST	FUTURE
reçois	recevais	reçus	recevrai
reçois	recevais	reçus	recevras
reçoit	recevait	reçut	recevra
recevons	recevions	reçûmes	recevrons
recevez	receviez	reçûtes	recevrez
reçoivent	recevaient	reçurent	recevront
COMPOUND PAST	**PLUPERFECT**	**PAST ANTERIOR**	**FUTURE PERFECT**
ai reçu	avais reçu	eus reçu	aurai reçu
as reçu	avais reçu	eus reçu	auras reçu
a reçu	avait reçu	eut reçu	aura reçu
avons reçu	avions reçu	eûmes reçu	aurons reçu
avez reçu	aviez reçu	eûtes reçu	aurez reçu
ont reçu	avaient reçu	eurent reçu	auront reçu
CONDITIONAL	**IMPERATIVE**	**SUBJUNCTIVE**	
Pres Conditional		**Present**	**Imperfect**
recevrais		reçoive	reçusse
recevrais	reçois	reçoives	reçusses
recevrait		reçoive	reçût
recevrions	recevons	recevions	reçussions
recevriez	recevez	receviez	reçussiez
recevraient		reçoivent	reçussent
Past Conditional		**Past**	**Pluperfect**
aurais reçu		aie reçu	eusse reçu
aurais reçu		aies reçu	eusses reçu
aurait reçu		ait reçu	eût reçu
aurions reçu		ayons reçu	eussions reçu
auriez reçu		ayez reçu	eussiez reçu
auraient reçu		aient reçu	eussent reçu

Indicative of the Verb "avoir"

PRESENT	IMPERFECT	SIMPLE PAST	FUTURE
ai	avais	eus	aurai
as	avais	eus	auras
a	avait	eut	aura
avons	avions	eûmes	aurons
avez	aviez	eûtes	aurez
ont	avaient	eurent	auront
COMPOUND PAST	**PLUPERFECT**	**PAST ANTERIOR**	**FUTURE PERFECT**
ai eu	avais eu	eus eu	aurai eu
as eu	avais eu	eus eu	auras eu
a eu	avait eu	eut eu	aura eu
avons eu	avions eu	eûmes eu	aurons eu
avez eu	aviez eu	eûtes eu	aurez eu
ont eu	avaient eu	eurent eu	auront eu
CONDITIONAL	**IMPERATIVE**	**SUBJUNCTIVE**	
Pres Conditional		Present	Imperfect
aurais		aie	eusse
aurais	aie	aies	eusses
aurait		ait	eût
aurions	ayons	ayons	eussions
auriez	ayez	ayez	eussiez
auraient		aient	eussent
Past Conditional		Past	Pluperfect
aurais eu		aie eu	eusse eu
aurais eu		aies eu	eusses eu
aurait eu		ait eu	eût eu
aurions eu		ayons eu	eussions eu
auriez eu		ayez eu	eussiez eu
auraient eu		aient eu	eussent eu

Indicative of the Verb "être"

PRESENT	IMPERFECT	SIMPLE PAST	FUTURE
suis	étais	fus	serai
es	étais	fus	seras
est	était	fut	sera
sommes	étions	fûmes	serons
êtes	étiez	fûtes	serez
sont	étaient	furent	seront
COMPOUND PAST	**PLUPERFECT**	**PAST ANTERIOR**	**FUTURE PERFECT**
ai été	avais été	eus été	aurai été
as été	avais été	eus été	auras été
a été	avait été	eut été	aura été
avons été	avions été	eûmes été	aurons été
avez été	aviez été	eûtes été	aurez été
ont été	avaient été	eurent été	auront été
CONDITIONAL	**IMPERATIVE**	**SUBJUNCTIVE**	
Pres Conditional		**Present**	**Imperfect**
serais		sois	fusse
serais	sois	sois	fusses
serait		soit	fût
serions	soyons	soyons	fussions
seriez	soyez	soyez	fussiez
seraient		soient	fussent
Past Conditional		**Past**	**Pluperfect**
aurais été		aie été	eusse été
aurais été		aies été	eusses été
aurait été		ait été	eût été
aurions été		ayons été	eussions été
auriez été		ayez été	eussiez été
auraient été		aient été	eussent été

APPENDIX B

ANSWER KEY

Answers to Questions in Lesson One

2) Linguistic interference is defined as the use of elements of one language while speaking or writing the other.

Phoenetic refers to the sound system acceptable to a given linguistic community. Phone = sound or tone.

Morphology is the study of forms. Greek "morpho" means form. Morphology is defined as that branch of linguistic study which deals with the history and functions of inflections and derivational forms.

Context is defined as the part or parts of a discourse preceding or following a "text" or passage or a word, or so intimately associated with it as to throw light upon its meaning.

Cognition is defined as any mental operation by which we become aware of objects, of thought or perception.

Lexicon refers to words; dictionary.

Semantics refers to the branch of the study of language concerned with meanings.

Syntax is that branch of linguistics which deals with sentence construction; the grammatical arrangement of words.

3) Cognates are words which have the same or similar spellings and meanings in two or more languages. Partial cognates are words whose meanings overlap in some senses but not in others. Deceptive cognates are words which have the same or similar spellings but different meanings in two or more languages.

Answers to Questions in Lesson Two

1) a) The French "-té" word-ending corresponds to the English "-ty" word-ending.

b) The French "-ie" word-ending corresponds to the English "-y" ending.

c) The French "-nce" word-ending corresponds to the English "-nce" or "-ncy" ending.

d) The French "-iste" word-ending corresponds to the English "-ist" ending.

2) The "-té" cognate word-endng appies to 542 english-French cognates.

3) "-iste" has the meaning of a person who does something. The gender is determined by the sex of the person in question.

4) For example, if you eliminate the noun suffix "-té" from "beauté" you hav the adjective "beau." Suffixes which determine the part of speech of words d not necessarily affect the essential meaning of the word. e.g., "rapide" is a adjective, "rapidité" a noun, and "rapidement" an adverb. Thus, from knowledge of the primary word you could understand derived words.

5) The cognates for the excerpt "La Renaissance italienne" are: Renaissance, italienne, riche, Médicis, Florence, Italie, protectrice, sculpteurs, désireux, harmonie, magnificence, art, gréco-romain, cité, splendeur, monuments, Venise, Rome, humanistes, culture, universelle, botanique, zoologie, anatomie, géologie, astrologie, navigation, étude, textes, anciens, sources, inspiration, période.

6) Counting only those English-French cognates with identical spelling, one letter difference in the spelling, or any of the cognate word-ending regularities, there are 33.

7) famille = family, règne = rules or reigns (verb), ville = town, peintres painters, palais = palace, rivalise = (to) rival, fêtes = celebrations, festivities.

8a) XVe siècle; 8b) la riche famille des Médicis; 8c) Ce sont des hommes de culture universelle; 8d) Florence; 8e) dans les textes anciens; 8f) riche;

9) a) "protectrice" refers to a person; it is a noun; b) the "-trice" is the feminine noun ending of "protecteur"; c) "protectrice" is preceded by the definite feminine article "la"; d) you can form the plural by adding an "s" "la protectrice - les protectrices"

10) articles and/or adjectives

11) You generally form the plural of French nouns in a similar manner as in English; you add an "s."

Answers to Questions in Lesson Three

1) a) The French "-eur" word-ending corresponds to the English "or" or "-er" word-ending.

b) The French "-isme" word-ending corresponds to the English "-ism" ending.

c) The French "-cien" word-ending corresponds to the English "-cian" endng.

d) The French "-re" word-ending corresponds to the English "-er" ending.

2) It indicates "belief in, doctrine or practice, profession, a system, a theory."

3) The "-eur" ending can be a noun or adjective ending. When the "-eur" ending is used as an adjective the word is not necessarily a cognate.

4) "one who" or in French "celui qui"

5) -isme = 302 English-French cognates
   -ie = 533 English-French cognates
   -re = 339 English-French cognates

6) The cognates for the excerpt "La Pollution" are: air, pollue, responsable, pollution, certainement, automobile, efforts, éliminer, ennemi, recours, requièrent, véhicule, effet, carbone, gouvernement, oblige, installer, systèmes, anti-pollution, informe, influence, dollars, diminuer, sévère, possible, indifférent, campagne, utilisation.

7) les fabricants = manufacturers, le coût = cost, expense, la bicyclette = bicycle.

8) rester = stay, remain; milliers = thousands

9a) l'automobile; 9b) On installe des systèmes anti-pollution sur tous les nouveaux véhicules. 9c) de la bicyclette, 9d) oui, 9e) le Gouvernement; 9f) les usines.

10) a) "véhicules" refers to a thing, it is a noun; b) preceded by an adjective "nouveaux;" c) plural ending "-s"

11) a) "ennemi" names a person, it is a noun, b) preceded by "cet," which is a demonstrative adjective.

12) The personal pronoun replaces a noun. The pronoun agrees in gender and number with the noun it replaces.

13) The French article ("le" or "la") indicates whether the noun is masculine or feminine.

14) The indefinite article does not determine or specify the object named.

15) The English definite article is "the" and the English indefinite article is "a" or "an", in the singulier. In the pluriel, it is unstressed "some" or ø.

Answers to Questions in Lesson Four

1) a) The French "=er" word-ending corresponds to the dropping in English of the "-er" or just the "r" cognate word-ending.

b) The French "-ier" word-ending corresponds to the English "-y" ending.

2) The "-cien" ending may be an adjective or noun ending, e.g., ancien, musicien.

3) "=ion" = 1,176; "-nce" = 274: "-iste" = 259; "-eur" =160; "-cien" = 10

4) There are 30 English-French cognates.

The cognates for the excerpt "L'Empire Inca" are: origine, humble, indienne, installée, océan, Pacifique, conquête, territoires, complètement, intégrait, société, communications, commerciales, rapidement, possible, accélérer, usage, concédé, diverses, classes, sociales, succession, royale, Incas, automatiquement, monarques, européens, empereur, statut, descendant.

5) peuplade = tribe; bords = borders; établi = established; échanges = exchanges; espèces = species; époque = epoch

6) propre = own

7) Did you recognize "corps" as meaning "groups"? (Think of airforce corps, or drum and bugle crops). In this excerpt "corps" does not mean "dead body" (corpse).

8a) sur les bords de l'océan Pacifique, 8b) Les vaincus étaient intégrés dans la société des Incas; 8c) à diverses classes sociales, 8d) pour accélérer toutes espèces d'échanges, 8e) tous les fils de l'empereur, 8f) En Europe le fils aîné régnait, mais pas nécessairement chez les Incas.

9) a) verbs are words that imply an action or a situation; b) "intégrait" expresses an action, it is a verb; c) - "ait" shows that the verb is in the imperfect tense, third person singular; d) the verb is preceded by a direct object "les."

10) A simple tense is one without any use of auxiliaries. There are seven simple tenses and seven compound tenses.

11a) "avait" is an auxiliary, b) "avait" appears next to the verb "entrepris," and c) "avoir" is frequently used as an auxiliary.

Answers to Questions in Lesson Five

1a) The French "-ique" word-ending corresponds to the English "-ic" endng.
b) The French "-if" word-ending corresponds to the English "-ive" ending.
c) The French "-eux, euse" word-ending corresponds to the English "-ous" ending.
d) the French "-tiel, elle" word-ending corresponds to the English "-tial" ending.
e) The French "-é" word-ending corresponds to the English "-ed" ending.
2) -phone = qui parle, qui est enregistré; - phile = qui aime; logie = science; -mètre = qui mesure
3) -é = 104 English-French cognates; -eux = 161 English-French cognates; -tiel = 16 English-French cognates
4) préférentiel = adj., préférence = noun; courageux = adj., courage = noun; certainement = adv., certain = adj.
5) There are 25 English-French cognates.
The cogantes for the excerpt "Les Dinosaures" are: lézards, terribles, Canada, passe, peuplé, immense, territoire, classe, émergées, population, Canadiens, Québec, Montréal, dinosaure, étrange, animal, millions, planète, diverses, Alberta, variété, spécimens, période, supérieur, différentes.
6) fait = fact; découverts = uncovered, discovered; nombre = number; nombreuse = numerous; rassurez = (to) reassure; autoroute = highway; grec = Greek, peuplé = peopled, populated; espèces = species
7) partie = part <u>not</u> party; anciens = former <u>not</u> ancient; chances - luck <u>not</u> opportunity
8a) jeune; 8b) en Alberta; 8c) Je m'enfuirais à toutes jambes; 8d) lézard terrible; 8e) plus de 65 espèces différentes; 8f) les dinosaures.
9) a) adjectives describe nouns, peuplé is an adjective. The French adjectival ending "-é" corresponds to the English "-ed" ending. The adjective agrees in number and gender with the noun it modifies, in this example "pays." Descriptive adjectives follow the noun e.g., "pays jeune et peuplé."
9) b) Verbs are words that imply an action or a situation; "passe" is a verb. The verb shows a change in tense by a change in sound and spelling; in this example it is in the present indicative tense and the third person singular. The verb "passe" is preceded by a noun (subject).
9) c) A noun names a person, place or thing; territoire is a noun; "territoire" is preceded by an adjective, "immense." The French "-oire" noun-

ending corresponds to the English "-ory" ending. "Territoire" would form the plural with an "s".

9) d) Adjectives modify nouns; "émergées" is an adjective; it agrees in number and gender with the noun it modifies, "terres émergées;" "émergées" follows the noun "terres" it modifies; the French adjective "-é" corresponds to the English "-ed" ending.

10) The French adjective agrees in number and gender with the noun it modifies.

11) The plural of the French adjective is generally formed by adding an "s" to the singular, e.g., vert - verts, verte - vertes.

12) Adjectives, with a few exceptions, can change their form to show comparison or to indicate the superlative. In addition, adjectives are words that will fill the blank in the test sentence: The (any suitable noun) is/ar very ----.

Answers to Questions in Lesson Six

1) The French "-ment" word-ending corresponds to the English "-ly" ending.

2) There are 34 English-French cognates. The cognates for the excerpt "L'Avenir de l'Amérique Centrale" are: Amérique, centrale, Costa Rica, véritable, paradis, misères, capable, économique, réel, conditions, actuelles, international, nations, développées, révisent, politique, accordent, favorables, développement, offrent, avantageuses, produits, correspond, acte, charité, contraire, justice, sociale, humaine, payons, bananes, tracteurs, Nicaragua, canadien.

3) Isthme = isthmus; agricole (adj.) = agricultural; échange = exchange; prix = price; sommes = sums; admettrons = (we will) admit.

4) Vendre = to sell, not to vend; travailler = to work not to travail

5a) The future of Central America, 5b) la pauvreté, 5c) Les nations en train de se développer et les nations développées paient le même prix pour les produits. 5d) en payant plus cher nos bananes et en vendant moins cher nos tracteurs, 5e) non, pas encore d'après cet extrait 5f) le travailleur agricole du Nicaragua.

6a) A verb expresses an action or a state of being; faudrait = verb; "faudrait" is the present conditional; third person singular; "faudrait" is preceded by a pronoun "il"

6b) A noun names a person, place or thing; démarrage = noun; it is preceded by an indefinite article "un," the plural could be formed by adding an "s."

6c) An adjective describes a noun; centrale = adjective; "centrale" agrees in number and gender with the noun it modifies; in this example "Amérique;" the descriptive adjective follows the noun.

7) Puisque = since; quand = when; si = if; parce que = because; à condition que = on condition that; dès que = as soon as; même si = even if; malgré que = even though, in spite of; pourvu que = provided that; attendu que = seeing that

8) "pour," "jusqu'à," etc., are prepositions; "et" is a conjunction

9) A preposition attaches or links a noun or pronoun used as a modifier to some other word in the sentence. Coordinate conjunctions join words, groups of words, or sentences that are grammatically equal.

10a) definition; 10b) restatement

Answers to Questions in Lesson Seven

1) There are four types of sentences: statement, question, command, exclamation.

2) The subject precedes the verb.

3) The order is verb - direct object - indirect object. In general, pronoun exhibit differences regarding order when compared with nouns. For example, "Je vois l'homme." But "je le vois," that is, the pronoun object precedes, whereas the noun object follows the verb.

4) You cannot command something to be done in a time already past.

5) The general rule is that the verb agrees in number with the subject of th sentence.

6a) The article, adjective, noun, pronoun, and verb (also the participles)

b) The conjunctions, prepositions, adverbs.

7) The subject is obmitted.

8) Questions are signalled in the following way: a) inversion of the subject and the verb or auxiliary, b) the interrogative pronouns or adverbs signal a question when they appear at the beginning of a sentence, c) the use of "est-ce que." The question mark is written at the end of each interrogative sentence.

9) In a compound sentence two independent clauses are joined by a coordinate conjunction. In a complex sentence an independent and a dependent clause are joined by a subordinate conjunction.

10a) "Mais rassurez-vous: il y a bien peu de chances de croiser, sur l'autoroute Québec-Montréal, . . . un dinosaure!"

b) The exclamation mark is an indicator since in written material there is n intonation of a speaker.

11a) "Informe-toi auprès de plusieurs garagistes pour savoir si les dispositifs anti-pollution ont une influence . . ."

b) 1. no subject, 2. the verb "informe" is used in the imperative form.

12a) "Et toi, que feras-tu?"

b) "Quand l'admettons-nous?"

13a) la (riche) famille (des Médicis) règne . . .

(subject) (verb)

b) (une humble) peuplade avait entrepris la conquête ...

(subject) (verb) (direct object)

14) Please hand in your excerpt.

APPENDIX C

French Frequency Ratings of the English-French Cognates

English-French Cognates Rated with *Le français fondamental*

(S), (M), (FF) accident m Accident, mishap.

(S), (FF) adieu adv. Adieu, Farewell. (Ku 1-01-001)

(FF) âge m Age. He is of age = "il est majeur."

(M), (FF) aider v. tr., intr. To aid.

(S), (FF) arriver v. tr. 1 To arrive, to come.

(S), (FF), (M) artiste s. Artist, performer.

(S), (M), (FF) atelier m Studio, atelier (d'artiste).

(S), (M), (FF) attention f Attention, observing, heed.

(S), (M), (FF) auto f Autom. Motor-car, car. U.S. auto.

(S), (M), (FF) avenue f Avenue.

(M), (FF) avion m Aviat. Aeroplane, plane, avion.

(S), (M), (FF) balcon m Balcony.

(S), (M), (FF) balle f Sports. Ball as well as bullet

(S), (M), (FF) ballon m Ball, football. Geogr. Ballon.

(S), (FF) blond, onde adj. Fair, blond, flaxen,

(S), (M), (FF) boulevard m Boulevard (v. Avenue).

(M), (FF) branche f Bot. Branche, bough (d'arbre).

(FF) bravo m Bravo (spadassin).

(S), (M), (FF) cabine m Cabin (on a ship).

(M), (FF) cent m Fin. Cent (monnaie).

(S), (FF) centime m Centime.

(M), (FF) champagne f Geogr. Champagne, Comm. Champagne.

(S), (FF) changer v. tr. 7 to change.

(S), (M), (FF) chanson f Mus. Song. Fam. Chansons!

(S), (M), (FF) chauffeur m Autom. Chauffeur, driver.

(S), (M), (FF) chemise f Chemise, shirt, wrapper.

(S), (M), (FF) chocolat m. Chocolat (barre, boisson).

(S), (M), (FF) cigarette f Cigarette.

(S), (M), (FF) cinéma m. Theatr. Cinema (art, édifice).
(S), (M), client m A dependent. Comm. Customer, client.
(FF) compliment m Compliment. Congratulation. Pl. Regards.
(S), (M), (FF) concierge m s. House-porter, concierge.
(S), (FF) continuer v. tr. 1 To pursue, to continue.
(S), (M), (FF) cours m Course, flow (d'un fleuve).
(S), (FF) cousin, ine s. Cousin as well as a gnat.
(S), (M), (FF) couturière f Dressmaker, couturière.
(S), (M), (FF) cravate f Neck-tie, tie (d'homme), cravat.
(FF) crayon m Pencil as well as crayon.
(S), (M), (FF) crème f Cream (de lait). Crème (liqueur).
(S), (FF) curieux, euse adj. Curious, inquisitive, prying.
(S), (FF) dangereux, euse adj. Dangerous, perilous.
(S), (FF) date f English senses of "date".
(S), (FF) décider v. tr. 1 To persuade, to decide.
(S), (FF) descendre v. intr. 4 To descend (de, from).
(S), (M), (FF) dessert m Culin. Dessert, sweet.
(S), (M), (FF) deviner v. tr. 1 To guess, to divine.
(S), (M), (FF) dîner v. intr. To dine (de, off, on).
(M), (FF) employé m Employee. (Ku 24-05-008)
(S), (FF) ensemble adj. Together. m. Ensemble (costume).
(S), (FF) enveloppe f Envelope (de lettre). (Ku 21-06-013)
(S), (FF) excuser v. tr. 1 To excuse, to extenuate.
(S), (FF) exemple m Example except as in par exemple.
(S), (M), (FF) face f Face (de l'homme). (Ku 371-15-189)
(S), (M), (FF) facteur, trice s. Maker. Comm. Factor,
(S), (FF) fatigue adj. Fatigue, tiredness, weariness.
(S), (M), (FF) film m. Cinem. Film, motion picture.
(M), (FF) filtre m Filter, strainer (cornet). (Ku 9-03-005)
(M), (FF) football m Sports. Football, European "soccer."
(FF) franc m Franc (monnaie). (Ku 1-01-001)
(M), (FF) France f Geogr. France. (Ku 74-12-039)
(S), (M), (FF) fruit m Fruit. (Ku 35-11-022)
(S), (FF) gai, gaie adj. Gay (cheerful), merry.
(S), (M), (FF) garage m Autom. Garage.
(S), (FF) gourmand, ande adj. Gourmand, greedy, gluttonous.

(S), (FF) grave adj. Grave, sedate, solemn, staid (air).
(M), (FF) hors-d'oeuvre m invar. Culin., Fam. Hors-d'oeuvre.
(S), (M), (FF) hôtel m Hotel, as well as town mansion,
(S), (FF) identité f Identity, sameness. (Ku 55-10-028)
(S), (FF) inviter v. tr. 1 To invite. (Ku 11-09-010)
(M), (FF) Italie f Geogr. Italy. (Ku 34-11-023)
(S), (M), (FF) journal m Paper, newspaper, journal.
(S), (FF) justice f Justice, fairness, right. (Ku 114-12-062)
(M), (FF) kilo, kilogramme m Kilogram, kilogramme.
(S), (M), (FF) lettre f Letter. (Ku 145-15-070)
(S), (M), (FF) lion m Zool. Lion. Astron. Leo. (Ku 17-04-006)
(S), (M), (FF) litre m Litre.
(S), (FF) long, ongue adj. Long. (Ku 755-15-338)
(FF) Louis m Lewis (prénom). Louis, twenty-franc piece
(M), (FF) Lyon m Geogr. Lyons. (Ku 3-02-002)
(S), (FF) mademoiselle (pl. mesdemoiselles) f Miss,
(S), (M), (FF) mandat m. Mandate. Fin. Money-order.
(M), (FF) Marie f Mary. (Ku 6-04-006)
(S), (FF) Mars m Mars. (Ku 21-05-010)
(M), (FF) mathématique adj. Math. Mathematical.
(FF) Maurice m Maurice (nom). (Ku 7-04-006)
(S), (FF) merci f Favour (v. Miséricorde). Mercy.
(S), (M), (FF) milieu m Middle, midst. Environment, milieu.
(S), (FF) minute f Minute. (Ku 53-13-049)
(S), (FF) moment m. Moment, instant, second.
(S), (M), (FF) moteur, trice adj. Motive, driving. m Techn. Motor.
(S), (FF) national, ale adj. National. (Ku 375-13-143)
(S), (FF) nationalité f Nationality. (Ku 3-03-003)
(S), (FF) obliger v. tr. 7 To oblige, to compel, to bind
(S), (FF) oncle m Uncle. (Ku 57-11-027)
(S), (M), (FF) opéra m Theatr., Mus. Opera. (Ku 47-11-023)
(S), (M), (FF) orange f Bot. Orange. (Ku 23-10-020)
(S), (M), (FF) orchestre m Mus. Band, orchestra.
(S), (M), (FF) page f Page, leaf. (Ku 66-14-046)
(S), (M), (FF) papa m Fam. Dad, daddy, papa, pa.
(S), (M), (FF) parc m Park (de château, de ville).

(S), (FF) pardon m Forgiveness, pardon. (Ku 8-07-008)

(S), (M), (FF) parent m pl. Parents as well as relative.

(M), (FF) Paris m Geogr, Paris. (Ku 67-12-040)

(FF) parisien, enne adj. Parisian. (Ku 3-02-002)

(S), (M), (FF) passer v. intr. 1 To pass.

(S), (M), (FF) payer v. tr. 9b To pay (qqn.) (de, for).

(S), (FF) permanent, ente adj. Permanent (v. Continuel).

(S), (M), (FF) pharmacie f. Med. Pharmacy, pharmaceutics.

(S), (M), (FF) photo f Photography. (Ku 5-02-003)

(S), (FF) politique adj. Political (parti), politic.

(S), (FF) poser v. tr. 1 To lay, to put, to pose.

(S), (FF) possible adj. Possible (v. Faisable, réalisable).

(S), (FF) postal, ale adj. Postal. (Ku 7-02-006)

(S), (M), (FF) pot m Pot. Jug, U.S. pitcher. (Ku 28-10-018)

(S), (FF) préférer v. tr. 5 To prefer, to like better.

(S), (M), (FF) préparer v. tr. 1 To prepare, to get ready.

(S), (FF) présenter v. tr. 1 To present, to offer.

(FF) pressé, ée adj. Pressed, crowded, close together

(S), (M), (FF) programme m Programme, syllabus.

(S), (M), (FF) promenade f Walking. Promenade. (Ku 3-01-001)

(S), (M), (FF) pyjama m Pyjamas, U.S. pajamas.

(FF) Quasimodo m Quasimodo (personnage). (Ku 3-01-001)

(S), (M), (FF) queue f Tail (d'animal), queue.

(S), (M), (FF) radio m Radio. (Ku 120-14-043)

(S), (M), (FF) rang m Row. Milit., Fig. Rank. (Ku 21-05-017)

(S), (M), (FF) ranger v. tr. 7 To range (v. Arranger).

(S), (M), (FF) rapide adj. Rapid, swift (courant), fast.

(S),(FF) recommencer v. tr. 6 To recommence, to begin again.

(S), (FF) reposer v. intr. 1 To rest, to repose.

(S), (FF) république f Jur. Republic. Fig. Republic

(FF) résolution f Med., Math. Resolution, resolve.

(S), (FF) ressembler v. intr. 1 To resemble, to look alike

(S), (M), (FF) restaurant m Comm. Restaurant.

(S), (FF) réunion f Reunion. Uniting (for the first time)

(S), (M), (FF) revue f Review as well as revue.

(S), (FF) rose f Bot. Rose. (Ku 86-13-065)

(S), (M), (FF) route f Road as well as route, path, way.

(M), (FF) rugby m Sports. Rugby.

(S), (M), (FF) sac m Sack, bag. (Ku 8-05-007)

(S), (M), (FF) salade f Culin. Salade as well as lettuce.

(S), (M), (FF) sandwich m Culin. Sandwich. (Ku 10-06-009)

(M), (FF) sardine f Zool. Sardine, pilchard. (Ku 2-02-002)

(S), (FF) sérieux, euse adj. Serious, grave.

(S), (M), (FF) service m Service (assistance).

(S), (M), (FF) serviette f Feeder, bib, serviette, napkin.

(S), (FF) signer v. tr. 1 To sign, to put one's name to

(S), (FF) sombre adj. Dark as well as sombre. (Ku 2-01-002)

(S), (M), (FF) sou m Sou. (Ku 1-01-001)

(FF) sûr, ûre adj. Sure, reliable, true (ami)

(S), (M), (FF) table f Table (meuble) as well as a slab

(S), (M), (FF) taxi m Autom. Taxi-cab, taxi, cab.

(S), (FF) télégraphier v. intr., tr. 1 To telegraph.

(S), (M), (FF) téléphone m Electr. Telephone, phone.

(S), (FF) téléphoner v. tr., intr. 1 To telephone, to phone.

(S), (M), (FF) télévision f Radio, Television, T.V.

(FF) tendre v. tr. 4 To stretch, to strain, to tend.

(M), (FF) tennis m Sports. Tennis as well as lawn-tennis.

(S), (M), (FF) timbre m Bell, stamp. Mus. Timbre.

(S), (M), (FF) tomate adj., invar., f. Bot., Culin. Tomato.

(S), (M), (FF) train m Ch. de f. Train as well as speed,

(FF) tranquille adj. Still, peaceful, tranquil.

(S), (M), (FF) transport m Transport, conveyance.

(S), (FF) traverser v. tr. 1 To go across, to traverse

(S), (M), (FF) tricot m Knitting (action). Tricot.

(M), (FF) tulipe f Bot. Tulip. (Ku 4-03-004)

(S), (M), (FF) tunnel m Tunnel. (Ku 10-05-005)

(M), (FF) Valentin m, Valentine f Valentine. (Ku 2-02-002)

(S), (M), (FF) valise f Suit-case, valise, bag.

(S), (M), (FF) village m Village. (Ku 72-13-045)

(S), (FF) voter v. intr. 1 To vote.

(S), (M), (FF) zéro m Zero, naught, cipher.

English-French Cognates Rated With
Les indices d'utilité du vocabulaire fondamental français

(S) absence f Absence (de, from), non-attendance.
(S) absent, ente adj. Absent (non présent), away.
(S) absorber v. tr. To absorb, to imbibe. (Ku 13-08-011)
(S) accent m Accent, emphasis (oratoire), stress (tonique)
(S) accepter v. tr. To accept (un cadeau, une invitation).
(S), (M), (FF) accident m Accident, mishap.
(S) accuser v. tr. To reveal, to acknowledge, to accuse.
(S), (M) acide adj. Acid. Fig. Tart. (Ku 13-06-009)
(S) actif, ive adj. Busy, alert, active (vie). Med. Active
(S) action f Act, action (en général).
(S) activité f Activity, diligence, briskness.
(S) adapter v tr. To adapt, to accomodate, to conform.
(S) addition f Addition (v. augmentation). Bill (restaurant).
(S), (FF) adieu adv. Adieu, farewell. (Ku 1-01-001)
(S) adjectif, ive adv. Adjectival, m adjective.
(S), (M) administration f Administration, management
(S) admirable adj. Admirable, wonderful, Excellent.
(S) admiration f Admiration, wonder. (Ku 10-05-007)
(S) admirer v. tr. To wonder as well as to admire.
(S) adopter v. tr. Jur. to adopt (un enfant), to pass
(S) adresse f Address (sur une lettre).
(S) adresser v tr. To address, to send (une lettre).
(S) adulte adj. Adult. (Ku 25-08-016)
(S) adverbe m Gramm. Adverb. (Ku 1-01-001)
(S), (M) affaire f Affair, business, matter, job.
(S) affection f Affection, liking. (v. Attachement).
(S) affirmation f Affirmation, assertion, asseveration,
(S) affirmer v. tr. To affirm, to assert, to state
(S), (M) agriculture f Agriculture, farming, husbandry,
(S), (M) aide f Aid, help (assistance), rescue
(S), (M) air m Air, appearance, aspect (aspect).
(S) alimentation f Alimentation, food, feeding.
(S) alphabet m Alphabet. Spelling-book, U.S. Speller

(S) altitude f Altitude, height. (Ku 4-03-003)

(S), (M) aluminium m Aluminium, U.S. aluminum.

(S) amateur m Lover of books as well as amateur.

(S) ambassadeur m Ambassador. Fam. Messenger.

(S), (M) ambulance f Ambulance, a military field hospital

(S) ample adj. Ample, abundant, wide.

(S), (M) amuser v. tr. (1) To amuse, to entertain

(S) analogue adj. Analogous (à, to). (Ku 1-01-001)

(S), (M) angle m Angle. Math. Angle. Fig. Point of view

(S), (M) animal m Zool. Animal (v. bête).

(S) antique adj. Antique (v. Ancien). Old-fashioned,

(S) antiquité f Antiquity (période, qualité),

(S) aptitude f Aptitude, fitness, tendency, inclination

(S), (M) arme f Milit. Arm, weapon (moyen de défense).

(S) armer v. tr. 1 To arm, to equip (qqn.).

(S), (FF) arriver v. tr. 1 To arrive, to come.

(S), (M) art m Art. English senses except "A work of art)"

(S) article m Comm., Gramm. Article. (Ku 68-10-035)

(S) artillerie f Milit. Artillery, ordnance.

(S), (M) artisan m Craftsman, artisan. Fig. Architect,

(S), (FF), (M) artiste s. Artist, performer.

(S) aspect m Astron., Gramm. Aspect. Look, appearance.

(S) assassin, ine adj. Murderous. m Assassin, murderer.

(S) assembler v. tr. 1 To assemble, to gather, to collect.

(S) assister v. tr. 1 To assist, to help (v. Aider).

(S) association f Association (pr. et fig.).

(S), (M) assurance f Assurance (v. Certitude). Insurance.

(S) assurer v. tr. To assure as well as to insure.

(S), (M), (FF) atelier m Studio, atelier (d'artiste).

(S) atome m Chim., Phys. Atom. Fig. Atom, particle, jot.

(S) attacher v. tr. 1 To attach, to fasten, to tie (lier)

(S), (M), (FF) attention f Attention, observing, heed.

(S) attitude f Attitude (pr. et fig.) "envers" = towards.

(S) augmentation f Augmentation, increase, rise.

(S) augmenter v tr. 1 To augment, to enlarge.

(S), (M), (FF) auto f Autom. Motor-car, car. U.S. auto.

(S) autocar m Autom. Motor coach, charabanc, autocar.
(S), (M) automobile adj. Self-propelling, automobile.
(S) autorité f Authority. (Ku 93-12-059)
(S) avance f Advance, progress, progression.
(S) avantage m Advantage, benefit, profit.
(S), (M) aventure f Adventure, enterprise.
(S), (M), (FF) avenue f Avenue (allée).
(S), (M) aviation f Aviat. Aviation, flying. Air force,
(S) avril m April. (Ku 71-11-041)
(S), (M) balance f Balance, scales. Fin. Balance.
(S), (M), (FF) balcon m Balcony.
(S), (M), (FF) balle f Sports. Ball as well as bullet
(S), (M), (FF) ballon m Ball, football. Geogr. Ballon.
(S) bande f Rout (de fêtards), band, troop.
(S), (M) barrage m Barrage, dam, weir (de rivière).
(S), (M) base f Base, basis, foundation, bottom (fond).
(S) beauté f Beauty (le beau). Beauteousness,
(S) beige adj., m Beige. (Ku 1-01-001)
(S), (M) béret m Beret (basque), tam-o'-shanter
(S) bizarre adj. Bizarre, odd, queer, peculiar, quaint.
(S), (M) bloc m Block, lump (only as in a block of wood)
(S), (FF) blond, onde adj. Fair, blond, flaxen,
(S), (M) bonbon m Sweet, bonbon, comfit, U.S. candy.
(S), (M) bouillon m Culin. Broth, bouillon cube.
(S), (M) boule f Ball (de billard), boule (de casino)
(S), (M), (FF) boulevard m Boulevard (v. Avenue).
(S), (M) boutique f Shop, U.S. store. Booth, stall, boutique.
(S), (M) boxer v. intr. 1 Sports. To box.
(S), (M) bracelet m Bracelet (en général), anklet,
(S), (M) brochure f Brochure, pamphlet, tract. (Ku 2-02-002)
(S) bruit m Fig. Turmoil, noise, report, rumour, bruit.
(S) brusque adj. Sudden, short, sharp, brusque, gruff, rough.
(S) brutal, ale adj. Savage, brutal (instinct, personne),
(S) budget m Fin. Budget (de l'état), estimates.
(S), (M) buffet m U.S buffet, sandwich-counter.
(S) bulletin m Bulletin, gazette, report, list.

(S), (M), (FF) cabine m Cabin (on a ship).

(S), (M) cabinet m An office, study, cabinet.

(S) cachet m Price of a lesson, meal ticket, Med. Cachet.

(S) cadavre m Corpse, dead body, cadaver.

(S), (M) cadre m Milit. Cadre, skeleton, nuleus.

(S), (M) cage f Cage (d'animaux), hutch (à lapins),

(S), (M) cahier m Copy-book, exercise-book, cahier,

(S) calme m Peace, order, calm, quiet, quietness.

(S), (M) camp m Faction, side (in games). Milit., Sports. Camp

(S), (M) camper v. intr. 1 Milit. To encamp, to camp,

(S), (M) canal m Canal (artificiel), channel.

(S), (M) candidat m Candidate, examinee. (Ku 34-09-020)

(S), (M) canon m Arts., Fig. Canon. Eccles. Canon,

(S) capable adj. Capable, able, competent, efficient.

(S), (M) capitaine m Milit. Captain. Sports. Captain,

(S), (M) capital, ale adj. Capital, outstanding, essential

(S), (M) caporal m Milit. Corporal. Comm. Caporal

(S) caprice m Caprice, whim, fancy, capriciousness,

(S), (M) carafe f Water-bottle, carafe (à eau),

(S) cardinal, ale adj. m Math., Zool., Eccles. Cardinal.

(S), (M) carton m Carton (boîte). (Ku 1-01-001)

(S), (M) cas m Case (an instance) not a legal case

(S), (M) casque m Casque, helmet (d'armure). Milit. Helmet

(S) catégorie f Class, category, division, sort. type.

(S), (M) cathédrale adj. f Cathedral. (Ku 8-06-008)

(S) cause f Cause, Reason, consideration, motive, ground.

(S), (M) causer v. tr. 1 To cause, to bring about.

(S) cavalerie f Milit. Cavalry, horse cavalry.

(S) céder v. tr. 5 To yield, to cede, to give up.

(S), (FF) centime m Centime.

(S), (M) central, ale adj. Central, principal, head, chief.

(S), (M) centre m Centre, U.S. center.

(S), (M) certificat m Med. Certificate (de médecin).

(S) certifier v. tr. 1 To certify, to assure. (Ku 5-02-002)

(S), (M) chaîne f Chain (de chien), (Ku 50-10-025)

(S), (M) champignon m Bot., Culin. Mushrom, champignon.

(S) champion m Champion, supporter. Sports. Champion.
(S), (FF) changer v tr. 7 To change.
(S), (M), (FF) chanson f Mus. Song. Fam. Chansons! rubbish!
(S) charge f Load, burden (v. Fardeau). Milit. Charge
(S), (M) charger v. tr. 7 to exaggerate, to take charge of
(S), (M) charme m Spell, charm, enchantment.
(S) charmer v. tr. 1 To charm, to enchant, bewitch,
(S), (M) château m Castle (féodal), château.
(S), (M), (FF) chauffeur m Autom. Chauffeur, driver.
(S), (M), (FF) chemise f Chemise, shirt, wrapper.
(S), (M), (FF) chèque m Fin. Cheque, U.S. check (de, for). (Ku 88-12-057)
(S) chic m Knack. Style, chic. (Ku 7-03-007)
(S) chimiste m Chim. Chemist. (Ku 4-04-004)
(S), (M), (FF) chocolat m Chocolat (barre, boisson, bonbon)
(S), (M), (FF) cigarette f Cigarette, fag. weed.
(S), (M), (FF) cinéma m Theatr. Cinema (art, édifice, film)
(S), (M) cinématographe m Cinematograph.
(S) circuit m Circuit, circumference. Roundabout way, detour.
(S), (M) circulation f Circulation, traffic (des gens).
(S), (M) cirque m Circus. Geogr. Cirque. (Ku 7-05-006)
(S) citer v. tr. 1 To quote, to cite (un auteur, une autorité)
(S) civil, ile adj. Civil. Milit. Civil (guerre). Fig. Civil
(S) civilisation f Civilization. (Ku 42-09-026)
(S), (M) classe f Class, category, sort, rank.
(S) classer v. tr. 1 To file papers as well as to classify,
(S) classique adj. Classic (auteur, beauté, litterature)
(S), (FF) client m A dependent. Comm. Customer, patron, client
(S) clientèle f Clientage, Patronage. Clientèle.
(S), (M) climat m Climate (conditions atmosphériques)
(S), (M) clinique adj. Med. Clinic, clinical.
(S), (M) coiffeur m Hairdresser, coiffeur.
(S), (M) col m Neck (cou). Geogr. Pass, col. Med. neck.
(S) collectif, ive adj. Collective (acte, contrat).
(S), (M) collection f English senses of collection
(S), (M) collège m College. Secondary grammar school.
(S), (M) colonel m Milit. Colonel. (Ku 37-07-020)

(S), (M) combat m Fight, struggle. Milit. Combat, battle.
(S) combiner v. tr. 1 To scheme, to arrange, to combine.
(S), (M) comédie f Theatr. Comedy (genre), play (pièce),
(S) comique adj. Theatr. Comic (acteur, opéra).
(S) commander v. tr. 1 To order, to command (qqch., qqn.).
(S) commencer v. tr. 6 To begin, (sens général), to commence
(S), (M) commerce m Comm. Trade (intérieur), commerce
(S) commercial, ale adj. Comm. Commercial.
(S), (M) commission f Errand (course), message. Commission
(S) communication f Communication, information.
(S) communisme m Communism. (Ku 70-09-024)
(S), (M) communiste adj., m Communist. (Ku 97-09-042)
(S) comparer v. tr. 1 To compare (à, to; avec, with),
(S), (M) compartiment m Square (d'un damier), compartment
(S) complément m Complement. (Ku 21-05-009)
(S), (M) complet, ète adj. Complete, entire, whole.
(S), (M) composer v. tr. 1 To compose (to calm).
(S) composition f Composition, a term paper.
(S), (M) concert m Mus. Concert. Fig. concert, concord.
(S), (M), (FF) concierge m s. House-porter, concierge.
(S) conclusion f Conclusion, decision, settlement.
(S), (M) concours m Competition, help, concourse.
(S) condition f A social status, condition.
(S), (M) conducteur, trice adj. Driving. Electr. Conductive.
m Electr. Conductor.
(S) conférence f A lecture, conference.
(S) confirmer v. tr. 1 To support, to confirm (une accusation).
(S) confortable adj. Med. Strengthening, capable of comfort.
(S) confusion f Confusion.
(S) conjonction f Conjunction, connection, union.
(S) conquérir v. tr. 13 To conquer (un pays). Fig. To win.
(S) conscience f Consciousness, perception, conscience.
(S) consentir v. intr. 93 To consent, to agree (à, to).
(S) conséquence f Consequence, inference, result.
(S) conséquent, ente adj. Logical (esprit). Phys. Consequent
(S) considérable adj. Substantial, considerable (aide).

(S) considérer v. tr. 5 To consider, to esteem, to reckon.
(S) consoler v. tr. 1 To comfort (de, for), to console,
(S) consommation f Consumption (use), drinks, consummation
(S) constitution f Constitution (sens général)
(S) construction f Construction, building.
(S) consul m Consul. (Ku 3-01-003)
(S) consulat m Consulate (bureaux), consulship (fonction).
(S) contenter v tr. 1 To content, to please (qqn.) To suit
(S), (FF) continuer v. tr. 1 To pursue, to continue.
(S) contrat m Contract, agreement (en général).
(S), (M) conversation f Conversation, talk. (Ku 50-12-037)
(S) coopératif, ive adj. Co-operative. (Ku 20-06-010)
(S), (M) copie f An exercise, composition (school). Copy
(S), (M) corde f Rope as well as cord. (Ku 6-05-006)
(S), (M) corps m Med. A live body as well as a corpse.
(S), (M) correspondance f A transfer. Correspondence.
(S), (M) costume m Clothes as well as a costume.
(S), (M) courage m Courage (v. Bravoure, vaillance), heart
(S) courageux, euse adj. Courageous, gallant (v. Brave).
(S), (M), (FF) cours m Course, flow (d'un fleuve).
(S), (M) court m Sports. Court (de tennis). (Ku 230-13-064)
(S), (FF) cousin, ine s. Cousin.
(S), (M) couture f Sewing (action), seam (résultat), couture.
(S), (M) couturière f Dressmaker, couturière.
(S), (M), (FF) cravate f Neck-tie, tie (d'homme), cravat.
(S) création f Eccles. Creation (acte, résultat).
(S) crédit m English senses of credit.
(S), (M), (FF) crème f Cream (de lait). Crème (liqueur).
(S) crime m Crime. Jur. Felony, Fam. Sin, shame, crime.
(S) critique adj. Critical
(S), (M) crochet m Hook (in general) as well as crochet
(S) cruel, elle adj. Cruel (acte, personne). (Ku 15-07-014)
(S), (M) cube adj. Cubic (centimètre, mètre). m Math. Cube.
(S), (M) cultivateur, trice adj. Agricultural m Agric. Cultivator.
(S), (FF) curieux, euse adj. Curious, inquisitive, prying.
(S), (M) cycliste s. Cyclist.

(S) danger m Danger (pour, to), (v. Pēril), risk.

(S), (FF) dangereux, euse adj. Dangerous, perilous.

(S), (FF) date f English senses of "date"

(S), (FF) dēcider v. tr. 1 To persuade, to decide.

(S) dēcision f Decision, determination, resolution.

(S) dēclaration f Declaration, statement.

(S) dēclarer v. tr. 1 To declare, to state.

(S), (M) dēcoration f Arts. Decoration, ornamentation.

(S) dēcourager v. tr. 7 To discourage, to dishearten,

(S) dēfaut m Lack, defect, want. Jur. Default.

(S) dēfense f Defence, U.S. defense (sens gēnēral).

(S) dēficit m Fin. Deficit. Comm. Shortage. (Ku 12-05-008)

S) dēfinition f Definition (en gēnēral). (Ku 38-08-026)

(S) degrē m Rank (de la hiērarchie), degree.

(S) dēlai m Delay (retard). (Ku 21-09-019)

(S) dēlicat, ate adj. Finnicky, delicate.

(S) dēmonstratif, ive adj. Demonstrative, conclusive

(S), (M) dentiste m Med. Dentist. (Ku 12-04-006)

(S) dēpendre v. intr. To depend.

(S) dēplacement m Transfer, displacement, shift.

(S) dēposer v. tr. 1 To deposit, to lay down, to depose.

(S), (FF) descendre v. intr. 4 To descend (de, from).

(S) descente f Coming down, invasion, raid, descent.

(S) dēsirer v. tr. 1 To desire, to wish, to want.

(S) dēsordre m Moral laxity, disorder.

(S), (M), (FF) dessert m Culin. Dessert, sweet.

(S) destin m Destiny, Fate, fortune. (Ku 22-07-018)

(S) destiner v. tr. 1 To destine, to design, to intend.

(S) dētacher v. tr. 1 To unfasten. To detach.

(S) dētail m Comm. Retail (commerce, vente). Detail,

(S) dēterminatif, ive adj., m Gramm. Determinative.

(S) dēterminer v. tr. 1 To persuade, to determine

(S) dētester v. tr. 1 To nauseate (un plat), to detest.

(S) dēvelopper v. tr. 1 To spread out, to develop.

(S), (M), (FF) deviner v. tr. 1 To guess, to feel, to divine.

(S) diffērence f Senses of English "difference"

(S) différent, ente adj. Different, unlike, dissimilar.
(S) difficulté f Difficulty (sens général),
(S) diminution f Diminution, shortening, decrease.
(S), (M), (FF) dîner v. intr. To dine (de, off, on).
(S), (M) directeur, trice adj. Directional, managing. m Director, manager
(S), (M) direction f Direction as well as instruction,
(S) discours m Speech, address, discourse (sur un sujet).
(S) discussion f Discussion, debate, argument.
(S) dispute f Debate, disputation. Dispute, quarrel.
(S) disputer v. tr. 1 To dispute, to contest (à, with).
(S), (M) disque m Disc, disk as well as Mus. Record, disc.
(S) distance f Distance (espace). (Ku 108-14-074)
(S) distribution f Distribution, allotment, supply.
(S), (M) divan m Divan, couch (meuble). Divan (en Orient).
(S) divers, erse adj. Changeful, varying. Diverse, various,
(S), (M) division f Division, partition (en, into).
(S) divorce m Jur. Divorce (d'avec, from). (Ku 29-10-16)
(S) divorcer v. intr. 6 To obtain a divorce, to be divorced
(S), (M) docteur m Doctor. (Ku 100-11-044)
(S) document m Outside of court usage, the English and French "document" have the same meaning.
(S) domaine m Domain, lands, Fig. Range, scope, domain
(S) domicile m Residence, abode, domicile, home.
(S), (M) double adj. Double, twofold. (Ku 56-12-040)
(S) doubler v. intr. 1 To double, to increase twofold.
(S), (M) éclair m Flash of lightening. Culin. Eclair.
(S) économie f Economy except "les économies" = savings
(S) économique adj. Economic, economical, cheap.
(S), (M) édifice m Archit. Building, edifice.
(S), (M) effacer v. tr. 6 To efface, to blot out,
(S) effet m Effect, result, consequence.
(S) effort m Effort, exertion, strain.
(S), (M) électeur m Elector, constituent, voter.
(S), (M) élection f Election as well as choice.
(S), (M) électricien m Electr. Electrician.

(S), (M) électricité f Electr. Electricity. (Ku 26-08-016)
(S), (M) électrique adj. Electric (courant, lumière)
(S), (M) électronique adj. Electronic (action).
(S) électrophone m Electrophone.
(S) élégance f Elegance, smartness. (Ku 10-05-009)
(S) élégant, ante adj. Elegant, dressy, stylish.
(S) élément m Element (corps, principe). Component,
(S), (M) éléphant m Zool. Elephant. (Ku 7-05-005)
(S) embarrasser v. tr. 1 To perplex, to hamper, to embarrass
(S) émission f Emission (de chaleur, de vapeur, d'un son).
(S) émotion f Commotion (or a crowd), emotion.
(S) empereur m Emperor. (Ku 19-05-009)
(S) empire m Empire (état, style). Power, control,
(S) employer v. tr. 9a To use, to employ, to make use
(S) employeur s. Employer. (Ku 15-08-013)
(S) encourager v. tr. 7 To encourage, to cheer up.
(S) énergie f Energy. Techn., Electr., Phys. energy.
(S) ennui m Nuisance, annoyance. Boredom, weariness, ennui
(S) enrichir v. tr. 2 To enrich, to make rich (de, with).
(S), (FF) ensemble adj. Together. m Ensemble (costume)
(S), (M) entrée f Entering, incoming, entry, entrée.
(S), (FF) enveloppe f Envelope (de lettre). (Ku 21-06-013)
(S) envelopper v. tr. 1 To envelop, to wrap up (qqn, qqch).
(S) envie f Want, craving, desire, envy.
(S) environ adj. About, or so, m pl. Environs.
(S) envisager v. tr. 7 To face, to envisage (le danger).
(S) équipage m Retinue, suite, equipage (du roi).
(S) équipement m Equipment, outfit, gear, appurtenances.
(S) équiper v. tr. 1 Techn., Milit. To equip, to fit
(S) erreur f Error (de, of, in), mistake. (Ku 36-08-027)
(S), (M) espace m Space (indéfini). (Ku 184-14-082)
(S) essai m Trial, test as well as an essay. (Ku 19-05-013)
(S), (M) essence f Essence, essential element. Gasoline.
(S) essentiel, elle adj. Essential. (Ku 81-13-059)
(S) éternel, elle adj. Eccles., Fig. Eternal,
(S) éternité f Eternity. Fam. Ages, eternity.

(S) évident, ente adj. Evident, obvious. (Ku 56-12-043)

(S) évolution f Evolution

(S) exact, ate adj. Punctual. Exact, right. Strict.

(S), (M) examen m Examination, investigation. Exam (fam.).

(S) examiner v. tr. 1 To examine, to survey. (Ku 33-10-031)

(S) excellent, ente adj. Excellent, First-class.

(S) exceptionnel, elle adj. Exceptional, outstanding.

(S), (M) excursion f Excursion, hiking, walk. (Ku 2-02-002)

(S) excuse f Excuse except in "les excuses" = apology.

(S), (FF) excuser v. tr. 1 To excuse, to extenuate.

(S) exécution f Execution, carrying out, fulfilment,

(S), (FF) exemple m Example except as in par exemple.

(S), (M) exercice m Exercise (du corps). Training.

(S) exigence f Exigency, exigence (nécessité),

(S) existence f Existence, being (être).

(S) exister v. intr. 1 To exist, to be in existence.

(S) expérience f Experiment as well as experience.

(S) explication f Explanation, exposition. Explication.

(S) (M) exploitation f Exploitation, management.

(S), (M) exploiter v. tr. 1 To exploit.

(S), (M) explosion f Blowing up, explosion, bursting.

(S) exportation f Comm. Exportation, export. Pl. Exports.

(S) exposer v. tr. 1 To explain, to display, to expose.

(S) exposition f Display, exposure, exposition.

(S), (M) express adj. Comm., Ch. de f. Express.

(S), (M) expression f Expression (de la pensée).

(S) extérieur, eure adj. Exterior (à, to).

(S) extrême adj. Extreme, farthest, intense, deep.

(S) extrémité f Extremity, end. (Ku 4-03-004)

(S) fable f Fable (genre littéraire). Tale, lie.

(S), (M) façade f Façade, front, Fig. Façade.

(S), (M), (FF) face f Face (de l'homme). (Ku 371-15-189)

(S) facile adj. Easy (ascension, travail). Facile, fluent,

(S) facilité f Facility, easiness (d'un travail).

(S), (M), (FF) facteur, trice s. Maker, Comm. Factor,

(S) fameux, euse adj. Famous, outstanding, great, Excellent.

(S) familier, ère adj. Familiar, domestic, inimate.
(S), (FF) fatigue adj. Fatigue, tiredness, weariness.
(S) faveur f Favour (bienveillance). (Ku 78-13-061)
(S) favorable adj. Favourable, propitious, suitable, kind.
(S) fédération f Federation. (Ku 15-06-012)
(S) féminin, ine adj. Feminine (monde, sexe, grâce),
(S), (M) figure f Figure (forme). Gramm., Arts. Figure
(S) figurer v. tr. 1 English senses of "to figure."
(S), (M), (FF) film m Cinem. Film, motion picture.
(S) fin, ine adj. Fine, finely.
(S) final, ale (pl. finals) adj. Last (lettre, mot), final
(S), (M) finance f Fin. Finance, money, cash. (Ku 31-09-022)
(S) financier, ère adj. Fin. Financial.
(S) fixer v. tr. 1 To fasten, to stare, to fix (les yeux)
(S) fonction f English senses of "function."
(S), (M) force f Strength, power, force. English "force"
(S) forcer v. tr. 6 To force except as in "forcer la dose"
(S), (M) forêt f Bot. Forest. (Ku 66-09-021)
(S), (M) forge f Forge, smithy (atelier), forge (feu).
(S), (M) forger v. tr. 7 To forge (le fer). Fig. To forge
(S) formation f Formation. Milit., Aviat. Formation.
(S), (M) forme f Form, shape (configuration). (Ku 370-14-171)
(S) former v. tr. 1 To form (un corps, un chiffre).
(S) formidable adj. Extraordinary, wonderful, formidable.
(S) formule f Form. Jur., Med., Chim., Math. Formula.
(S) fortune f Fortune, fate (sort). Fortune, wealth,
(S), (M) foulard m Foulard (étoffe), scarf (fichu).
(S) fragile adj. Fragile, brittle (cassant). Fig. Weak,
(S), (M) fraise f Fraise, ruff (collet). Culin. Frill.
(S) franc, anque adj. Free, complete, real, franc.
(S) fraternal, elle adj. Brotherly, fraternal.
(S) fraternité f Brotherhood, fraternity. (Ku 6-04-005)
(S) fréquent, ente adj. Frequent. (Ku 34-10-031)
(S) fréquenter v. t . 1 To frequent (un lieu), to visit.
(S), (M), (FF) fruit m Fruit. (Ku 35-11-022)
(S) furieux, euse adj. Furious, in a rage. (Ku 8-04-006)

(S), (M) futur adj. Future (à venir).
(S), (FF) gai, gaie adj. Gay (cheerful), merry.
(S), (M) gamin m Urchin, gamin, kid, street-boy.
(S), (M), (FF) garage m Autom. Garage.
(S), (M) gaz m Gas. (Ku 98-11-039)
(S), (M) géant, ante adj. Giant, gigantic. m Giant.
(S), (M) général, ale adj. General, universal.
(S) généreux, euse adj. Courageous, noble, generous.
(S) génie m Genius (v. Talent). (Ku 23-08-016)
(S), (M) géographie f Geogr. Geography (science).
(S), (M) géographique adj. Geogr. Geograpic(al).
(S), (M) globe m Globe (s. Sphère), orb (du soleil).
(S), (M) golf m Sports. Golf (jeu). (Ku 34-08-014)
(S), (M) gorge f Throat, neck (cou). Archit. Quirk, gorge.
(S), (FF) gourmand, ande adj. Gourmand, greedy, gluttonous.
(S) gourmet m Gourmet, epicure. (Ku 2-01-001)
(S), (M) gouvernement m Government. (Ku 1-01-001)
(S) grâce f Grace, gracefulness, charm, attractiveness
(S) gracieux, euse adj. Graceful, gratuitous, gracious.
(S), (M) grain m Bot. Grain (d'avoine, de blé).
(S), (M) gramme m Gramme, gram. (Ku 10-02-004)
(S) grandeur f Size (dimension) as well as grandeur,
(S), (FF) grave ad. Grave, sedate, solemn, staid (air).
(S), (M) grille, f Grating, railing. Eccless. Grille.
(S) grippe f Med. Grippe, influenza, flu (fam.).
(S) groupe m Group (d'amis, d'objets). (Ku 390-15-190)
(S) grouper v. tr. 1 To group, to arrange in groups.
(S), (M) guide m Guide, cicerone (dans une musée).
(S) guider v. tr. 1 To steer (un bateau), to guide.
(S), (M) hangar * m Shed. Aviat. Hangar.
(S) hasard * m Risk, danger, as well as hazard.
(S) hectare m Hectare (2.47 acres).
(S), (M) hélicoptère m Aviat. Helicopter. (Ku 1-01-001)
(S), (M) hôpital m Med. Hospital. (Ku 27-12-048)
(S) horizon M Horizon, sky-line. (Ku 27-12-022)
(S), (M), (FF) horrible adj. Horrible, horrid (v. Affreux). Hideous,

(S), (M), (FF) hôtel m Hotel, a well as town mansion,
(S) humanité f Humanity, human nature. Humaneness.
(S) humide adj. Wet, damp, humid. (Ku 1-01-001)
(S), (M) hygiène f Hygiene, sanitation (propreté),
(S) idéal, ale (pl. idéals, idéaux), adj. Ideal.
(S), (FF) identité f Identity, sameness. (Ku 55-10-028)
(S) idiot, ote adj. Idiotic, absurd. (Ku 2-02-002)
(S) illustration f Illustriousness, making illustrious.
(S), (M) image f Image, picture (représentation).
(S) imagination f Imagination (faculté). Fig. Fancy,
(S) imaginer v. tr. 1 To imagine, to fancy, to picture.
(S) imbécile adj. Imbecile, half-witted, idiotic.
(S) imitation f Imitation, imitating, copying.
(S) immédiat, ate adj. Immediate, near (avenir).
(S) immense adj. Immense, huge, vast. (Ku 14-07-013)
(S) immobile adj. Immobile, motionless, still.
(S) immoral, ale adj. Immoral. (Ku 5-04-005)
(S) impatient, ente adj. Impatient, intolerant. Eager
(S) impératif, ive adj. Imperious (air), imperative
(S) impérialisme m Imperialism. (Ku 2-02-002)
(S) impérialiste adj. Imperialist(ic).
(S), (M) imperméable adj. Impermeable, waterproof (à l'eau).
(S) impersonnel, elle adj. Impersonal. (Ku 14-07-010)
(S) importance f Importance, consequence, gravity.
(S) importation f Comm. Importing, importation. (Ku 2-02-002)
(S) importer v. tr. 1 Comm. To import (des denrées).
(S) impossible adv. Impossible, not possible. (Ku 84-15-073)
(S) impression f Impression, impress, mark, imprint.
(S) incapable adj. Incapable, unfit, incompetent.
(S) incident, ente adj. Incidental. (Ku 49-13-037)
(S) incliner v. tr. 1 To incline, to slope, to tilt.
(S) indépendence f Independence (v. Liberté). (Ku 70-08-032)
(S) indicatif, ive adj. Indicative (de, of).
(S) indication f Indication, indicating. Information,
(S) indifférence f Indifference, coolness, unconcern.
(S) indifférent, ente adj. Indifferent, unconcerned

(S) indirect, ecte· adj. Gramm., Milit. Indirect.
(S) indispensable adj. Indispensable, essential
(S) individuel, elle adj. Individual. (Ku 239-11-131)
(S), (M) industrie f Comm. Industry, manufacture.
(S), (M) industriel, elle adj. Industrial. (Ku 143-11-057)
(S) inférieur, eure adj. Fig. Inferior, lower, poorer.
(S) infinitif, ive adj., m Gramm. Infinitive. (Ku 1-01-001)
(S) infirme adj. Infirm, weak, feeble. (Ku 1-01-001)
(S) infirmité Med. Infirmity, illness, disability.
(S) infirmité f Influence (des astres). Fig. Influence
(S) information f Jur. Investigation. Information
(S) informer v. tr. 1 To inform, to tell. (Ku 7-06-007)
(S) initiative f Initiative. (Ku 32-09-017)
(S) injustice f Injustice, unfairness. (Ku 16-05-008)
(S) innocent, ente adj. Inocent, guiltness. (Ku 37-11-022)
(S) inondation f Flood, inundation. (Ku 1-01-001)
(S) inquiétude f Restlessness, inquietude (agitation).
(S) inscription f English senses of "inscription."
(S), (M) insecte m Zool. Insect. (Ku 14-06-009)
(S) insister v. intr. 1 To insist, to lay stress (sur, on).
(S) inspecter v. tr. 1 To inspect (une école), to survey
(S), (M) inspecteur m English "inspector."
(S) inspection f Inspection, examination, survey.
(S), (M) installation f Tech. Installation. (Ku 12-02-007)
(S) instant, ante adj. Instant. (Ku 38-10-026)
(S) instinct m Instinct. (Ku 14-05-011)
(S), (M) instituteur s. School-teacher, institutor.
(S) instruction f Schooling, education, instruction.
(S), (M) instrument m Instrument, tool. Mus. Instrument
(S) intact, acte adj. Untouched as well as English intact.
(S) intellectuel, elle adj. Intellectual, mental.
(S), (M) intelligence f Intelligence, intellect.
(S) intelligent, ente adj. Intelligent, smart, brainy,
(S) intense adj. Intese. (Ku 40-10-037)
(S) intention f Intention, purpose (dessein, désir).
(S) intérêt m Interest, advantage, profit. (Ku 330-15-170)

(S) interjection f Gramm. Interjection.

(S) international, ale adj. m Geogr., Sports. International

(S) interprête s. Interpreter (homme).

(S) intervention f Intervention, intervening.

(S), (M) intestin, ine adj. Intestine.

(S) intransitif, ive adj. Gramm. Intransitive.

(S) inventer v. tr. 1 To invent, to contrive (une machine).

(S) inventeur, trice adj. Inventive.

(S) invention f Invention, discovery, contrivance.

(S) invitation f Invitation. (Ku 20-09-018)

(S), (FF) inviter v. tr. 1 To invite. (Ku 11-09-010)

(S) islam m Islam. (Ku 3-03-003)

(S) islamique adj. Islamic. (Ku 3-02-002)

(S) israëlite adj. Israelite, Israeli, Jewish. (Ku 1-01-001)

(S), (M) joie f Joy, mirth, gladness. (Ku 40-12-032)

(S), (M), (FF) journal m Paper, newspaper, journal.

(S), (M) journaliste m Journalist, reporter, correspondent.

(S), (FF) justice f Justice, fairness, right (Ku 114-12-062)

(S) justifier v tr. 1 To justify, to vindicate.

(S), (M) kēpi m Milit. Kēpi.

(S) kilomètre m Kilometre. (Ku 8-01-001)

(S) lampe f Lamp. (Ku 18-07-010)

(S), (M), (FF) lettre f Letter. (Ku 145-15-070)

(S) liaison f Linking, joining, liaison. Fig. Connection,

(S) libēration f Liberation, delivery. (Ku 5-03-004)

(s), (M) libertē f Liberty, freedom. (Ku 46-11-027)

(S) lieutenant m Milit. Lieutenant. (Ku 29-08-012)

(S) limite f Limit, boundary (d'un pays). Limit, margin.

(S) limiter v. tr. 1 To bound, to limit (v. Borner).

(S), (M), (FF) lion m Zool. Lion, Astron. Leo. (Ku 17-04-006)

(S), (M) liquide adj. liquid, fluid. (Ku 48-07-018)

(S) liste f List, register, roll. (Ku 133-15-067)

(S), (M) (FF) litre m Litre.

(S) littērature f Literature. (Ku 133-12-053)

(S), (M) local, ale adj. Local (intērêt, heure).

(S), (M) locomotive f Ch. de f. Locomotive, engine.

(S) logique adj. Logical, consistent.
(S), (M) long, ongue adj. Long. (Ku 755-15-338)
(S), (M) machine f Machine as well as Ch. de f. Locomotive
(S), (M) maçon m Archit. Mason, bricklayer. (Ku 23-06-007)
(S), (M) madame (pl. mesdames) f Mrs., Madam.
(S), (FF) mademoiselle (pl. mesdemoiselles) f Miss,
(S), (M) majeur adj. Major, important. Mus. Major (tierce).
(S) majorité f Majority, greater part. (Ku 57-10-039)
(S) maladie f Med. Illness, sickness, malady.
(S) maladroit, oite adj. Heavy, clumsy, awkward, maladroit
(S) mâle adj. Male, bull. Fig. Masculine, strong.
(S), (M), (FF) mandat m Mandate. Fin. Money-order
(S) manifester v tr. 1 To manifest, to show, to evince
(S) manoeuvre f Manoeuvring, handling, Milit. Manoeuvre.
(S), (M) merchandise f Comm. Merchandise, goods, wares.
(S), (M) mariage m Marriage, match (union). Wedding.
(S), (M) marine f Naut. Marine, navy. (Ku 55-08-013)
(S) maritime adj. Naut. shipping, seaborne, maritime.
(S), (FF) Mars m Mars. (Ku 21-05-010)
(S) masculin, ine adj. Masculine (genre, rime). Male
(S), (M) masse f Mass, heap, bulk. Mass, mob, crowd.
(S) masser v. tr. 1 To mass as well as to massage.
(S), (M) matériel, elle adj. Material, physical.
(S), (M) maternel, elle adj. Maternal, motherly.
(S) matinée f Morning, forenoon. Theatr. Matinée,
(S) mauve adj., m Mauve, light purple. (Ku 1-01-001)
(S) maximum adj. Greatest, maximum. (Ku 79-10-042)
(S) mécanisme m Techn. Mechanism, works (de, of).
(S) médical, ale adj. Med. Medical. (Ku 172-13-049)
(S), (M) médicament m Med. Medicine, medicament.
(S), (M) membre m Med. Limb, member. Fig. Member.
(S) menace f Threat, menace (threatening word or act).
(S) menacer v. tr. 6 To threaten, to menace (de, with).
(S), (M) menu m Culin. Bill-of-fare, menu.
(S), (FF) merci f Favour (v. Miséricorde). Mercy.
(S) mérite m Merit, desert, worth (v. Valeur).

(S) mériter v. tr. 1 To merit, to deserve.

(S), (M) métal m Metal. (Ku 61-13-039)

(S) métallurgie f Metallurgy.

(S), (M) métallurgiste m Metallurgist.

(S) méthode f Method, system, way. (Ku 142-12-081)

(S), (M) mètre m Metre, U.S. meter. (Ku 1-01-001)

(S), (M), (FF) milieu m Middle, midst. Environment, milieu.

(S) milliard m Milliard, U.S. billion.

(S) millimètre m Millimeter. (Ku 3-03-003)

(S) million m Million. (Ku 204-14-073)

(S), (M) mine f Mine, mine de houille = colliery, coal-mine.

(S) minéral, ale adj. Mineral. Chim. Inorganic.

(S), (M) mineur, eure adj. Minor, lesser. Mus. Minor.

(S) minimum m Minimum. (Ku 64-10-045)

(S), (M) ministre m Minister, agent. (Ku 12-06-010)

(S) minorité f Minority (en politique).

(S), (FF) minute f Minute. (Ku 53-13-049)

(S) miracle m Eccles. Miracle. Fig. Wonder, miracle.

(S) misérable adj. Miserable, wretched, unfortunate.

(S) mode m Mode, form, method. Mus. mode, mood.

(S) moderne adj. Modern, up-to-date (maison, style).

(S) moderniser v. tr. 1 To modernize, to bring up-to-date.

(S) modeste adj. Modest, unassuming, unobtrusive, quiet.

(S) modestie f Modesty, unpretentiousness, bashfulness.

(S) modifier v. tr. 1 to modify, to alter, to change.

(S), (M) modiste f Milliner, modiste.

(S), (FF) moment m Moment, instant, second.

(S), (M) monument m Monument, memorial, a notable building.

(S) moral, ale adj. Moral (loi, sens).

(S), (M), (FF) moteur, trice adj. Motive, driving. m Techn. Motor.

(S), (M) moustache f Whiskers (de chat), moustache.

(S) mouvement m Impulse, emotion, movement.

(S) multiplication f Math. Multiplication. fig. Increase.

(S) multiplier v. tr. 1 Math., Fig. To multiply.

(S) municipal, ale adj. Municipal. (Ku 1-01-001)

(S) murmure m Murmuring, murmur, whispering. (Ku 3-02-003)

(S) murmurer v. intr. 1 To murmur, to whisper.

(S), (M) muscle m Med. Muscle. (Ku 42-08-017)
(S), (M) musical, ale adj. Mus. Musical. (Ku 85-13-032)
(S), (M) musicien, enne adj. Mus. Musical. s. Musician.
(S), (M) musique f Mus. Music. (Ku 216-15-064)
(S) mystérieux, euse adj. Mysterious. (Ku 26-10-024)
(S) naif, ive adj. Ingenuous, naive, unsophisticated,
(S) nation f Nation as well as tribe. (Ku 139-13-073)
(S), (FF) national, ale adj. National. (Ku 375-13-143)
(S), (FF) nationalité f Nationality. (Ku 3-03-003)
(S) naturaliser v. tr. 1 To naturalize, to nationalize
(S), (M) nature f Nature (cours des choses, tempérament).
(S) naturel, elle adj. Natural (inné), innate (dons),
(S) nécessité f Necessity, need (v. Besoin).
(S) négligent, ente adj. Negligent, neglectful, careless.
(S) nerveux, euse adj. Med. Nerve, sinewy, nervous.
(S), (M) net, nette adj. Clean, spotless. Fin. Net.
(S), (M) nickel m Nickel. (Ku 7-03-005)
(S) nièce f Niece. (Ku 8-04-005)
(S) noble adj. Noble. Fig. Noble, generous (sentiments),
(S) normal, ale adj. Normal, ordinary, usual.
(S), (M) note f Note (observation, billet, instructions).
(S) noter v. tr. 1 To note, to remark, to take notice of.
(S) novembre m November. (Ku 74-15-042)
(S), (M) nylon m Nylon. (Ku 1-01-001)
(S) objectif, ive adj. Objective, unbiased.
(S) objection f Objection (à, to). (Ku 18-09-011)
(S), (M) objet m Object (chose visible). Object, thing.
(S), (FF) obliger v. tr. 7 To oblige, to compel, to bind
(S) obscur, ure adj. Dark (chambre, forêt, grotte), obscure
(S) obscurité f Obscurity as well as darkness, gloom.
(S) observation f Observation, observance (d'une loi).
(S) observer v. tr.1 To observe, to keep (la loi).
(S) obstacle m Obstacle. Fig. Obstacle, impediment.
(S) occasion f Occasion (conjoncture, cas). Comm. Bargain.
(S) Occident m West (direction), Occident. (Ku 2-01-001)
(S) occidental, ale adj. Occidental, western.
(S) occupation f Milit. Occupation <u>not</u> occupation

(S), (M) océan m Ocean. Fig. Sea, ocean. (Ku 34-12-022)

(S) officiel, elle adj. Official. (Ku 75-15-060)

(S), (M) olive f Bot. Olive. (Ku 5-04-004)

(S), (M) omnibus m Ch. de f., Autom. Omnibus, bus.

(S), (FF) oncle m Uncle. (Ku 57-11-027)

(S), (M), (FF) opéra m Theatr., Mus. Opera. (Ku 47-11-023)

(S) opération f Eccles. Philos. Comm. Milit. Med. Operation

(S) opinion f Opinion, notion, point of view, judgment,

(S) opposer v. tr. 1 To oppose, to place opposite.

(S) opposition f Opposition as well as contrast.

(S), (M), (FF) orange f Bot. Orange. (Ku 23-10-020)

(S), (M), (FF) orchestre m Mus. Band, orchestra.

(S) ordinal, ale adj., m Ordinal.

(S) ordonnance f Order, ordonnance, arrangement.

(S), (M) ordre m Order, course (de la nature).

(S), (M) organe m Med. Organ. Mus. Voice.

(S) organisation f Organization, set-up (fam.).

(S) organiser v. tr. 1 To organize, to arrange, to get up.

(S) Orient m East, Orient. (Ku 4-03-004)

(S) oriental, ale adj. Eastern, oriental. (Ku 16-08-013)

(S), (M) ornement m Ornament, adornment, embellishment.

(S), (M) ouverture f Opening, aperture. Mus. Ouverture.

(S), (M), (FF) page f Page, leaf. (Ku 66-14-046)

(S) paire f Pair (d'amis, de bas). (Ku 50-13-043)

(S), (M) panier m Basket. Pannier (de jupe).

(S), (M) panne f Techn. Breakdown. Arts. Daub. Panne,

(S), (M), (FF) papa m Fam. Dad, daddy, papa, pa.

(S), (M) parachute m Aviat. Parachute. (Ku 1-01-001)

(S), (M) paradis m Eccles., Fig. Paradise. (Ku 12-08-011)

(S), (M), (FF) parc m Park (de château, de ville).

(S), (FF) pardon m Forgiveness, pardon. (Ku 8-07-008)

(S), (M), (FF) parent m pl. Parents as well as relative.

(S) parfumerie f Perfumery (magasin, métier), scent.

(S), (M) passage m Passage, way, ferry crossing.

(S) passeport m Passport. (Ku 6-03-003)

(S), (M), (FF) passer v. intr. 1 To pass.

(S), (M) passion f Passion. Eccles. Passion.

(S) pasteur m Shepherd as well as Eccles. Pastor.

(S), (M) patience f bot. Patience (plant), or spinachdock.

(S) patient, ente adj. Patient, enduring, long-suffering.

(S), (M) pâturage m pasture, grazing-ground.

(S), (M), (FF) payer v. tr. 9b To pay (qqn.) (de, for).

(S), (M) pédale f Pedal (de bicyclette), treadle.

(S) pension f Pension, allowance. Boarding school or house.

(S) péril m Peril, jeopardy (v. Danger). (Ku 8-06-007)

(S) période f Era, time, period (époque).

(S) périodique adj. Periodic, periodical. (Ku 9-05-009)

(S), (FF) permanent, ente adj. Permanent (v. Continuel).

(S) permission f Permission as well as leave of absence.

(S), (M), personnage m Personage, person of rank.

(S), (M), (FF) pharmacie f Med. Pharmacy, pharmaceutics.

(S), (M) phono, phonographe m Phonograph, gramophone.

(S), (M), (FF) photo f Photography. (Ku 5-02-003)

(S) photographique adj. Photographic.

(S) piété f Piety, devotion. Eccles. Piety, godliness.

(S) pieux, euse adj. Dutiful (enfant), pious, godly

(S), (M) pigeon m Zool. Pigeon. (Ku 3-02-003)

(S), (M) pile f Pile, stack (de bois), heap (d'objets).

(S), (M) pilote m Naut., Aviat. Pilot. (Ku 44-10-019)

(S), (M) pipe f Pipe (pour fumer), <u>not</u> pipe (tuyau).

(S), (M) piquet m Piquet (aux cartes).

(S) pitié f Pity (v. Compassion). (Ku 14-07-012)

(S), (M) placer v. tr. 5 To place, to put, to set (sur, on)

(S), (M) plaine f Plain, flat country. (Ku 48-13-038)

(S), (M) plan m Archit. Plan. Fig. Plan (d'action, de vie)

(S), (M) plante f Bot. Plant as well as Med. Sole (du pied)

(S), (M) planter v tr. 1 Agric. To plant, to set.

(S), (M) plastique adj. Plastic (art). (Ku 31-07-017)

(S), (M) plateau m Geogr. Plateau, high plain.

(S) pneumatique adj. Pneumatic.

(S), (M) poète m Poet. (Ku 99-12-038)

(S), (M) pointe f Point (d'aiguille, d'épingle, de clou).

(S), (M) poison m Poison. (Ku 10-05-008)

(S), (M) police f Police (maintien de l'ordre).

(S), (FF) politique adj. Political (parti), politic.
(S), (M) pompe f Pomp, display, state, ceremony, array.
(S) population f Population. (Ku 136-09-053)
(S), (M) port m Naut. Harbour (bassin). Geogr. Port
(S), (M) portrait m Portrait. Arts. Portrait, face.
(S), (FF) poser v. tr. 1 to lay, to put, to pose.
(S) position f Position, place. (Ku 241-15-146)
(S) possessif, ive adj. Gramm. Possessive. Fig. Grasping
(S) possibilité f Possibility (d'un fait), feasibility
(S), (FF) possible adj. Possible (v. Faisable, réalisable).
(S), (FF) postal, ale adj. Postal. (Ku 7-02-006)
(s) poste m Post (employé). Station (de police).
(S), (M), (FF) pot m Pot. Jug, U.S. pitcher. (Ku 28-10-018)
(S) précaution f Precaution (mesure) as well as caution.
(S) précéder v. tr. 5 to precede, to antecede.
(S) précieux, euse adj. Precious (objet), invaluable.
(S) précis, ise adj. Accurate, exact, precise.
(S) précision f Precision, preciseness, accuracy.
(S), (FF) préférer v. tr. 5 To prefer, to like better.
(S) préparation f Preparation, preparing. (Ku 54-09-031)
(S), (M), (FF) préparer v. tr. 1 To prepare.
(S) préposition f Gramm. Preposition. (Ku 2-01-001)
(S) présence f Presence (à, at). Med. Presence, trace
(S) présent, ente adj. Present, at hand. Gramm. Present.
(S), (FF) présenter v. tr. 1 To present, to offer.
(S) présidence f Presidency (d'une nation), chairmanship
(S), (M) président, ente s. Chairman, president.
(S) présider v. intr. 1 To preside (à, at, over).
(S), (M) presse f Press, crowd, throng (foule).
(S) presser v. tr. 1 To press, to squeeze (une éponge).
(S) prétexte m Pretext (v. Excuse). (Ku 3-03-003)
(S), (M) prince m Prince. (Ku 33-06-014)
(S), (M) principal, ale adj. Principal, chief, leading,
(S), (M) prison f Jur. Prison, gaol, jail (lieu).
(S) probable adj. Probable, likely. (Ku 24-10-022)
(S), (M) problème m Problem, enigma, puzzle, riddle.
(S) procurer v. tr. 1 To procure, to get, to furnish.

(S) production f Agric. Production, growing (de blé).
(S), (M) professeur m Teacher, professor.
(S) profit m Advantage, profit. fig. Profit, benefit,
(S) profiter v. intr. 1 Comm. To profit, to benefit
(S), (M), (FF) programme m Programme, syllabus.
(S) progrès m Progress in the sense of "improvement"
(S) projectivle m Projectile, missile (Ku 1-01-001)
(S), (M) project m Project, plan (v. Dessein).
(S) prolonger v. tr. 7 To prolong, to extend (une rue).
(S), (M), (FF) promenade f Walking. Promenade. (Ku 3-01-001)
(S) prononciation f Pronunciation (v. Accent). Delivery
(S) propagande f Propaganda. (Ku 30-08-021)
(S) proposer v tr., intr. 1 English senses of "to propose."
(S) proposition f Proposition, suggestion. (Ku 16-07-013)
(S) protection f Protection. Jur. Protection.
(S) proverbe m Proverb. Theatr. Proverb. (Ku 5-04-005)
(S), (M) province f Province. (Ku 15-06-011)
(S) provision f Provision, store, supply, stock.
(S) prudence f Prudence, caution, discretion.
(S) prudent, ente adj. Prudent, cautious, wary.
(S) psychologie f Psychology. (Ku 14-06-013)
(S) public, ique adj. Public (Ku 438-14-180)
(S) publicité f Publicity, advertisement. (Ku 27-12-023)
(S) pur, ure adj. Pure, unalloyed (sans mélange).
(S), (M) purée f Culin. Mash, puree.
(S) pureté f Purity, pureness, Chastity, innocence.
(S), (M), (FF) pyjama m Pyjamas, U.S. pajamas.
(S) qualité f Quality (v. Attribut, propriété).
(S) quantité f Quantity, amount (nombre). Math. Quantity.
(S), (M) question f Question (v. Demande). Question, point.
(S), (M), (FF) queue f Tail (d'animal), queue.
(S) quotidien, enne adj. Daily, Med. Quotidian (fièvre).
(S), (M) race f Race, ancestry, descent, species.
(S), (M) radiateur m Autom., Electr. Radiator.
(S), (M), (FF) radio m Radio. (Ku 120-14-043)
(S), (M), (FF) rang m Row. Milit., Fig. Rank. (Ku 21-05-017)
(S), (M), (FF) ranger v. tr. 7 To range (v. Arranger).

(S), (M), (FF) rapide adj. Rapid, swift (courant), fast.
(S) rapprochement m Bringing together. Rapprochement.
(S) rare adj. Rare (peu commun), unusual, sparse.
(S), (M) rat m Zool. Rat. (Ku 6-05-006)
(S) ravager v. tr. 7 To harry, to lay waste, to ravage
(S), (M) réaction f Chim. Reaction, Fig. Response
(S) réalisation f Senses of "realization."
(S) réalité f Reality, actuality, fact. (Ku 79-11-049)
(S) récent, ente adj. Recent, new (événement), fresh.
(S) réception f Receipt (d'une lettre). Reception
(S) recommander v. tr. 1 To recommend (qqch., qqn.) (à, to).
(S), (FF) recommencer v. tr. 6 To recommence, to begin again
(S) récompense f Recompense, reward (de, for). Retribution
(S) recompenser v. tr. 1 To recompense, to reward.
(S), (M) récréation f Recreation (v. Amusement).
(S), (M) rectangle dj. Math. Right-angled. m. Rectangle.
(S) réduction f Reduction, decrease (d'une quantité).
(S) réforme f Reform (des abus). (Ku 30-07-017)
(S) reformer v. tr. 1 To re-form. (Ku 30-07-017)
(S), (M) réfrigérateur m Refrigerator, fridge.
(S) refuge m Refuge, sanctuary, asylum, retreat.
(S) refuser v. tr. 1 To refuse, to decline, to reject.
(S) régime m Regime, mode of living. (Ku 23-07-018)
(S), (M) régiment m Milit. Regiment. (Ku 25-06-008)
(S), (M) région f Geogr. Region, district, area.
(S) regret m Longing for as well as "regret," remorse.
(S) relatif, ive adj. Relative, relating (à, to).
(S) relation f Relation (entre, between), connection,
(S), (M) religieux, euse adj. Eccles. Religious (cérémonie),
(S), (M) religion f Eccles. Religion. (Ku 119-14-044)
(S) remarquable adj. Remarkable, noteworthy. (Ku 47-11-040)
(S) remarque f Remark, comment. (Ku 31-09-019)
(S), (M) remède m Med. Remedy (à, for), a medicine.
(S), (M) réparation f Repair as well as reparation
(S), (M) repasser v. tr. 1 To repass, to pass by again.
(S) réponse f Answer, reply (à, to). Response.
(S), (M) repos m Repose, rest. (Ku 2-02-002)

(S), (FF) reposer v. intr. 1 To rest, to repose.
(S) représentation f Representation. Theatr. Performance.
(S) représenter v. tr. 1 To produce, to show. to represent,
(S) républicain, aine adj. s. Jur. Republican
(S), (FF) république f Jur. Republic. Fig. Republic
(S) réserve f Reserve. Fin., Milit., Naut. Reserve.
(S) réserver v. tr. 1 To reserve, to set aside.
(S) résistance f Resistance, opposition (à, to).
(S) résister v. intr. 1 To hold out, to endure, to resist.
(S) respect m Respect, reverence, regard. (Ku 125-13-079)
(S) respecter v. tr. 1 To respect, to esteem, to reverence.
(S) responsabilité f Responsibility, accountability.
(S) ressemblance f Resemblance (avec, to), likeness.
(S), (FF) ressembler v. intr. 1 To resemble, to look alike.
(S) ressource f Resource, resourcefulness. (Ku 9-07-008)
(S), (M), (FF) restaurant m Comm. Restaurant.
(S) reste m Rest, remainder. (Ku 163-15-119)
(S), (FF) réunion f Reunion. Uniting (for the first time)
(S) révolution f Math. Revolution. Fig. Change, revolution.
(S), (M), (FF) revue f Review as well as revue.
(S) riche adj. Senses of English "rich" except for food.
(S), (M) rideau m Curtain, screen. Milit. Rideau.
(S) ridicule adj. Ridiculous, laughable, absurd. m Ridicule.
(S) robuste adj. Med. Robust, strong (corps, personne).
(S), (FF) rose f Bot. Rose. (Ku 86-13-065)
(S), (M) rouleau m Roller, coil (de corde), rouleau (d'or)
(S), (M) roulette f Small wheel, roulette. Math. Cycloid,
(S), (M), (FF) route f Road as well as route, path, way.
(S) ruche f Bee-hive as well as ruche, ruching (d'une robe).
(S), (M) rue f bot. Rue. (Ku 6-05-005)
(S) ruine f Ruin, collapse. (Ku 14-07-013)
(S) ruiner v. tr. 1 to ruin, to destroy, to demolish.
(S) rural, ale adj. Rural, country (vie). (Ku 54-09-027)
(S) ruse f Ruse as well as trick, craftiness, guile.
(S) rythme m Rhythm as well as tempo (or) rate.
(S), (M) sable m Sable (animal). Blas. Sable, black.
(S), (M) sabot m Sabot, clog. Milit. Sabot (de projectile).

(S), (M), (FF) sac m Sack, bag. (Ku 8-05-007)

(S) sage adj. Sage, wise, shrewd as well as well-behaved

(S), (M) saint, ainte adj. Eccles. Saint as well as holy.

(S), (M), (FF) salade f Culin. Salad as well as lettuce.

(S), (M), (FF) sandwich m Culin. Sandwich (Ku 10-06-009)

(S) satisfaction f Watisfaction, contentment.

(S), (M) sauce f Culin. Sauce as well as gravy.

(S), (M) savant; ante adj. Critical, savant, learned.

(S), (M) scène f Theatr. Stage, scene (d'un acte).

(S), (M) science f Science, knowledge, learning.

(S) scientifique adj. Scientific. (Ku 86-09-047)

(S), (M) sculpteur m Arts. Sculptor. (Ku 6-03-003)

(S), (M) sculpture f Arts. Sculpture. (Ku 11-05-007)

(S) seconde f Second (time). Ch. de f. Second (classe).

(S) secret m Secret (chose cachée) as well as secrecy.

(S), (M) secrétaire s. Secretary. (Ku 191-13-066)

(S) secteur m Astron., Math., Techn., Naut. Sector.

(S) section f Section, part as well as cutting.

(S) seigneur m Lord, master, Seigneur, lord, noble.

(S) sénat m senate (assemblée), senate-house (lieu).

(S) sénateur m Senator. (Ku 40-10-026)

(S) sense m Direction, way as well as sense (faculté),

(S) septembre m September. (Ku 56-12-038)

(S) série f Series (de couleurs, de nombre), succession

(S), (FF) sérieux, euse adj. Serious, grave.

(S), (M) serpent m Zool. Serpent, snake, Mus. Serpent.

(S), (M), (FF) service m Service (assistance).

(S), (M), (FF) serviette f Bib (d'enfant), serviette.

(S) sexe m Sex. (Ku 84-12-030)

(S), (M) siège m Seat (d'une chaise). Milit. Siege.

(S) signal m Signal. (Ku 63-12-032)

(S) signature f Signing (action), signature (nom).

(S), (M) signe m Sign, gesture (geste). Math. Sign.

(S), (FF) signer v. tr. 1 to sign, to put one's name to

(S) signifier v. tr. 1 To signify as well as to notify.

(S) silence f Silence, still, hush. (Ku 52-10-041)

(S) simple adj. Simple, guileless, naive, innocent.

(S) sincère adj. Candid (opinion), sincere, frank.
(S) situation f Senses of English "situation."
(S) social, ale adj. Social (contrat, science).
(S) socialisme m Socialism. (Ku 20-06-010)
(S) socialiste adj. Socialist, socialistic.
(S) société f Society, gathering, company.
(S), (M) sol m invar. Mus. Sol, G. (Ku 3-03-003)
(S) solidarité f Fig. Solidarity, fellowship.
(S) solitude f Solitude, isolation, loneliness (état).
(S) solution f Phys., Math., Med. Solution. (Ku 59-11-047)
(S), (FF) sombre adj. Dark as well as sombre. (Ku 2-01-002)
(S), (M) sorte f Kind, sort (espece) as well as manner,
(S), (M) sortie f Exit, outburst, tirade. Milit. Sortie.
(S), (M), (FF) sou m Sou. (Ku 1-01-001)
(S), (M) souffle m Breath, blast. Med. Souffle.
(S), (M) source f Source, spring (v. Fontaine).
(S), (M) souvenir m Memory, remembrance, souvenir.
(S), (M) speaker (f. speakerine) Radio announcer, speaker.
(S) spécial, ale adj. Special, particular (Ku 250-14-155)
(S), (M) spécialiste s. Specialist (v. Technicien).
(S) spécialité f Speciality, specialty.
(S) spectacle m Spectacle, sight (v. Scène).
(S), (M) spectateur, trice s. Spectator, onlooker.
(S), (M) statue f arts. Statue. (Ku 17-05-009)
(S) style m Bot., Gramm. Style. Arts. Stylus, style.
(S) subjonctif, ive adj. Gramm. Subjunctive.
(S) substance f Substance, matter, stuff. Fig. Essence,
(S) succès m Success, issue, result (résultat).
(S), (M) supérieur, eure adj. Higher (in space), superior.
(S) supplément m Supplement, addition. Math. Supplement.
(S) supposer v. tr. 1 To suppose (admettre, impliquer).
(S) supposition f Supposition, conjecture, surmise.
(S) suprême adj. Supreme, sovereign (autorité).
(S) sûreté f Sureness, surety, soundness, security.
(S), (M) surface f Surface. Math. Surface. Fig. Appearance.
(S) surprise f Surprise (action), astonishment.
(S) suspendre v. tr. 4 to suspend, to hang up (un lustre).

(S) syndical, ale adj. Jur. Underwriting (acte), syndical

(S), (M) système m system, scheme, plan. (Ku 416-14-133)

(S), (M), (FF) table f Table (meuble) as well as a slab

(S) talent m Talent (v. Aptitude, capacité, don).

(S), (M), (FF) taxi m Autom. Taxi-cab, taxi, cab.

(S), (M) technicien, enne s. Technician, technicist,

(S), (M) technique adj. Techn. Technical. f. Technique.

(S), (M) télégramme m Telegram, wire. (Ku 8-02-006)

(S), (M) télégraphe m Electr. Telegraph. (Ku 21-05-007)

(S), (FF) télégraphier v. intr., tr. 1 To telegraph,

(S) télégraphique adj. Telegraphic (adresse, mandat).

(S), (M), (FF) téléphone m Electr. Telephone, phone.

(S), (FF) téléphoner v. tr., intr. 1 To telephone, to phone.

(S) téléphonique adj. Telephonic.

(S), (FF) télévision f Radio. Television, T.V.

(S), (M) température f Temperature, weather.

(S) temple m Eccles. Temple, place of worship.

(S), (M) tente f Booth (d'un marché). Sports. Tent.

(S) terme m Limit, end, terminus. Math., Jur. Term.

(S) terminus adj., m Ch. de f., Autom. Terminus.

(S), (M) terrain m Ground, piece of land. Milit. Terrain.

(S) terreur f Terror, fear, dread. (Ku 25-11-022)

(S) terrible adj. Terrible, dreadful, frightful.

(S) testament m Eccles., Jur. Testament, will.

(S) texte m Text. (Ku 60-10-020)

(S) textile adj. Textile. (Ku 28-05-008)

(S), (M) théâtre m Stage (of a theater), theater.

(S) théorie f Theory as well as Fam. Procession, line.

(S), (M) thermomètre m Phys. Thermometer. (Ku 10-04-004)

(S), (M), (FF) timbre m Bell, stamp. Mus. Timbre.

(S) timide adj. Shy, retiring, timid. (Ku 5-04-005)

(S), (M) tissu m Texture (d'une étoffe), tissue, cloth.

(S), (M), (FF) tomate adj., invar., f Bot., Culin. Tomato.

(S) ton m Tone, intonation. Med., Mus., Arts. Tone

(S), (M) tonneau m Barrel, cask, keg. Autom. Tonneau.

(S), (M) torchon adj. Torchon (papier).

(S), (M) torrent m Torrent. Fig. Torrent, stream (d'injures)

(S) total, ale adj. Total, entire, whole, complete.
(S), (M) tourisme m Tourism.
(S) touriste s. Tourist. (Ku 16-05-012)
(S) trace f Trace as well as trail, path, track.
(S) tradition f Tradition. (Ku 94-10-053)
(S) tragédie f Theatr. Tragedy. Fig. Tragic event.
(S) tragique adj. Theatr. Tragic. Fig. Tragic, Tragical.
(S), (M), (FF) train m Ch. de f. train as well as speed,
(S), (M) transformer v. tr. 1 To transform, to convert,
(S) transitif, ive adj. Gramm. Transitive.
(S), (M), (FF) transport m Transport, conveyance.
(S), (M) transporter v. tr. 1 To transport, to convey.
(S), (M) traverser v. tr. 1 to go across, to traverse.
(S) trembler v. intr. To shake. Fig. To tremble, to fear.
(S), (M) triangle m Math., Mus., Astron. Triangle.
(S), (M) tribunal m Tribunal (siège). Jur. Law-court.
(S), (M), (FF) tricot m Knitting (action). Tricot.
(S) triple adj. Triple, treble, three-fold
(S), (M) tube m Tube (de vaseline). Milit., Bot., Med. Tube
(S), (M), (FF) tunnel m Tunnel. (Ku 10-05-005)
(S), (M) type m Type, model, pattern. Zool., Techn. Type.
(S) union f Union as well as agreement. (Ku 182-13-071)
(S) unique adj. Only, sole, single as well as Fig. Unique,
(S) unité f Math. Unit (de mesure) as well as unity.
(S), (M) université f University. (Ku 214-13-086)
(S) usage m Use (v. Emploi) as well as usage. (Ku 14-04-008)
(S) utilisation f Utilization. (Ku 9-03-006)
(S) utiliser v. tr. 1 To utilize, to make use of.
(S) utilité f Utility, usefulness (v. Profit).
(S) vague adj. Vacant, empty (regard). Vague, sketchy,
(S) vain, aine adj. Vain, conceited (personne). Futile.
(S), (M), (FF) valise f Suit-case, valise, bag.
(S) varier v. intr. 1 To change (temps, vent). To vary,
(S) variété f Variety, diversity. (Ku 85-12-071)
(S), (M) vase m Vase (à fleurs) as well as vessel, dish.
(S) vaste adj. Vast, huge (v. Ample, spacieux.).
(S), (M) veine f Med., Bot. Vein. Fig. Vein, humour.

(S) vengeance f Vengeance, revenge. (Ku 10-06-009)

(S), (M) verbe m Gramm. Verb as well as tone of voice,

(S) vérifier v. tr. 1 to verify as well as to audit.

(S) véritable adv. True, veritable (ami), genuine, real.

(S) vérité f Verity, truth. (Ku 1-01-001)

(S) vice m Vice, corruption, depravity as well as flaw.

(S) victime f Victim, sacrifice (offrande). Sufferer.

(S), (M) villa f Villa, cottage, country house.

(S), (M), (FF) village m Village. (Ku 72-13-045)

(S) violence f Violence (en général), force, severity

(S) violent, ente adj. Violent, furious (attaque), severe

(S), (M) violet, ette adj. Violet, purple. (Ku 7-02-003)

(S), (M) visage m Face, visage. (Ku 2-02-002)

(S), (M) visite f Visit, call as well as inspection.

(S) visiter v. tr. 1 To visit (les malades, les pauvres).

(S), (M) voile m Veil (de tête). Voile (étoffe).

(S), (M) volume m Volume, mass, bulk, volume (d'un son).

(S) vote m Vote, voting, ballot, pol (aux élections).

(S), (FF) voter v. intr. 1 To vote.

(S), (M), (FF) zéro m Zero, naught, cipher.

(S) zone f Zone (frontière, postale). Milit., Astron. Zone.

(S), (M) zoo m Zoo. (Ku 9-05-007)

English-French Cognates Rated with
Le vocabulaire disponible du français

(M) abdomen m Méd. Abdomen. (Ku 6-05-006)
(M) abréviation f Abbreviation.
(M) acacia m Bot. Acacia, locust-tree. "the black locust."
(S), (M), (FF) accident m Accident, mishap.
(M) acétylène m Chim. Acetylene.
(S), (M) acide adj. Acid. Fig. Tart. (Ku 13-06-009)
(M) acteur m Theatr. Actor.
(M) administrateur m Administrator. (Ku 15-06-012)
(S), (M) administration f Administration, management
(M) adrénaline f Med. Adrenalin.
(M) aérodrome m Aviat. Aerodrome, U.S. airport.
(M) aéroplane m Aviat. Aeroplane, airplane, plane
(S), (M) affaire f Affair, business, matter, job.
(S), (M) agriculture f Agriculture, farming, husbandry,
(S), (M) aide f Aid, help (assistance), rescue
(M), (FF) aider v. tr., intr. To aid.
(S), (M) air m Air, appearance, aspect (aspect).
(M) ajusteur m Techn. Adjuster, fitter.
(M) albatros m Zool. Albatross.
(M) Alberta f Alberta.
(M) album m Scrap-book (de découpures), album
(M) aliment m Food, aliment, nutriment, nourishment.
(M) alligator m Zool. Alligator. (Ku 4-02-002)
(M) alpiniste s. Sports. Alpinist, mountaineer.
(S), (M) aluminium m Aluminium, U.S. aluminum.
(S), (M) ambulance f Ambulance, a military field hospital.
(M) amusement m Amusement, entertainment (v. Distraction).
(S), (M) amuser v. tr. (1) To amuse, to entertain, to deceive.
(M) ananas m Bot. Pineapple, ananas.
(M) anémone f Bot. Anemone, windflower.
(S), (M) angle m Angle. Math. Angle. Fig. Point of view.
(S), (M) animal m Zool. Animal (v. bête).
(M) annonceur m Comm. Advertiser. Radio. Announcer.
(M) annuel, elle adj. Annual, yearly. (Ku 93-11-060)
(M) anorak m Anorak, wind-jacket, wind-cheater.

(M) anus m Med. Anus.
(M) aquarelle f Arts. Aquarelle, water-color.
(M) aquarium m Aquarium.
(M) araignée f Zoo. Spider, Milit. Araignée.
(M) arcade f Arcade, passageway (d'une rue).
(M) architecte m Architect (pr. et. fig.). (Ku 22-07-015)
(M) architecture f Archit., Fig. Architecture.
(M) arène f Arena, amphitheater. (Ku 7-01-006)
(M) arithmétique f Math. Arithmetic (science).
(S), (M) arme f Milit. Arm, weapon (moyen de défense).
(S), (M) art m Art. English senses escept "A work of art"
(M) (M) articulation f Med. Knuckle (des doigts), articulation
(M) artificiel, elle adj. Artificial. (Ku-17-08-017)
(S), (M) artisan m Craftsman, artisan, Fig. Architect,
(S), (M), (FF) artiste s. Artist, performer.
(M) arum m Bot. Arum.
(M) aspic m Zool. Aspic.
(M) aspirine f Med. Aspirin. (Ku 3-03-003)
(M) assemblage m Assemblage, assembling, gathering,
(S), (M) assurance f Assurance (v. Certitude), insuranace.
(M) astronaute m Astronaut. (Ku 2-01-002)
(S), (M), (FF) atelier m Studio, atelier (d'artiste).
(M) athlète m Sports. Athlete. (Ku 9-05-008)
(M) atlas m Geogr., Med. Atlas. (Ku 12-03-005)
(M) atmosphère f Phys., Fig. Atmosphere. (Ku 79-14-061)
(S), (M), (FF) attention f Attention, observing, heed.
(M) auditorium m Auditorium, auditory. (Ku 14-07-010)
(M) aurochs m Zool. Aurochs.
(S), (M), (FF) auto f Autom. Motor-car, car. U.S. auto.
(M) automatique adj. Automatic (appareil, arme, machine).
(S), (M) automobile adj. Self-propelling, automobile.
(S), (M) aventure f Adventure, enterprise, venture.
(S), (M), (FF) avenue f Avenue.
(M) aviateur m Aviat. Aviator, airman, flier.
(S), (M) aviation f Aviat. Aviation, flying, Air force,
(S), (FF) avion m Aviat. Aeroplane, plane, avion.
(M) azote m Chim. Nitrogen, azote.

(M) babouche f Babouche, Turkish slipper.

(M) badminton m Sports, Badminton. (Ku 1-01-001)

(S), (M) balance f Balance, scales. Astron. The Balance.

(M) balancer v. intr. To balance. to waver.

(S), (M), (FF) balcon m Balcony.

(S), (M) balle f Sports. Ball as well as bullet

(M) ballet m Théâtr. Ballet. (Ku 45-10-017)

(S), (M), (FF) ballon m Ball, football. Geogr. Ballon.

(M) banane f Bot. Banana. (Ku 4-03-004)

(M) bandage m Med. Bandaging (action), bandage.

(M) bande f Band, stretch, belt, strip (de terre).

(M) banderole f Banderole. Pennant.

(M) bandit m Bandit, gangster. Fam. Scoundrel.

(M) banjo m Mus. Banjo. (Ku 2-02-002)

(M) baobab m Bot. Baobab.

(M) bar m Zool. Bar, sea-dace, bass.

(M) baromètre m Phys. Barometer.

(S), (M) barrage m Barrage, dam, weir (de rivière).

(M) barrette f Small bar. Bar (de broderie), U.S. Barrette.

(M) bascule f Bascule, rocker (de berceau, de fauteuil).

(S), (M) base f Base, basis, foundation, bottom (fond).

(M) baseball m Sports. Baseball. (Ku 57-09-015)

(M) batterie f Milit. Battery (armes). Naut. Battery,

(M) bégonia m Bot. Begonia.

(M) belote f Belote (jeu).

(S), (M) béret m Beret (basque), tam-o'-shanter

(M) berline Autom. Berline, four-door saloon.

(M) bibelot m Bibelot, trinket, knick-knack, curio.

(M) Bible f Bible. (Ku 59-11-028)

(M) biceps adj., m Med. Biceps. (Ku 3-01-001)

(M) bidet m Zool. Nag (v. Canasson). Bidet.

(M) bikini m Bikini. (Ku 1-01-001)

(M) bile f Med. Bile, gall. Fig. Bad temper, anger, worry

(M) bise f Bise, north wind. Fig. Winter, the wintry blast.

(M) bison m Zool. Bison, U.S. Buffalo. (Ku 1-01-001)

(M) blanquette f Culin. Blanquette (ragoût, vin).

(S), (M) bloc m Block, lump (only as in a block of wood).

(M) bluff m Bluff. (Ku 8-06-006)

(M) boa m Boa (fourrure, serpent. (Ku 7-01-001)

(M) boléro m Bolero (danse, veste).

(M) bombardement m Milit. Bombing, bombardment,

(M) bombardier m Milit. Bombardier. Aviat. bomber.

(M) bombe f Milit. Bomb, block-buster.

(S), (M) bonbon m Sweet, bonbon, comfit, U.S. candy.

(M) boom m Fin. Boom. (Ku 8-06-008)

(K) bordure f Skirt, border except that of a country.

(M) Boston m Geogr. Boston. Boston (jeu).

(M) boudoir m Boudoir.

(S), (M) bouillon m Culin. Broth, bouillon cube.

(S), (M) boule f Ball (de billard), boule (de casino).

(S), (M), (FF) boulevard m Boulevard (v. Avenue).

(S), (M) boutique f Shop, U.S. store. Booth, stall, boutique.

(M) bovin, ine adj. m Zool. Bovine. (Ku 2-01-002)

(M) box m Cubicle, U.S. box, stall. (Ku 70-15-041)

(S), (M) boxer v. intr. 1 Sports. To box.

(M) boxeur m Sports. boxer. (Ku 1-01-001)

(S), (M) bracelet m Bracelet (en général).

(M), (FF) branche f Bot. Branch, bough (d'arbre).

(M) brancher v. tr 1 Electr. To branch, to connect.

(M) bridge m Bridge (dentier, jeu).

(M) brio m Brio, spirit, dash, pep.

(M) brioche f Culin. Brioche.

(M) briquette f Briquette, briquet, compressed slack.

(S), (M) brochure f Brochure, pamphlet, tract. (Ku 2-02-002)

(M) bronche f Med. Bronchus (pl. bronchi, bronchia),

(M) bronchiole f Med. Bronchiole (Ku 4-01-001)

(S), (M) buffet m U.S. Buffet, sandwich-counter.

(M) bulbe m Bot., Med., Archit. Bulb.

(M) bulldozer m Bulldozer.

(M) bureaucrate m Bureaucrat. (Ku 1-01-001)

(M) burnous m Burnous, U.S. burnoose.

(M) butane m Chim. Butane. (Ku 1-01-001)

(M) butte f Knoll, hillock, mound, U.S. butte.

(S), (M), (FF) cabine m Cabin (on a ship).

(S), (M) cabinet m An office, study, cabinet.
(M) câble m Cable, rope. Naut., Archit., Electr. Cable.
(M) cabriolet m Cabriolet.
(M) cacao m Bot. Cacao. (Ku 1-01-001)
(M) cactus m Bot. Cactus.
(M) cadet m Younger (of two), (fils, frère). Milit. Cadet.
(S), (M) cadre m Milit. Cadre, skeleton, nucleus.
(S), (M) cage f Cage (d'animaux), hutch (à lapins),
(S), (M) cahier m Copy-book, exercise-book, cahier,
(M) caiman m Zool. Cayman, caiman.
(M) calèche f Calash, calèche.
(M) calotte f Eccles. Calotte, skull-cap (bonnet).
(M) caméra f Cine-camera. (Ku 36-11-017)
(M) cameraman m Camera-man. (Ku 1-01-001)
(M) camisole f Camisole, loose jacket.
(S), (M) camp m Faction, side. Milit., Sports. Camp.
(S), (M) camper v. intr. 1 Milit. To encamp, to camp,
(M) camping m Sports. Camping.
(M) Canada m Geogr. Canada. (Ku 34-11-026)
(S), (M) canal m Canal (artificiel), channel.
(M) canapé m Sofa, settee. Culin. Canapé
(M) canari m Zool. Canary.
(S), (M) candidat m Candidate, examinee. (Ku 34-09-020)
(M) canoe m Canoe. (Ku 7-04-004)
(S), (M) canon m Arts., Fig. Canon. Eccles. Canon,
(M) canton m Canton, district, U.S. Township, section.
(M) cape f Cloak, cape as well as hood. (Ku 20-10-016)
(S), (M) capitaine m Milit. Captain. Sports. Captain,
(S), (M) capital, ale adj. Capital, outstanding, essential
(S), (M) caporal m Milit. Corporal. Comm. Caporal (tabac)
(M) capot m Capot (jeu).
(M) capote f Capote (manteau). (Ku 1-01-001)
(M) capsule f Med., Bot., Chim. Capsule.
(S), (M) carafe f Water-bottle, carafe (à eau),
(M) caramel m Caramel, butter-scotch, toffee, bonbon.
(M) caravane f A gypsy cart, a caravan.
(M) carie f Med. Decay, caries (des dents).

(M) carillon m Carillon, chimes, peal (cloches),
(S), (M) carton m Carton (boîte). (Ku 1-01-001)
(M) cartouche m Archit. Cartouche.
(S), (M) cas m Case (an instance) not a legal case
(M) casaque f Casaque, a wide sleeved overcoat, jumper,
(M) cascade f Cascade, waterfall. Fig. Cascade, shower.
(M) casino m Casino. (Ku 2-02-002)
(S), (M) casque m Casque, helmet (d'armure).
(M) catalogue m Catalogue. Comm. Price-list (Ku 8-05-006)
(M) cataracte f Waterfall, cataract. Med. Cataract.
(M) catéchisme m Catechism. (Ku-2-02-002)
(S), (M) cathédrale adj. f Cathedral. (Ku 8-06-008)
(S), (M) causer v. tr. 1 To cause, to bring about.
(M) caverne f Cave, cavern. "Homme des cavernes" = cavemen.
(M) céleri m Bot. Celery. (Ku 4-03-004)
(M) cellule f Zool., Med., Electr., Jur. Cell. Bot. Cellule.
(M), (FF) cent m Fin. Cent (monnaie).
(M) centimètre m Centimetre (or) centimeter. (Ku 2-01-001)
(S), (M) central, ale adj. Central, principal, head, chief.
(S), (M) centre m Centre, U.S. center.
(S), (M) certificat m Med. Certificate (de médecin).
(S), (M) chaîne f Chain (de chien). (Ku 50-10-025)
(M) châlet m Swiss chalet. Chalet (maison).
(M) chalumeau m Straw (pour boire). Mus. Pipe, chalumeau.
(M) chamois m Chamois (animal). (Ku 1-01-001)
(M), (FF) champagne f Geogr. Champagne. Comm. Champagne (vin)
(S), (M) champignon m Bot., Culin. Mushroom, champignon.
(S), (M), (FF) chanson f Mus. Song. Fam. Chansons!
(S), (M) chaperon m Hood. Fig. Chaperon. (Ku 1-01-001)
(M) charade f charade. Fig. Puzzle.
(S), (M) charger v. tr. 7 To exaggerate. Electr. To charge.
(M) Charlemagne m Charlemagne.
(M) Charlotte f Charlotte, Lottie. (Ku 13-04-006)
(S), (M), (FF) charme m Spell, charm, enchantment.
(M) châssis m Frame. Milit. Slide, chassis.
(M) chasuble f Eccles. Chasuble.
(S), (M) château m Castle (féodal), château.,

(S), (M), (FF) chauffeur m Autom. Chauffeur, driver.
(S), (M), (FF) chemise f chemise, shirt, wrapper.
(M) chemisette f Front, chemisette (blouse).
(M) chevron m Milit. Chevron, service stripe.
(M) chiffonnier m Rag-picker, ragman. Chiffonnier.
(M) chimpanzé m Zool. Chimpanzee
(M) chinchilla m Zool. Chinchilla.
(M) chiné, ée, adj. Mottled, clouded, chiné.
(S), (M), (FF) chocolat m Chocolat (barre, boisson).
(M) cigare m Cigar, weed (fam.). (Ku 10-06-009)
(S), (M), (FF) cigarette f Cigarette.
(M) cilice m Cilice, hair-shirt.
(S), (M) cinéma m Theatr. Cinema (art, édifice).
(S), (M) cinématographe m Cinematograph.
(S), (M) circulation f Traffic, circulation.
(S), (M) cirque m circus. Geogr. Cirque. (Ku 7-05-006)
(M) cité f City, large town (ville). (Ku 393-15-156)
(M), claque f Slap, crack, a clog (wooden soled shoe), claque.
(S), (M) classe f Class, category, sort, rank.
(M) clef, clé f Key. Mus. Clef, key-signature.
(S), (M) climat m Climate (conditions atmosphériques).
(S), (M) clinique adj. Med. Clinic, clinical.
(M) clip m Clip (bijou). (Ku 6-04-006)
(M) clique f Clique (a contemptible set of people).
(M) clown m Theatr. Clown. (Ku 3-03-003)
(M) club M Club. Sports. Club (de golf). (Ku 145-14-065)
(M) cobra M Zool. Cobra. (Ku 3-02-003)
(M) coca f Bot. Coca. Coca-Cola. (Ku 1-01-001)
(M) cocktail m cocktail (boisson). (Ku 25-09-015)
(M) cocotte f Culin. Stew-pan, U.S. sauce-pan. Fam. Cocotte
(S), (M) coiffeur m Hairdresser, coiffeur.
(M) coiffeuse f Hairdresser. Coiffeuse (meuble).
(M) coke m Coke. (Ku 4-02-002)
(S), (M) col m Neck (cou). Geogr. Pass, Col. Med. neck.
(M) collage m Gluing. Arts. Collage. (Ku 15-01-001)
(M) collation f The conferring of a degree, collation.
(S), (M) collection f English senses of collection

(S), (M) collège m College. Secondary grammar school.
(S), (M) colonel m Milit. Colonel. (Ku 37-07-020)
(S), (M) combat m Fight, struggle. Milit. Combat, battle.
(S), (M) comédie f Theatr. Comedy (genre), play (pièce),
(M) comédien m Theatr. Comedian as well as Fig. Actor
(M) comète f Astron. Comet.
(M) commandant m Milit. Commandant as well as any army major
(S), (M) commerce m Comm. Trade (intérieur), commerce
(S), (M) commission f Errand (course), message, Commission.
(S), (M) communiste adj., m Communist. (Ku 97-09-042)
(S), (M) compartiment m Square (d'un damier), compartment
(M) compendium m Compendium. (Ku 1-01-001)
(S), (M) complet, ète adj. Complete, entire, whole.
(S), (M) composer v. tr. 1 To compose (to calm).
(M) compote f Culin. Compote (de fruits). (Ku 1-01-001)
(S), (M) concert m Mus. Concert. Fig. Concert, concord.
(S), (M) concierge m s. House-porter, concierge.
(S), (M) concours m Competition, help, concourse.
(M) condor m Zool. condor.
(S), (M) conducteur, trice adj. Driving. Electr. Conductive.
m Electr. Conductor.
(M) conduit m Techn. Conduit, pipe, channel (Ku 1-01-001)
(M) cône m Math. cone. Geol., Bot., Astron. Cone.
(M) conifère adj. Bot. Coniferous. m Bot. Conifer.
(M) console f console-table (meuble). Archit., Mus. Console.
(M) constellation f Astron. Constellation. (Ku 4-02-003)
(M) constructeur m Manufacturer, builder, constructor
(M) continental, ale adj. Continental. (Ku 19-07-014)
(S), (M) conversation f conversation, talk. (Ku 50-12-037)
(S), (M) copie f An exercise, composition, copy.
(M) cordage m cordage, rope. Naut. Rigging.
(S), (M) corde f Rope as well as cord. (Ku 6-05-006)
(M) cordon m Small cord, braid, ribbon, cordon.
(M) cordon-bleu m Culin. First-rate cook, cordon-bleu.
(M) cornet m Mus. A little horn as well as English cornet.
(S), (M) corps m Med. A live body as well as a corpse.
(S), (M) correspondance f A transfer, correspondence.

(M) corridor m Corridor (v. Passage). (Ku 17-05-011)
(M) corselet m Corselet. Zool. Corslet.
(M) corset m Corset, stays.
(S), (M) costume m Clothes as well as a costume.
(M) cotillon m Petticoat (jupe) as well as Cotillon (danse).
(M) coupe f Cutting (in general). Sports. Coupe, trophy,
(S), (M) courage m Courage (v. Bravoure, vaillance), heart
(S), (M) (FF) cours m course, flow (d'un fleuve).
(S), (M) court m Sports. Court (de tennis). (Ku 230-13-064)
(S), (M) couture f Sewing (action), seam (résultat), couture.
(M) couturier m Couturier, ladies' tailor (Ku 1-01-001)
(S), (M), (FF) Couturière f Dressmaker, couturière
(M) coyote M Zool. Coyote. (Ku 1-01-001)
(M) crabe m Zool. Crab. (Ku 2-02-002)
(M) crasse adj., f Crass (ignorance). (Ku 2-02-002)
(S), (M) (FF) cravate f Neck-tie, tie (d'homme), cravat.
(M) crèche f Agric. Manger, crib. Eccles. Crib, crèche.
(M) crédence f Eccles. Credence table (altar side-table).
(S), (M), (FF) crème f Cream (de lait). Crème (liqueur).
(M) crêpe m Crape. Crepe, crepe-rubber (pour semelle).
(M) Crète f Geogr. Crete.
(M) crinoline f Crinoline.
(M) cristallin, ine adj. Crystalline. (Ku 5-02-003)
(S), (M) crochet m Hook (in general) as well as crochet
(M) crocodile m Zool. Crocodile (Ku 1-01-001)
(M) croquet m Sports. Croquet (jeu).
(M) croupe f croup, crupper, hindquarters (du cheval).
(M) crucifier v. tr. 1 to crucify (pr. et. fig.).
(M) crucifix m Eccles. Crucifix. (Ku 3-02-002)
(S), (M) cube adj. Cubic (centimètre, mètre). m Math. Cube.
(M) cubitus m Med. Ulna, cubitus.
(S), (M) cultivateur, trice adj. Agricultural m Agric. Cultivator
(M) cumin m Bot. Cumin. (Ku 1-01-001)
(M) cutter m Naut. Cutter. (Ku 4-02-002)
(M) cycle m Cycle (bicyclette). Cycle. Course (des études).
(S), (M) cycliste s. Cyclist.
(M) dahlia m Bot. Dahlia.

(M) dard m Dart, sting, a snake's tongue. Fig. Dart.

(M) D.D.T. m Chim. D.D.T.

(M) décamètre m Decametre.

(M) décimètre m Decimetre. (Ku 1-01-001)

(M) décorateur, trice s. Arts. Decorator. (Ku 5-05-005)

(S), (M) décoration f Arts. Decoration, ornamentation.

(M) dentelle f Lace. Techn. Dentelle (en reliure).

(S), (M) dentiste m Med. Dentist. (Ku 12-04-006)

(S), (M), (FF) dessert m Culin. Dessert, sweet.

(S) détective m Detective as well as a box-camera.

(M) détergent adj. Detergent.

(S), (M), (FF) deviner v. tr. 1 To guess, to feel, to divine.

(M) diaphragme m Sound box, diaphragm (en photo).

(M) diesel m Techn. Diesel engine. (Ku-1-01-001)

(M) digestif, ive adj. Med. Digestive.

(M) digestion f Med. Digestion (de la nourriture).

(M) diligence f Diligence, application, care. Speed,

(M) dîme f Eccles. Tithe as well as Fin. U.S. dime.

(S), (M), (FF) dîner v. intr. To dine (de, off, on).

(M) diplôme m Diploma, certificate.

(M) direct, ecte adj. Direct (action, cause, intérêt).

(S), (M) directeur, trice adj. directional, managing.
m Director.

(S), (M) direction f Direction as well as instruction,

(S), (M) disque m Disc, disk as well as Mus. Record, disc.

(S), (M) divan m Divan, couch (meuble). Divan (en Orient).

(S), (M) division f Division, partition (en, into).

(M) dock m Naut. Dock (bassin). (Ku 8-04-005)

(S), (M) docteur m Doctor. (Ku 100-11-044)

(M) domino m Domino (jeu, vêtement).

(S), (M) double adj. Double, twofold (Ku 56-12-040)

(M) draperie f drapery (drapé, étoffe, manufacture).

(M) drink m Fam. drink. (Ku 82-11-044)

(M) drive m Sports. Drive (au tennis). (Ku 105-15-079)

(MK) dune f Dune. Pl. Downs (crayeuses), dunes (sableuses).

(M) dynamite f Dynamite. (Ku 5-04-004)

(M) dynamo f Electr. Dynamo. (Ku 2-02-002)

(S), (M) éclair m Flash of lightening. Culin. Eclair.
(M) edelweiss m Bot. Edelweiss.
(S), (M) édifice m Archit. Building, edifice.
(M) éducateur, trice adj. Educative, educational. m Educator.
(S), (M) effacer v. tr. 6 To efface, to blot out,
(S), (M) électeur m Elector, constituent, voter.
(S), (M) élection f Election as well as choice.
(S), (M) électricien m Electr. Electrician.
(S), (M) électricité f Electr. Electricity. (Ku 26-08-016)
(S), (M) électrique adj. Electric (courant, lumière).
(S), (M) électronique adj. Electronic (action)
(S), (M) éléphant m Zool. Elephant. (Ku 7-05-005)
(M) embrasure f Embrasure. Milit. Embrasure.
(M) embryon m Embryo. (Ku 1-01-001)
(M), (FF) employé m Employee. (Ku 24-05-008)
(M) encyclopédie f Encyclopedia. (Ku-1-01-001)
(M) encyclopédiste m Encyclopedist.
(M) ensiler, ensiloter v. tr. 1 Agric. To ensile, to silo.
(S), (M) entrée f Entering, incoming, entry.
(M) équilibriste m Equilibrist.
(M) équitation f Riding, horsemanship, equitation
(M) escalader v. tr. 1 To scale, to climb. Milit. To escalade.
(S), (M) espace m space (indéfini). (Ku 184-14-082)
(M) espadrille f Canvas shoe, U.S. espadrille.
(M) espagnolette f Espagnolette. (Ku 1-01-001)
(S), (M) essence f Essence, essential element. Gasoline.
(M) éther m Ether (espace). Chim. ether. (Ku-1-01-001)
(M) étiquette f Label, U.S. sticker, etiquette.
(S), (M) examen m Examination, investigation. Exam (fam.).
(S), (M) excursion f Excursion, hiking, walk. (Ku 2-02-002
(S), (M) exercice m Exercise (du corps). Training.
(M) exhibition f Exhibition, display. (Ku 22-06-016)
(S), (M) exploitation f Exploitation, management.
(M) exploration f Exploration. (Ku 25-07-013)
(S), (M) explosion f Blowing up, explosion, bursting.
(S), (M) express adj. Comm., Ch. de F. Express.
(S), (M) expression f Expression (de la pensée).

(M) extension f Extension, stretching. Prolongation.

(M) extirpateur m Extirpator.

(M) fabrication f Manufacture (industrielle). Fabrication

(S), (M) façade f Façade, front. Fig. Façade.

(S), (M), (FF) face f Face (de l'homme). (Ku 371-15-189)

(S), (M), (FF) facteur, trice s. Maker. Comm. Factor,

(M) fakir m Fakir.

(M) fanal m Lantern, lighthouse lamp, fanal, beacon light.

(M) fémur m Med. Femur.

(M) ferry m Naut. Ferry-boat. (Ku 11-05-006)

(M) ferry-boat m Naut. Train-ferry.

(M) fertiliser v. tr. 1 to fertilize.

(M) fiancé, ée s. Fiancé. (Ku 1-01-001)

(S), (M) figure f Figure (forme). Gramm., Arts. Figure

(M) file f File (of people), rank (line).

(S), (M), (FF) film m Cinem. Film, motion picture.

(M), (FF) filtre m Filter, strainer (cornet). (Ku 9-03-005)

(S), (M) finance f Fin. Finance, money, cash. (Ku 31-09-022)

(M) flamme f Flame. Love, passion. Fig. Fire.

(M) fluorescent, ente adj. Fluorescent. (Ku 4-03-003)

(M) flûte f Mus. flute. (Ku 1-01-001)

(M) fondation f Foundation, founding (action). (Ku 38-07-024)

(M), (FF) football m Sports. Football, European "soccer."

(M) footballeur m Sports. Footballer. (Ku 1-01-001)

(S), (M) force f Strength, power, force. English "force"

(S), (M) forêt f Bot. Forest. (Ku 66-09-021)

(S), (M) forge f Forge, smithy (atelier), forge (feu).

(S), (M) forger v. tr. 7 to forge (le fer). Fig. To forge

(S), (M) forme f Form, shape (configuration). (Ku 370-14-171)

(M) forum m Forum. Fam. Politics. (Ku-10-06-006)

(S), (M) foulard m Foulard (étoffe), scarf (fichu).

(M) foyer m Hearth, fire-place, home, foyer.

(S), (M) fraise f Fraise, ruff (collet). Culin. Frill.

(M), (FF) France f Geogr. France. (Ku 74-12-039)

(M) frégate f Naut. Frigate.

(M) frigorifique adj. Frigorific, refrigerating.

(M) frontal, ale adj. Med. Frontal (os). (Ku 3-02-003)

(S), (M), (FF) fruit m fruit. (Ku 35-11-022)

(M) fusillade f fusillade. (Ku 1-01-001)

(S), (M) futur adj. Future (à venir).

(M) gabardine f Gabardine (tissu), twill raincoat (vêtement)

(M) gain m Gain, profit, winnings (au jeu), earnings.

(M) gala m Festivity, gala. (Ku 7-03-006)

(M) galène f Galena, sulphide of lead. (Ku 2-02-002)

(M) gallon m Gallon (mesure). (Ku 6-02-004)

(S), (M) gamin m Urchin, gamin, kid, street-boy

(S), (M), (FF) garage m Autom. Garage.

(M) garrot m Med. Garrot. Techn. Tongue (d'une scie),

(M) gascon, onne adj. s. Gascon.

(S), (M) gaz m Gas. (Ku 98-11-039)

(S), (M) géant, ante adj. Giant, gigantic. m Giant.

(M) gendarmerie f Gendarmerie, constabulary.

(S), (M) général, ale adj. General, universal.

(M) Genève m Geogr. Geneva. (Ku 17-04-008)

(S), (M) géographie f Geogr. Geography (science).

(S), (M) géographique adj. Geogr. Geographic(al).

(M) géomètre m Math. Geometer, geometrician.

(M) géométrie f Math. Geometry. (Ku 9-04-006)

(M) géranium m Bot. Geranium, pelargonium.

(M) germe m Med. Germ. Fig. Principle, source, origin, seed

(M) girafe f Zool. Giraffe.

(M) glande f Bot. Gland, kernel, acorn. Med. Gland.

(M) glasse m Fam. Glassful (contenu), glass (verre).

(M) glissade f Slip, slipping, slide, Glide, glissade

(S), (M) globe m Globe (s. Sphère), orb (du soleil).

(M) globule m Globule (d'air), drop (d'eau). Globule,

(S), (M) goal m Sports. Goal (but). (Ku 60-11-044)

(M) goitre m Med. Goitre. (Ku 3-01-001)

(S), (M) golf m Sports. Golf (jeu). (Ku 34-08-014)

(S), (M) gorge f Throat, neck (cou). Archit. Quirk, gorge.

(M) gorille m Zool. Gorilla.

(S), (M) gouvernement m Government. (Ku 1-01-001)

(M) gouverneur m Governor (de banque, de province).

(S), (M) grain m Bot. Grain (d'avoine, de blé).

(S), (M) gramme m Gramme, gram. (Ku 10-02-004)

(M) gramophone m Gramophone. (Ku 1-01-001)

(M) granite m Geol. granite. (Ku 3-02-002)

(M) grapefruit m Bot. Grapefruit. (Ku 3-02-003)

(M) grenadine f Culin. Grenadine.

(S), (M) grille f Grating, railing. Eccles. Grille.

(M) grotte f Grotto (artificielle), cave (naturelle).

(M) guēpard m Zool. Cheetah, guepard.

(S), (M) guide m Guide, cicerone (dans une musēe).

(M) guidon m Handlebars (d'une bicyclette). Milit. Guidon.

(M) guimpe f Eccles. Wimple (de religieuse). Guimpe, tucker.

(M) guitare f Mus. Guitar. (Ku 19-06-010)

(M) guitariste s. Mus. Guitarist. (Ku 2-02-002)

(M) gymnastique adj. Gymnastic. (Ku 4-01-001)

(M) habitant m Inhabitant, dweller, occupant. Habitant

(M) haddock * m Zool. Haddock. (Ku 1-01-001)

(M) hall * m Hall, entrance hall (d'entrēe), lobby.

(M) hand-ball * m Sports. Hand-ball.

(S), (M) hangar * m Shed, hangar.

(S), (M) hélicoptère m Aviat. Helicopter. (Ku 1-01-001)

(M) herbage m Grass, meadow, pasture, herbage.

(M) herbeux, euse adj. Bot. Grassy. Herbous, herby.

(M) herboriste m Bot. Herborist, herbalist.

(M) historien s. Historian. (Ku 30-06-012)

(M) hockey * m Sports. Hockey. (Ku 1-01-001)

(M) Hollande * f Geogr. Holland. (Ku 8-05-006)

(S), (M) hōpital m Med. Hospital. (Ku 110-12-048)

(M), (FF) hors-d'oeuvre m invar. Culin., Fam. Hors-d'oeuvre.

(M) hospice m Hospice, home, poor house, almshouse.

(S), (M), (FF) hōtel m Hotel, as well as town mansion,

(M) humērus m Med. Humerus.

(M) humiditē f Humidity, moisture, dampness, wetness.

(M) hydraulique adj. Hydraulic. (Ku 1-01-001)

(M) hydrographie f Hydrography.

(S), (M) hygiēne f Hygiene, sanitation (propretē),

(M) ibis m Zool. Ibis.

(M) igloo m Igloo.

(M) ignorant, ante adj. Ignorant, uneducated. (Ku 12-06-010)
(S), (M) image f Image, picture (représentation).
(M) impasse f Blint-alley, cul-de-sac, impasse.
(S), (M) imperméable adj. Impermeable, waterproof (à l'eau).
(M) imposte f Transom (moveable or fixed). Archit. Impost.
(M) index m Forefinger, index-finger. Index (d'un livre).
(M) indien adj. s. Geogr. Indian. (v. Hindou).
(M) indigence f Indigence (v. Besoin). Fig. Lack, want,
(S), (M) industrie f Comm. Industry, manufacture.
(S), (M) industriel, elle adj. Industrial. (Ku 143-11-057)
(S), (M) insecte m Zool. Insect. (Ku 14-06-009)
(M) insecticide adj. Insecticide. (Ku 1-01-001)
(S), (M) inspecteur m English "inspector."
(S), (M) installation f Tech. Installation. (Ku 12-02-007)
(M) institut m Institute, institution. (Ku 1-01-001)
(S), (M) instituteur s. School-teacher, institutor.
(M) instructeur, trice m Instructor. (Ku 8-06-007)
(S), (M) instrument m Instrument, tool. Mus. Instrument.
(S), (M) intelligence f Intelligence, intellect.
(M) intendant m Intendant, manager. (Ku 1-01-001)
(M) interrupteur, trice adj. Interrupting. m Interruptor.
(S), (M) intestin, ine adj. Intestine.
(M) ire f Ire. (Ku 1-01-001)
(M) iris m Iris. Med. Iris (de l'oeil). Bot. Iris
(M) isard m Zool. Izard.
(M), (FF) Italie f Geogr. Italy. (Ku 34-11-023)
(M) jack m Jack (du téléphone). (Ku 92-11-033)
(M) jaguar m Zool. Jaguar. (Ku 5-02-002)
(M) jeep f Milit. Jeep. (Ku 16-05-005)
(M) Jésus m Eccles. Jesus Christ, Jesus. (Ku 66-06-018)
(M) jockey m Sports. Jockey. (Ku 5-04-005)
(S), (M) joie f Joy, mirth, gladness. (Ku 40-12-032)
(M) jongleur m Juggler (moderne). Jongleur, minstrel.
(S), (M), (FF) journal m Paper, newspaper, journal.
(M) journalisme m Journalism. (Ku 13-08-011)
(S), (M) journaliste m Journalist, reporter, correspondent.
(M) judo m Sports. Judo.

(M) jumper m Sweater, jumper. (Ku 1-01-001)

(M) jungle f Jungle. (Ku 20-05-008)

(S), (M) kēpi m Milit. Kēpi.

(M) kermesse f Kermesse, village fair.

(M), (FF) kilo, kilogramme m. Kilogram, Kilogramme.

(M) kimono m Kimono. (Ku 1-01-001)

(M) kirsch m Kirsch.

(M) klaxon m Autom. Motor-horn, klaxon. (Ku 1-01-001)

(M) lama m Zool. Llama.

(M) lance f Spear as well as lance (arme). (Ku 3-03-003)

(M) landau (pl. landaus) m Landau. (Ku 2-02-002)

(M) lanterne f Lantern. (Ku 13-03-006)

(M) larynx m Med. Larynx.

(M) leader m Leader (article, chef). (Ku 74-09-044)

(M) leggings f pl. Leggings. (Ku 1-01-001)

(M) lēgion f Milit. Legion. Lēgion ētrangēre,

(M) léopard m Zool. Leopard. (Ku 1-01-001)

(S), (M) lettre f Letter. (Ku 145-15-070)

(M) libērateur, trice adj. Liberating, rescuing. m Liberator.

(S), (M) libertē f Liberty, freedom. (Ku 46-11-027

(M) licence f Licence (permission). (Ku 36-10-022)

(M) lichen m Bot. Lichen.

(M) ligament m Med. Ligament. (Ku 1-01-001)

(M) lignite m Lignite, brown coal. (Ku 4-01-001)

(M) limousine f Long woollen cloak. Autom. Limousine.

(M) linolēum m Linoleum, oil-cloth. (Ku 1-01-001)

(S), (M) lion m Zool. Lion. Astron. Leo. (Ku 17-04-006)

(S), (M) liquide adj. liquid, fluid. (Ku 48-07-018)

(S), (M), (FF) litre m Litre.

(S), (M) local, ale adj. Local (intērēt, heure).

(M) locomotion f Locomotion.

(S), (M) locomotive f Ch. de. f. Locomotive, engine.

(M) loterie f Lottery.

(M) luge f Sports. Luge, tobaggan.

(M) luzerne f Bot. Lucerne; U.S. alfalfa.

(M) lynx m Zool. Lynx.

(M), (FF) Lyon m Geogr. Lyons. (Ku 3-02-002)

(M) macaron m Culin. Macaroon.

(M) macaroni m Culin. Macaroni.

(S), (M) machine f Machine as well as Ch. de f. Locomotive

(S), (M) maçon m Archit. Mason, bricklayer. (Ku 23-06-007)

(S), (M) madame (pl. mesdames) f Mrs., Madam.

(M) Madrid m Madrid. (Ku 1-01-001)

(M) magazine m Magazine. (Ku 39-14-028)

(M) magicien m Wizard, magician. (Ku 4-03-003)

(M) magie f Magic (v. Sorcellerie). Fig. Witchery.

(M) magique adj. Magic, magical. (Ku 12-04-005)

(S), (M) majeur adj. Major, important, Mus. Major (tierce).

(M) mammouth m Zool. Mammoth. (Ku 4-03-004)

(M) manager m Manager. (Ku 88-12-040)

(M) mandarine f Tangerine, mandarine.

(S), (M), (FF) mandat m Mandate. Fin. Money-order

(M) mandoline f Mus. Mandoline.

(M) manège m Riding school, manege, ring (d'équitation).

(M) manne f Eccles. Manna.

(S), (M) marchandise f Comm. Merchandise, goods, wares.

(M) margarine f Culin. Margarine.

(S), (M) mariage m Marriage, match (union). Wedding.

(M), (FF) Marie f Mary. (Ku 6-04-006)

(M) marinade f culin. Marinade. (Ku 1-01-001)

(S), (M) marine f Naut. Marine, navy. (Ku 55-08-013)

(M) marionnette f Puppet, marionette. (Ku 1-01-001)

(M) marmelade f Culin. Compote (de fruits), marmelade.

(M) Marseille f Geogr. Marseilles. (Ku 1-01-001)

(M) martingale f Martingale (harnais, jeu). Naut. Martingale

(S), (M) masse f Mass, heap, bulk. Mass, mob, crowd.

(M) masseuse f Med. Masseuse.

(M) matic m Mastic (résine).

(M) match (pl. matches) m Sports. Match. (Ku 41-12-032)

(S), (M) matériel, elle adj. Material, physical.

(S), (M) maternel, elle adj. Maternal, motherly.

(M) mathématicien s. Math. Mathematician. (Ku 2-02-002)

(M), (FF) mathématique adj. Math. Mathematical.

(M) mayonnaise f Culin. Mayonnaise. (Ku 2-02-002)

(M) mazout m Fuel oil;, oil, mazout, mazut.
(S), (M) médicament m Med. Medicine, medicament.
(M) melon m Bot. Melon. (Ku 1-01-001)
(S), (M) membre m Med. Limb, member. Fig. Member.
(M) ménagerie f Menagerie. (Ku 1-01-001)
(S), (M) menu m Culin. Bill-of-fare, menu.
(M) mercantile adj. Comom. Mercantile, commercial.
(M) mess m Milit. Mes. (Ku 22-09-013)
(S), (M) métal m Metal. (Ku 61-13-039)
(M) Métallurgique adj. Metallurgic.
(S), (M) métallurgiste m Metallurgist.
(M) métayer m Agric. Metayer, tenant farmer.
(M) métis adj. Half-bred, cross-bred (animal). m Metis.
(S), (M) mètre m Metre, U.S. meter. (Ku 1-01-001)
(M) métronome m Mus. Metronome. (Ku 3-02-002)
(M) microfilm m Microfilm. (Ku 2-02-002)
(M) microphone m Microphone. (Ku 4-03-004)
(M) microscope m Phys. Microscope. (Ku 8-04-004)
(S), (M), (FF) milieu m Middle, midst. Environment, milieu.
(M) mimosa f Bot. Mimosa.
(S), (M) mine f Mine, mine de houille = colliery, coal-mine.
(S), (M) mineur, eure adj. Minor, lesser. Mus. Minor.
(S), (M) ministre m Minister, agent. (Ku 12-06-010)
(M) mocassin m Moccasin.
(S), (M) modiste f Milliner, modiste.
(S), (M) monument m Monument, memorial, a notable building.
(M) morillon m Rough emerald (pierre). Bot. Morillon.
(M) morse m Morse (télégraphie). (Ku 29-04-005)
(M) mortel, elle adj. Mortal (sujet à la mort), deadly.
(M) mosaique f Arts. Mosaic. (Ku 4-04-004)
(M) motel m Motel. (Ku 24-06-010)
(S), (M), (FF) moteur, trice adj. Motive, driving. m Motor.
(S), (M) moustache f whiskers (de chat), moustache.
(M) mule f Mule, she-mule. (Ku 4-03-004)
(S), (M) muscle m Med. Muscle. (Ku 42-08-017)
(M) musette f Mus. Musette, country bagpipe.
(S), (M) musical, ale adj. Mus. Musical. (Ku 85-13-032)

(S), (M) musicien, enne adj. Mus. Musical, m. Musician.
(S), (M) musique f Mus. Music. (Ku 26-15-064)
(M) naja m Zool. Naja.
(M) natation f Sports. Swimming, natation.
(S), (M) nature f Nature (cours des choses, tempérament).
(M) navigateur, trice s. Naut. Navigator, sailor.
(M) navigation f Navigation, sailing. (Ku 6-05-006)
(S), (M) net, nette adj. Clean, spotless. Fin. Net.
(M) niche f Kennel (à chien). Archit. Niche, nook.
(S), (M) nickel m Nickel. (Ku 7-03-005)
(M) Normandie f Geogr. Normandy. (Ku 1-01-001)
(S), (M) note f Note (observation, billet, instructions).
(M) nougat m Culin. Nougat.
(S), (M) Nylon m Nylon. (Ku 1-01-001)
(S), (M) objet m Object (chose visible). Object, thing.
(S), (M) océan m Ocean. Fig. Sea, ocean. (Ku 34-12-022)
(M) ocelot m Zool. Ocelot.
(M) oculiste m Med. Oculist.
(M) ogre m Ogre.
(S), (M) olive f Bot. Olive. (Ku 5-04-004)
(M) omelette f Culin. Omelette, omelet. (Ku 3-01-001)
(S), (M) omnibus m Ch. de f., Autom. Omnibus, bus.
(M) omoplate f Med. Shoulder-blade, scapula, omoplate.
(S), (M), (FF) opéra m Theatr., Mus. Opera. (Ku 47-11-023)
(M) opérateur, trice s. Operator. (Ku 49-06-011)
(M) opticien m Optician (v. Occuliste).
(S), (M), (FF) orange f Bot. Orange. (Ku 23-10-020)
(M) orangeade f Orangeade.
(M) orang outan m Zool. Orang outang.
(M) orbite f Astron. Orbit. Fig. Orbit (d'une nation).
(S), (M) orchestre m Mus. Band, orchestra.
(S), (M) ordre m Order, course (de la nature).
(S), (M) organe m Med. Organ. Mus. Voice.
(M) organisme m Organism. Body (en politique).
(M) original, ale adj. Original (texte, version, etc.).
(S), (M) ornement m Ornament, adornment, embellishment.
(M) ortolan m Zool. Ortolan.

(M) osier m Osier, wicker.

(M) ossature f Med. Ossature, skeleton, frame.

(S), (M) ouverture f Opening, aperture, orifice. Ouverture.

(M) oxygène m Chim. Oxygen. (Ku 43-04-012)

(S), (M), (FF) page f Page, leaf. (Ku 66-14-046)

(M) pagne f Pagne, loin-cloth.

(M) paillasse f Straw mattress, paillasse.

(M) paillette f Spangle, paillette (ornement).

(M) Palestine f Geogr. Palestine. (Ku 7-02-003)

(M) palette f Arts. Palette (de peintre). (Ku 7-02-003)

(M) panache m Plume, panache (au chapeau).

(M) pancréas m Med. Pancreas.

(S), (M) panier m Basket. Pannier (de jupe).

(S), (M) panne f Techn. Breakdown. Arts. Daub. Panne,

(S), (M), (FF) papa m Fam. Dad, daddy, papa, pa.

(M) papille f med., Bot. Papilla.

(S), (M) parachute m Aviat. Parachute. (Ku 1-01-001)

(M) parachutiste s. Aviat. Parachutist, paratrooper.

(S), (M) paradise m Eccles., Fig. paradise. (Ku 12-08-011)

(M) paraffine f Paraffin.

(S), (M), (FF) parc m Park (de château, de ville].

(S), (M), (FF) parent m pl. Parents as well as relative.

(M), (FF) Paris m Geogr. Paris. (Ku 67-12-040)

(M) parodie f Parody, travesty. (Ku 4-03-003)

(M) parterre m Flowerbed, parterre (de jardin). Theatr. Pit

(S), (M) passage m Passage, way, ferry crossing.

(M) passant, ante adj. Well-trodden (rue). Blas. Passant.

(M) passe f Period, spell. Pass. (Ku 89-15-063)

(S), (M), (FF) passer v. intr. 1 To pass.

(S), (M) passion f Passion. Eccles. Passion. (Ku 28-08-065).

(M) pâte f Culin. Paste, dough, batter. (Ku 10-05-007)

(S), (M) patience f Bot. Patience (plant), or spinach-dock.

(M) patiner v. tr. 1 To patine, to give a patina to.

(M) patio m Patio. (Ku 2-01-002)

(S), (M) pâturage m Pasture, grazing-ground.

(M) pause f Pause, stop. Mus. Pause, rest. (Ku-21-10-017)

(S), (M), (FF) payer v. tr. 9b To pay (qqn.) (de, for).

(S), (M) pédale f Pedal (de bicyclette), treadle.
(M) pédaler v. intr. 1 To pedal, to cycle, to bike.
(M) peignoir m Peignoir, négligé, house-coat.
(M) pelage m Hair, coat, pelage, fur, pelt.
(M) pèlerine f Pelerine, tippet.
(M) pélican m Zool. Pelican.
(M) pénis m Med. Penis.
(M) pénitence f Penitence. Eccles. Penance. Penalty
(M) perche f Zool. Perch.
(M) percher v. intr. 1 To perch (oiseau), to roost.
(M) percolateur m Percolator. Culin. Coffee-percolator.
(M) périmètre m Math. Perimeter (v. Circonférence).
(M) Pernod m Pernod. (Ku 1-01-001)
(M) perron m Perron, flight of steps.
(M) persienne f Blind, persienne, slanted shutter.
(S), (M) personnage m Personage, person of rank.
(M) phaéton m Phaeton.
(S), (M), (FF) pharmacie f Med. Pharmacy, pharmaceutics.
(M) pharynx m Med. Pharynx.
(M) philosophie f Philosophy. (Ku 86-11-036)
(S), (M) phono, phonographe m Phonograph, gramophone.
(M) phosphate, m Chim. Phosphate. (Ku 7-02-003)
(S), (M), (FF) photo f Photography. (Ku 5-02-003)
(M) photographie f Photography as well as photograph,
(M) pianiste s. Mus. Pianist, piano-player. (Ku 14-05-008)
(M) piano s. Mus. Piano. Fam. Slowly, gently, quietly.
(M) pick-up m Pick-up, record-player. (Ku 14-06-010)
(S), (M) pigeon m Zool. Pigeon (Ku 3-02-003)
(S), (M) pile f Pile, stack (de bois), heap (d'objets).
(S), (M) pilote m Naut., Aviat. Pilot. (Ku 44-10-019)
(S), (M) pipe f Pipe (pour fumer), <u>not</u> pipe (tuyau).
(M) pique f Pike, spear. Fam. Pique, tiff (querelle).
(M) pique-nique m invar. Picnic. (Ku 15-06-008)
(S), (M) piquet m Piquet (aux cartes).
(M) pirate m Pirate. (Ku 4-03-003)
(M) pirouette f Pirouette (v. Cabriole). (Ku 4-2-003)
(M) pistole f Pistole. (Ku 27-08-016)

(M) piston m Piston as well as Fam. Pull, influence.

(S), (M) placer v. tr. 5 To place, to put, to set (sur, on)

(S), (M) plaine f Plain, flat country. (Ku 48-13-038)

(S), (M) plan m Archit. Plan. Fig. Plan (d'action, de vie)

(M) planchette f Small plank. Planchette.

(M) planète f Astron. Planet. (Ku 21-06-011)

(M) planisphère m Planisphere.

(M) plantation f Planting (action), plantation (résultat)

(S), (M) plante f Bot. Plant as well as Med. Sole (du pied)

(S), (M) planter v. tr. 1 Agric. To plant.

(S), (M) plastique adj. Plastic (art). (Ku 31-07-017)

(S), (M) plateau m Geogr. Plateau, high plain.

(M) pliant, ante adj. Folding as well as pliant.

(M) plinthe f Plinth (de colonne, de mur).

(M) pluviomètre m Pluviometer, raingauge.

(M) pochette f Envelope, pocket-case, pochette.

(S), (M) poète m Poet. (Ku 00-12-038)

(S), (M) pointe f Point (d'aiguille, d'épingle, de clou).

(S), (M) poison m Poison. (Ku 10-05-008)

(M) poker m Poker (cartes, jeu). (Ku 6-06-006)

(M) pôle m Geogr., Phys., Math., Electr. Pole.

(S), (M) police f Police (maintien de l'ordre).

(M) politician, enne s. Politician. (Ku 13-06-009)

(M) pollen m Bot. Pollen. (Ku 11-03-003)

(M) polo m Polo (jeu). (Ku 4-02-004)

(S), (M) pompe f Pomp, display, state, ceremony, array.

(M) pompon m Tassel. Milit. Pompon. (Ku 1-01-001)

(M) pore m Med. Pore. (Ku 2-01-001)

(S), (M) port m Naut. Harbour (bassin). Geogr. Port

(M) portion f Part, share, portion (partie). Fam. Portion.

(S), (M) portrait m Portrait. Arts. Portrait, face.

(M) pose f Fig. Posture, attitude, pose. (Ku 11-07-010)

(M) postérieur, eure adj. Later, posterior, subsequent.

(M) postillon m Postillion (cocher).

(M) posture f Posture as well as position, situation.

(S), (M), (FF) pot m Pot. Jug, U.S. pitcher. (Ku 28-10-018)

(M) pouf m Pouf, hassock, tuffet.

(M) préfecture f Prefecture. (Ku 1-01-001)
(S), (M), (FF) préparer v. tr. 1 To prepare, to get ready.
(M) presbytère m Eccles. Parsonage, rectory, presbytery.
(S), (M) président, ente s. Chairman, president.
(S), (M) presse f Press, crowd, throng (foule).
(S), (M) prince m Prince. (Ku 33-06-014)
(M) princesse f Princess. (Ku 10-05-007)
(S), (M) principal, ale adj. Principal, chief, leading.
(S), (M) prison f Jur. Prison, gaol, jail (lieu).
(S), (M) problème m Problem, enigma, puzzle, riddle.
(S), (M) professeur m Teacher, professor.
(S), (M), (FF) programme m Programme, syllabus.
(M) projecteur m Lecture-lantern, projector. (Ku 1-01-001)
(S), (M) projet m Project, plan (v. Dessein).
(S), (M), (FF) promenade f Walking. Promenade. (Ku 3-01-001)
(M) propane m Chim. Propane.
(M) prophète m Prophet. (Ku 5-03-005)
(M) prospecter v. tr. 1 To prospect. (Ku 25-10-019)
(M) prospecteur m Prospector.
(M) protestant, ante adj. s. Eccles. Protestant.
(S), (M) province f Province. (Ku 15-06-011)
(M) pull-over m Pullover, slip-on sweater. (Ku 2-01-001)
(M) puma m Zool. Puma, cougar.
(S), (M) purée f Culin. Mash, puree.
(M) purifier v. tr. 1 To purify. (Ku 2-02-002)
(S), (M), (FF) pyjama m Pyjamas, U.S. pajamas.
(M) pylône m Archit. Pylon, pillar.
(M) python m Zool. Python. (Ku 14-01-001)
(M) Québec m Geogr. Quebec.
(S), (M) question f Question (v. Demande). Question, point.
(S), (M), (FF) queue f Tail (d'animal), queue.
(M) quinquina m Med. Cinchona, quinquina. Quinquina.
(S), (M) race f Race, ancestry, descent, species.
(M) racoon m Zool. Racoon. (Ku 1-01-001)
(S), (M) radiateur m Autom., Electr. Radiator.
(S), (M), (FF) radio m Radio. (Ku 120-14-043)
(M) radiologie f Med. Radiology, X-ray treatment.

(M) ragoût m Culin. Stew, ragout.

(S), (M), (FF) rang m Row. Milit., Fig. Rank. (Ku 21-05-017)

(S), (M), (FF) ranger v. tr. 7 To range (v. Arranger).

(S), (M), (FF) rapide adj. Rapid, swift (courant), fast.

(M) rapine f Rapine, plundering, extortion, graft.

(S), (M) rat m Zool. Rat. (Ku 6-05-006)

(S), (M) réaction f Chim. Reaction. Fig. Response.

(M) récitation f Recitation (acte, texte), saying.

(S), (M) récréation f Recreation (v. Amusement).

(S), (M) rectangle adj. Math. Right-angled. m Math. Rectangle.

(M) rectum m Med. Rectum.

(M) réflecteur adj. Reflecting (mirror). m. Reflector.

(M) réflexible adj. Phys. Reflexible.

(S), (M) réfrigérateur m Refrigerator, fridge.

(S), (M) régiment m Milit. Regiment. (Ku 25-06-008)

(M) Regina m Geogr. Regina.

(S), (M) région f Geogr. Region, district, area.

(S), (M) religieux, euse adj. Eccles. Religious (cérémonie).

(S), (M) religion f Eccles. Religion. (Ku 119-14-044)

(S), (M) remède m Med. Remedy (à, for), a medicine.

(S), (M) réparation f Repair as well as reparation

(S), (M) repasser v. tr. 1 To repass, to pass by again.

(M) replanter v. tr. 1 Agric. To replant.

(S), (M) repos m Repose, rest. (Ku 2-02-002)

(M) réservoir m Reservoir, tank. (Ku 10-05-009)

(M) résidence f Residence, abode, dwelling. (Ku 29-10-021)

(M) résine, f Resin. (Ku 9-02-003)

(M) respiration f Med. Respiration, breathing.

(S), (M), (FF) restaurant m Comm. Restaurant.

(M) résumé m Résumé, summary, abstract. (Ku 16-07-013)

(M) revers m Reverse. (Ku 18-08-015)

(S), (M), (FF) revue f Review as well as revue.

(M) rhinocéros m Zool. Rhinoceros. (Ku 3-02-002)

(M) rhubarbe f Bot. Rhubarb.

(S), (M) rideau m Curtain, screen. Milit. Rideau.

(M) rillettes f pl. Culin. Rillettes, potted minced pork.

(M) Rimouski m Geogr. Rimouski.

(M) ring m Sports. Ring _not_ a ring in general.

(M) rite m Eccles. Rite (Ku 8-03-005)

(M) Rome m Geogr. Rome.

(S), (M) rouleau m Roller, coil (de corde), rouleau (d'or).

(S), (M) roulette f Small wheel, roulette. Math. Cycloid.

(S), (M), (FF) route f Road as well as route, path, way.

(S), (M), rue f Bot. Rue. (Ku 6-05-005)

(M), (FF) rugby m Sports. Rugby.

(M) rumeur f Confused (or) distant noise, rumor, report.

(M) Russie f Geogr. Russia. (Ku 72-11-044)

(S), (M) sable m Sable (animal). Blas. Sable, black.

(S), (M) sabot m Sabot, clog. Milit. Sabot (de projectile).

(M) sabre m Milit. Sabre, sword. (Ku 2-02-002)

(S), (M), (FF) sac m Sack, bag. (Ku 8-05-007)

(M) sachet m Small bag as well as sachet, packet.

(M) sacrifice m Eccles. Sacrifice. Fig. Sacrifice (dépense).

(M) sacrum m Med. Sacrum.

(S), (M) saint, ainte adj. Eccles. Saint as well as holy.

(S), (M), (FF) salade f Culin. Salade as well as lettuce.

(M) salamandre m Zool. Salamander. (Ku 2-01-001)

(M) salin, ine adj. Saline (concrétion), salt, salty.

(M) salive f Med. Saliva, spittle. (Ku 4-02-002)

(M) sanatorium (pl. sanatoriums) m Med. Sanatorium.

(M) sandale m Sandal. Sports. Gym-shoe. (Ku 5-03-004)

(S), (M), (FF) sandwich m Culin. Sandwich. (Ku 10-06-009)

(M), (FF) sardine f Zool. Sardine, pilchard. (Ku 2-02-002)

(M) satellite m Astron., Phys. Satellite. (Ku 8-05-007)

(S), (M) sauce f Culin. Sauce as well as gravy.

(M) sauté, ée adj. Culin. Sauté. (Ku 1-01-001)

(S), (M) savant, ante adj. Critical, savant, learned.

(S), (M) scène f Theatr. Stage, scene (d'un acte).

(S), (M) science f Science, knowledge, learning.

(M) scorpion f Zool., Milit., Astron. Scorpion.

(M) scout m Boy-scout, scout. (Ku 8-04-004)

(S), (M) sculpteur m Arts. Sculptor. (Ku 6-03-003)

(S), (M) sculpture f Arts. Sculpture. (Ku 11-05-007)

(M) sécateur m Pruning-scissors, secateurs.

(S), (M) secrétaire s. Secretary. (Ku 191-13-066)

(M) seiche, sèche f Seiche, tidal wave (d'un lac).

(M) séparateur, trice adj. Separative. m. Separator.

(M) serin s. Zool. Serin, canary.

(M) sermon m Eccles. Sermon. Fam. Sermon, lecture.

(S), (M) serpent m Zool. Serpent, snake. Mus. Serpent.

(M) servante f Servant, maid-servant (personne).

(S), (M), (FF) service m Service (assistance).

(S), (M), (FF) serviette f Feeder, bib, serviette, napkin.

(M) shérif m Sheriff. (Ku 20-05-009)

(M) short m Shorts. (Ku 212-15-158)

(S), (M) siège m Seat (d'une chaise). Milit. Siege.

(M) sieste f Siesta, nap (fam.). (Ku 2-01-001)

(S), (M) signe m Sign, gesture (geste). Math. Sign.

(M) silex m Silex, flint.

(M) silo m Agric. Silo. (Ku 1-01-001)

(M) sinus m Med. Sinus (drontal, maxillaire), antrum.

(M) sketch (pl. sketches) m Theatr. Sketch, playlet.

(M) ski m Sports. Ski. (Ku 5-02-002)

(M) skunks m Zool., Comm. Skunk. (Ku 1-01-001)

(M) slip m Slips (vêtement). Sports. Slip.

(M) sloop m Naut. Sloop. (Ku 1-01-001)

(M) soda m Soda, soda-water. (Ku 3-02-002)

(M) sofa m Sofa. (Ku 6-03-003)

(S), (M) sol m invar. Mus. Sol, G. (Ku 3-03-003)

(M) solarium m Solarium.

(M) sole f Sole (de sabot, d'un animal). Zool. Sole.

(M) sombrero m Sombrero.

(S), (M) sorte f Kind, sort (espèce) as well as manner.

(S), (M) sortie f Exit, outburst, tirade. Milit. Sortie.

(S), (M), (FF) sou m Sou. (Ku 1-01-001)

(S), (M) souffle m Breath, blast. Med. souffle.

(S), (M) source f Source, spring (v. Fontaine).

(M) soutane f Eccles. Cassock, soutane. (Ku 1-01-001)

(S), (M) souvenir m Memory, remembrance, souvenir.

(M) spaghetti m Culin. Spaghetti. (Ku 1-01-001).

(S), (M) speaker (f. speakerine) Radio announcer, speaker.

(S), (M) spécialiste s. Specialist (v. Technicien).
(S), (M) spectateur, trice s. Spectator, onlooker.
(M) sphère f Sphere, globe. Astron., Math., Fig. Sphere.
(M) stand m Stand, stall (à une exposition). Sports. Stand.
(S), (M) statue f Arts. Statue. (Ku 17-05-009)
(M) statuette f Arts. Statuette. (Ku 1-01-001)
(M) steamer m Naut. Steamer, steamboat. (Ku 1-01-001)
(M) steeple-chase m Sports. Steeplechase.
(M) stencil m Stencil.
(M) sternum m Med. Sternum, breastbone. (Ku 1-01-001)
(M) stop interj. Stop. (Ku 120-13-086)
(M) stylet m Stiletto, stylet. Med. Stylet.
(M) stylographe m Stylograph, fountain-pen.
(S), (M) supérieur, eure adj. Higher (in space), superior.
(S), (M) surface f Surface. Math., Fig. Surface.
(M) suspension f Fin., Chim., Autom., Suspension.
(M) sweater m Sweater. (Ku 14-05-006)
(M) sweat-shirt f Tee-shirt, U.S. sweat-shirt.
(M) syllabe f Syllable. (Ku 1-01-001)
(S), (M) système m System, scheme, plan. (Ku 416-14-133)
(S), (M), (FF) table f Table (meuble) as well as a slab.
(M) tamarin m Zool. Tamarin.
(M) tambour m Mus. Drum (instrument). Techn. Tambour.
(M) tandem m Tandem, tandem bicycle. (Ku 1-01-001)
(M) tank m Milit. Tank. (Ku 12-08-010)
(M) tapioca m Comm. Tapioca. Culin. Tapioca soup.
(M) tapir m Zool. Tapir as well as Fam. Private pupil.
(M) tare f Comm. Depreciation, loss in value, tare.
(M) taupe adj. Taupe (couleur).
(M) taverne f Café-restaurant. Tavern. (Ku 2-02-002)
(S), (M), (FF) taxi m Autom. Taxi-cab, taxi, cab.
(S), (M) technicien, enne s. Technician, technicist.
(S), (M) technique adj. Techn. Technical.
(S), (M) télégramme m Telegram, wire. (Ku 8-02-006)
(S), (M) télégraphe m Electr. Telegraph. (Ku 21-05-007)
(S), (M), (FF) téléphone m Electr. Telephone, phone.
(M) téléphoniste s. Telephonist, telephone operator.

(S), (M), (FF) télévision f Radio. Television, T.V.
(S), (M) température f Temperature, the weather.
(M) temporal, ale adj., m Med. Temporal. (Ku 5-02-002)
(M) tenaille f Techn. Pincers as well as Milit. Tenaille.
(M) tendon m Med. Tendon, sinew. (Ku 2-02-002)
(M), (FF) tennis m Sports. Tennis as well as lawn-tennis.
(S), (M) tente f Booth (d'un marché). Sports. Tent.
(S), (M) terrain m Ground, piece of land. Milit. Terrain.
(M) terrier m Hole, burrow (de lapin). Zool. Terrier (chien).
(M) terrine f Earthenware pan, pot, terrine.
(M) test m Med. Test. (Ku 119-13-071)
(M) tester v. tr. 1 To test.
(S), (M) théâtre m Stage (of a theater), theater.
(S), (M) thermomètre m Phys. Thermometer. (Ku 10-04-004)
(M) thermos m Thermos, thermos (or) vacuum flask.
(M) thermostat m Electr. Thermostat. (Ku 6-02-003)
(M) thorax m Med. Thorax, chest. Zool. Thorax.
(M) thym m Bot. Thyme.
(M) tibia m Med. Tibia, shin-bone
(M) tigresse f Zool. Tigress. (Ku 1-01-001)
(M) tilbury m Tilbury.
(M) timbale f Metal cup (or) mug as well as timbale.
(S), (M), (FF) timbre m Bell, stamp. Mus. Timbre.
(M) tirade f Theatr. Tirade, declamatory speech. Mus. Tirade.
(S), (M) tissu m Texture (d'une étoffe), tissue, cloth.
(M) toast m Toast. Culin. Toast. (Ku 19-09-013)
(S), (M), (FF) tomate adj., invar., f Bot., Culin. Tomato.
(S), (M) tonneau m Barrel, cask, keg. Autom. Tonneau.
(M) top m Radio. Pip (de l'horloge parlante), top.
(M) torche f Torche (flambeau) as well as straw-twist.
(S), (M) torchon adj. Torchon (papier).
(M) toréador m Toreador, bullfighter.
(S), (M) torrent m Torrent. Fig. Torrent, stream.
(S), (M) tourisme m Tourism.
(M) tracteur m Tractor. (Ku 24-04-006)
(M) traction f Traction as well as pulling, drawing.
(S), (M), (FF) train m Ch. de f. Train as well as speed.

(M) traîne f Train (d'une robe) as well as drag-net.
(M) tramontane f Tramontane, north wind (vent).
(M) tramway m Tramway (voie), U.S. streetcar. (Ku 1-01-001)
(M) transatlantique adj. Geogr. Transatlantic. (Ku 1-01-001)
(M) transfert m Transfer, transference.
(S), (M) transformer v. tr. 1 To transform, to convert.
(M) transplanter v. tr. 1 Agric. To transplant (trees).
(S), (M), (FF) transport m Transport, conveyance.
(S), (M) transporter v. tr. 1 To transport, to convey.
(M) transporteur adj. Techn. Conveying. Naut. Transport.
m Transporter, carrier.
(M) trapèze adj. Med. Trapezius (muscle), trapezium (os).
(M) trappeur m Trapper. (Ku 2-01-001)
(M) tresser v. tr. 1 To braid, to tress, to plait.
(S), (M) triangle m Math., Mus., Astron. Triangle.
(S), (M) tribunal m Tribunal (siège). Jur. Law-court.
(M) triceps m Med. Triceps.
(M) trick m Trick (aux cartes). (Ku 15-06-012)
(S), (M), (FF) tricot m Knitting (action). Tricot.
(M) tricycle m Tricycle, three-wheeled vehicle.
(M) trident m Trident. Agric. Three-pronged pitchfork.
(M) tringle f Rod. Archit. Tringle, square moulding.
(M) trio m Trio. Mus. Trio. (Ku 9-04-007)
(M) tripe f (généralement pl.) Culin. Tripe. (Ku 1-01-001)
(M) trolleybus m Autom. Trolleybus.
(M) tropique adj. Tropical.
(S), (M) tube m Tube (de vaseline). Milit. Bot. Med. Tube.
(M), (FF) tulipe f Bot. Tulip. (Ku 4-03-004)
(M) tunique f Tunic (des Anciens). Milit. Med., Bot. Tunic.
(S), (M), (FF) tunnel m Tunnel. (Ku 10-05-005)
(M) turbine f Techn. Turbine, centrifugal sugar refiner
(S), (M) type m Type, model, pattern. Zool., Techn. Type.
(M) uniforme adj. Uniform (en général), even, regular.
(S), (M) université f University. (Ku 214-13-086)
(M) urine f Urine. (Ku 1-01-001)
(M), (FF) Valentin m, Valentine f Valentine. (Ku 2-02-002)
(S), (M), (FF) valise f Suit-case, valise, bag.

(M) vampire m Zool. Vampire, vampire-bat. Fig. Vampire.
(M) vanille f Culin. Vanilla. (Ku 1-01-001)
(S), (M) vase m Vase (à fleurs) as well as vessel, dish.
(M) vedette f Milit. Vedette, mounted sentry.
(M) végétation f Vegetation as well as Med. adenoid
(S), (M) veine f Med., Bot. Vein. Fig. Vein, humour.
(M) ventilateur m Ventilator as well as electric fan.
(M) véranda f Veranda, U.S. porch, a bay window.
(S), (M) verbe m Gramm. Verb as well as tone of voice.
(M) verdure f Bot. Greenness, verdure (couleur).
(M) vertébral, ale adj. Med. Vertebral. (Ku 3-01-001)
(M) vertèbre f Med. Vertebra (pl. vertebrae).
(M) vestibule m Vestibule, hall, lobby, passage.
(M) vice-président m Vice-president, vice-chairman.
(M) Vichy m Geogr. Vichy. (Ku 1-01-001)
(S), (M) villa f Villa, cottage, country house.
(S), (M), (FF) village m Village. (Ku 72-13-045)
(S), (M) violet, ette adj. Violet, purple. (Ku 7-02-003)
(M) vipère f Zool. Viper, adder.
(S), (M) visage m Face, visage. (Ku 2-02-002)
(M) vision f Vision, sight, eye-sight, perception, seeing.
(S), (M) visite f Visit, call as well as inspection.
(M) vison m Zool. Vison, American mink. Comm. Mink.
(M) vitamine f Med. Vitamin. (Ku 5-04-004)
(S), (M) voile m Veil (de tête). Voile (étoffe).
(M) volley-ball m Sports. Volley-ball. (Ku 2-01-001)
(M) volt m Electr. Volt. (Ku 1-01-001)
(S), (M) volume m Volume, mass, bulk, volume (d'un son).
(M) water-polo m Sports. Water-polo.
(M) wharf m Wharf. (Ku 4-02-002)
(M) yacht m Naut. Yacht. (Ku 4-02-002)
(M) yo-yo m Yo-yo.
(M) zèbre m Zool. Zebra. (Ku 1-01-001)
(S), (M), (FF) zéro m Zero, naught, cipher.
(M) zinc m Chim. Zinc as well as Fam. Counter, bar.
(S), (M) zoo m Zoo. (Ku 9-05-007)

Linn B. Konrad

MODERN DRAMA AS CRISIS

The Case of Maurice Maeterlinck

American University Studies: Series II, (Romance Languages and Literature), Vol. 25

ISBN 0-8204-0222-2 206 pp. hardback US$ 39.25*

*Recommended price - alterations reserved

This book characterizes Maurice Maeterlinck as a «modern» writer by showing that his early rejection of language in favor of symbolic images and gestures to convey significant experience led to a methodological crisis by threatening silence and madness. This recognition caused the writer to turn back to language as a necessary, even if inadequate, means by which to carry out his artistic-philosophical quest.

An important work ... Cogent, well-researched, and sensitive, Linn B. Konrad's work is a must for those interested in theatre, in culture, in live! (Bettina L. Knapp, Hunter College and the Graduate Center of the City University of New York)

PETER LANG PUBLISHING, INC.
62 West 45th Street
USA - New York, NY 10036

Jeffrey T. Chamberlain

LATIN ANTECEDENTS OF FRENCH CAUSATIVE *FAIRE*

American University Studies: Series XIII, (Linguistics), Vol. 2
ISBN 0-8204-0258-3 195 pp. hardback US$ 29.50*

*Recommended price - alterations reserved

The factitive construction *faire faire quelque chose à quelqu'un,* a central problem in French syntax, differs in structure from its counterpart in Classical Latin, which typically expressed causation by means of a subordinate clause with its verb in the subjunctive. This examination of causative constructions in representative Late Latin and Old French texts offers evidence that the infinitive construction characteristic of the Romance languages in fact originated in Latin and was widespread by the sixth century. Additional syntactic features of the causative in French, however, including the generalization of the indirect object *à quelqu'un* and the fusion of *faire* with its dependent infinitive, are shown to be Romance developments that are not generalized in French until the fifteenth century.

Contents: Causation in Latin and in French - Examples in Latin (1st to 11th centuries) - Examples in Old French (11th to 15th centuries) - Chronological summary.

PETER LANG PUBLISHING, INC.
62 West 45th Street
USA - New York, NY 10036